Music in Esports

This book invites the reader to expand their idea of esports as an independent niche and consider it an integral part of a growing multi- and transmedia ecosystem that includes the global entertainment industry, where music plays an essential role.

The music present *in* and *around* esports games is an integral part of how they are communicated and mediated and, as such, holds a central role in binding their narratives cohesively and coherently to appeal to their audiences. Popular music theory is placed at the foundation of the issues raised in the chapters, as it is taken as a cornerstone for linking the esports international scene with the music industry. This text uses specific case studies from popular esports to support and illustrate each chapter, including *League of Legends*, *Counter-Strike*, and *Fortnite*.

This book will be of great interest to researchers and students in the fields of esports, game design and development, musicology, and media studies.

Eulalia Febrer-Coll is the Subdirector of the Music Department and Academic Coordinator of the MA in Musicology at Universidad Internacional de la Rioja (UNIR). She holds a PhD in Popular Music from Cardiff University.

Music in Esports

On the Convergence of the Music and Gaming Industries

Eulalia Febrer-Coll

CRC Press
Taylor & Francis Group
Boca Raton London New York

CRC Press is an imprint of the
Taylor & Francis Group, an **informa** business

First edition published 2026
by CRC Press
2385 NW Executive Center Drive, Suite 320, Boca Raton FL 33431

and by CRC Press
4 Park Square, Milton Park, Abingdon, Oxon, OX14 4RN

CRC Press is an imprint of Taylor & Francis Group, LLC

ISBN: 9781032625355 (hbk)
ISBN: 9781032625348 (pbk)
ISBN: 9781032625362 (ebk)

DOI: 10.1201/9781032625362

Typeset in Times
by codeMantra

To Jordi, Laia and Marc

Contents

Acknowledgments

When I first began actively working on music in video games, little did I know that I would eventually have the opportunity to combine several years of research, discussions, and interviews into a single contribution. In 2020, in the heist of the pandemic, my PhD supervisor, Professor Sarah Hill, brought up the idea that I should encompass the topic I had been researching since my thesis days, mainly involving esports, into this format. Although it took me several years to build the case—and confidence—to do so, I can only express my gratitude for that gentle push.

In the last few years, I have had the opportunity to immerse myself in gaming from both professional and academic perspectives, hand in hand with small startups and different institutions. I have had the pleasure of meeting key figures in today's music video game landscape—composers from Akira Yamaoka to Eduardo de la Iglesia, music strategists with experience at some of the biggest brands on the market, and, most and foremost, many influential international scholars in ludomusicology. Furthermore, I have had the space to discuss and elaborate on the influence of *League of Legends*, *Fortnite*, and other games converging with the music industry, in events and private conversations alike. To all of those who have engaged with me at some point, thank you for your kind recommendations and advise. The research group and colleagues at LudoSpain have been essential in providing continuous support to my research and, among them, I must especially thank Professor Lidia López, who has joined me in bringing ideas to life and always encouraged me to move and improve.

For the writing of this book, I was confident that bringing forward the voices of professionals in the gaming and music industries would enrich what I could offer academically, and after three dozen interviews, it became clear that I was not mistaken. I owe a special thanks to Mariana Migliore, Toa Dunn, Mike Ault, Eric Tan, and Mat Ombler, who have spent their time conversing with me on multiple occasions. I am most grateful to all other participants who have enriched these pages since the very beginning, including Tim Larkin, Carmen Rodríguez, Wilhelm Voutilainen, Gavin Johnson, Mike Morasky, Tommi Toivonen, Martin Schjøler, Anders Blume, Juandi, Alan Gai, and Ainhoa Campos. Also, content creators Moisés Nieto, Anikilo, Jay the Bard, Chewie Catt, and Elesky kindly offered their insight from both fan and professional standpoints, as have other players and industry agents.

Many of my colleagues at work, especially Beatriz Amorós, have been pillars in helping me bring these lines to fruition. But I most essentially thank my closest friends and, of course, my family for bearing with me during the several months of dedication to this project. To Jordi, I can only express my gratitude for his care, patience, and encouragement, and for being my rock throughout it all.

Introduction

When I first downloaded *League of Legends* in 2011, the game's esports scene was only beginning to unfold. It was the year of the game's first World Championship at *DreamHack Summer* in Sweden. The smaller concurrence of the gathering sparked an inside joke around the games' community, stating that it had taken place in former caster Phreak's basement, which underlines the significant growth of the event since, and the bonds developed by its followers. Although the event was attended by a small crowd, which witnessed team Fnatic's first World Cup win, it was the germ of a global phenomenon that, fifteen years later, gathers thousands of fans in person and millions virtually annually.

The broadcast was simple, and music was yet scarcely present as it briefly accompanied the introduction and final victory of the matches by using game motifs.[1] At this point, besides the soundtrack of the title's main map, character Sona featured music-based abilities, and (silent) character dances evoking popular music hits resonated with an interest that I only pursued years later, as there was not much music content to explore yet. There was no winning trophy but cash prizes for the third, second, and first-place winners, all of whom filed onto the stage to receive a giant check and welcoming applause from now-veteran followers. On that day, Fnatic won $50,000. In 2024, the prize had escalated to $445,000, including a total prize pool of $2,225,000,[2] which attests to the game's growing attractiveness for players, collaborating brands, multimedia companies, and global investors.

The rapid popularization of the title and the increased use of social media contributed to early artistic expressions from fans, who started sharing parodies and memes on platforms such as YouTube or Tumblr. Yet, it was not until the expansion of Riot Music Group that music began being explicitly exploited as a definitory product for the brand, which later placed it at the epicenter of a multi- and transmedia gaming panorama. During the following decade, many games benefitted from ever-expanding technologies and global access to the internet, incorporating sound and music as key marketing media—and expanding a whole field for (ludo)musicologists to explore.

League of Legends has been discussed in the past, as I do here, not only because it provides a gateway into the study of video games and esports, but also because it has maintained a distinct position as the most viewed competitive game worldwide for several years.[3] Scholars from diverse fields, from sports science and management to marketing and media studies,[4] have tackled the game from different angles to explore its presence in the current media panorama, its operative principles, and its effects on players and audiences. Although music has only been addressed tangentially, it can be expected that the transmedia presence of the industry provides new fields and case studies for closer analysis, as it has during the last lustrum.

The global esports scene, which is the tangent of this book, contributed additional strata to an already complex industry, mostly by edifying a media-focused sports system

DOI: 10.1201/9781032625362-1

around other media. In organizing video games as sports, multiple agents were added to the scene that contributed to the content and capital generated around them—including league organizations, professional teams, hosts, casters, influencers, and a long etcetera. Furthermore, the engagement of these contributors with the media environment in which they were embedded provided additional pathways for collaboration with the music industry.

Although partnerships between games and music brands have been essential to maximizing the potential of the music departments in developing companies, elements like licensing and music streaming integration have also been central to building the current, predominantly digital multimedia landscape. This was already noticed by Collins in her 2008 *Game Sound*, where she underlined the potential behind the intersection of both industries before the height of the internet, as "games are being used to promote and sell music, and recording artists are being used to market and sell games."[5] The popular music market has continued its growth, and esports reports forecasts have surpassed what could have been expected a few decades ago, yet the consideration of these niches as separate industries needs to be scrutinized in their bifurcations and collaborative endeavors.

According to Pillsbury's 2023 report, media rights will become the next major growth area for esports revenue,[6] which is hardly surprising, as the embeddedness of gaming in global media steadily contributes to our current trans- and cross-mediated environment, as I will discuss in the following epigraphs. In this context, endemic to younger generations and characteristic of digital capitalism,[7] users jump indistinctively between platforms and services, progressively erasing the distinction between what used to be well-defined entertainment fields. Music provides continuity and coherence to this connected world and, as such, continues to transform its uses and functions to adapt to new demands and forms of creating, sharing, and consuming culture.

In this light, this book invites the reader to expand their idea of esports as an independent niche and consider it an integral part of a growing multi- and transmedia ecosystem that includes the global entertainment industry, in which music plays an essential role. Despite the organized competitive nature at the basis of the definition of esports,[8] they can be understood as more than a category or a series of games surrounded by institutionalized sportive structures, as they have evolved into a whole ecosystem that permeates through multiple layers in the entertainment industry, and have come to include products and by-products profoundly intermingled with the music industry.

ABOUT THE ROLE OF MUSIC IN ESPORTS

The video game core that shapes esports implies, on the one hand, the necessity for understanding them as an integral part of the audiovisual media market and, on the other, their inherently participatory nature.[9] Through the intersection with popular culture from diverse fronts—as video games and as sports, but also as music products and even films—esports have become an integral part of our current multimediated environment. As an example, the television series *Arcane*, based on the *League of Legends* universe and with a soundtrack composed by multiple popular music artists, reached far beyond the games' audience when launched on Netflix in 2021, adding more than 34 million reproductions only in its first six days on broadcast.[10] The conversion of users was likewise significant, as many took it as the gateway into the game and, to an extent, to its related products and esports scene.[11] Is the show strictly esports content? Not necessarily. However, it contributes to the edification of the game's fictional universe, and is a key tool in promoting and maintaining its esports scene, as well as its derived music products.

Based on these premises and considering the multiple ways in which esports are ubiquitous in the daily lives of internet-connected users, I argue that music acts as a social binder for the media products encompassed under the esports umbrella. Since such games draw not only from original soundtracks but also from wider music inputs, the music industry inevitably comes to a crossroads with the inherently social nature of esports. This means a growing interest of esports agents in exploiting transmedia products, including popular music, which benefit from their users' internal connectedness.

Literature on the topic is brief as of 2024, but contributions such as those by Yaewon Jin and Tae-Jin Yoon on *Global Esports: Transformation of Cultural Perceptions of Competitive Gaming,*[12] or Andra Ivănescu's on *The Cambridge Companion to Video Game Music*,[13] have started illustrating the possible pathways of exploration for a niche of games that is strongly reliant on multi- and transmediation due to its social essentiality. Likewise, volumes such as the *Routledge Handbook of Esports*[14] afford key tools for understanding the complexity of the system created around and derived from the building of competitive scenarios around diverse titles on the market. In this handbook, the authors break down the structure and mechanics behind and around esports as part of the entertainment industry, and approach them internally—e.g., as a business, through their players, etc.—and externally—e.g., their applications to education or their influence on other media.

Here, I will adhere to the definition offered by Nothelfer, Jenny, and Besombes in the same volume, which is rooted in a thorough review of past descriptions, and according to whom "esports is an organized and codified competition between human players using video games."[15] The need for organization and codification is argued to include in-game and out-of-game rules, which is especially relevant for the discussion at hand, as it implies the intersubjective agreement of viewers and participants on the value of surrounding elements beyond gameplay—including music.

Therefore, when I tackle music in esports, I refer not only to the music present in the games or competitions but also to all the music and sound *in* and *around* diverse titles. Many of the musical expressions surrounding esports are not necessarily inserted in competitive events, but refer to the games at their core, creating an unavoidable codependence. Likewise, the globality of esports implies a need to explore the cultural expressions and approaches of widely diverse countries—a task that can prove complex to the Western eye, especially regarding language and idiosyncratic barriers. The growing presence of the Eastern market through music influences in K-pop, as well as in C- and J-pop, are steadily influencing global tendencies in and around the games discussed in the following, but they have also gained centrality capital-wise in the absorption of developing and publishing brands by bigger corporations, such as Tencent.

ESPORTS AS A (TRANS)MEDIATIC ECOSYSTEM

Transmediality is key to understanding the superimposition of music and esports, as agents on both parties travel from and through one medium to the other—now almost indistinctively. The presence of popular music in esports games, as well as of esports games in the creation of musical—and overall audiovisual—products, is part of the essence of their continuous collaboration, as it appeals to and allows the flow of audiences. As argued by Jenkins, "different media attract different market niches,"[16] but what happens when media boundaries are blurred? Considering the current digital sociocultural landscape, I will not only discuss the use of different entertainment channels to communicate esports but, more essentially, their intermingling in a continuous stream of content.

In 2019, Besombes already included media as a section of his schematic representation of the esports ecosystem, drawing it separately rather than as a transversal binding element to what is a media-based environment.[17] In a step further, Carrillos Vera and Antón considered content production as a wider, essential part of esports as a whole.[18] However, that esports are based on a form of media implies that they are dependent on sound and image production, audiovisual promotion, and communication—this includes teams, tournaments, games, and, most essentially, developers and publishers.

Like in other entertainment industries such as sports or cinema, social media and the participatory culture[19] that they afford imply an expansion of the narrative structure of the games and their scenes through storytelling,[20] which is not contained but continuously developed around the whole ecosystem. This does not mean that media production is at the center of esports or that music is indiscernible to gaming culture, but that "the music industry cannot be treated as being somehow apart from the sociology of everyday life – its activities are themselves culturally determined,"[21] and form an integral part of digital media.

This reinforces Cross' thesis, according to which music in the digital age becomes rooted in three pillars: commodity—it holds and creates value—community—it involves time sharing and the entrainment of participants—and communication—"as a component of the human communicative toolkit."[22] These three dimensions become indissociable as they are materialized into products such as virtual bands based on esports games, promotional music videos for competitions and teams, or fan-generated content contributing secondary markets to the scene.

I discuss these topics, among others, in the following six chapters, which offer a journey from the diverse games and genres contained under the label "esports"—from a musical perspective—to the appropriation and reinterpretation of game content through music means by prosumers. In awareness of the potential expansion of each chapter in future research and the wide variety of examples that could be quoted under each epigraph, I hope that the reader will find a point of reference for mapping the intersection of the esports and music industries. In other words, I do not pretend to cover all games and expressions related to esports, but provide some insight into a transmedia panorama that is growingly tending toward convergence and the different ways in which it manifests.[23]

The case studies used throughout are diverse but mostly focused on a smaller array of titles that have shown specific attention to music development. These include MOBAs such as *DotA 2* and *League of Legends*; shooters like *Counter-Strike* or *Fortnite*; sports games like *Rocket League* or *EA Sports FC*; fighting games like *Street Fighter*; and card games such as *Hearthstone*, as well as other titles like *Pokémon GO* or *Brawl Stars*. In this vein, I consider games that can be accessed through different consoles, from PC to mobile devices, especially taking into account the growing weight of games aimed at hand-held devices.[24] Nevertheless, since the ability to invest in music products and development is essential to become embedded into the industry, most of the focus relies on companies with a strong presence in the market, like Epic Games or Riot Games, which illustrate the potential behind the continuous conversation between entertainment media.

CHAPTER BREAKDOWN

The main six chapters in this book are structured to provide a comprehensive understanding of the presence of music—especially popular music—in esports games. Each opens with contextualizing epigraphs aimed at deepening the knowledge and relevance of the contents later discussed, and closes with a brief conclusion that recaps and reflects on its main arguments. Furthermore, the inclusion of short excerpts from in-depth interviews with music, esports, and overall gaming agents provides further contrast and a deeper insight into the videoludic—and overall commodifiable—content from which they participate, bringing additional hands-on value to the discussion.

I find it essential to emphasize the relevance of social and digital media as key resources, as they contribute academic and industry media that inform, recreate, and help interpret the development of the scenes around the games. In this sense, as suggested by Michiel Kamp, digital (auto)ethnography is implicit as a method contending "that the scholarly explication of experiences can be similar to the way in which we relate many of our daily experiences: by recounting them,"[25] essential to address the field firsthand.

Chapter 1 opens with an approach to the musical gears behind the games addressed in this book. Using Collins' *Game Sound*[26] and Summer's *Understanding Video Game Music*[27] as reference, among other works, I discuss the different ways in which music can be incorporated into esports games, differentiating between original soundtracks and licensed contributions, as well as their possible placements within different titles. I offer a tentative categorization to allow a general analysis of the strategies used in diverse genres, to help differentiate *grosso modo* the sound morphology of each group. Following this, I refer to the commodification of music in esports to create alternative routes for developers and publishers to exploit commercially and dialogue with their users. In this light, I reinterpret the value network behind the video game industry to include music industry agents in the equation, as a means to understand their growing ties.

This chapter includes an in-depth discussion of each priorly established category, which uses specific case studies to illustrate their commonness and particularities. More specifically, I use *League of Legends* and *DotA 2* to address MOBAs; *Counter-Strike* and *Fortnite* to discuss shooters; *FIFA* (now *EA Sports FC*) and *Rocket League* to tackle sports games; and games such as *Street Fighter*, *Hearthstone*, and *Pokémon GO* in reference to fighting games, card games, and other miscellaneous titles, respectively. I conclude with a reflection based on the theoretical frame initially outlined, reinforcing the need for understanding each game genre as a wide category: each title holds particularities that can be traced back to the strategic plan formulated by its developers.

Chapter 2 focuses on narrativity and the development of character identities in esports titles, as they have become relevant in and outside of games, especially regarding the creation of derived music products. I explore the convergence between media as a way of providing continuity for game brands, and delve into how music affords constancy and consistency to a cohesive discourse between fictional worlds and real-life events. For this purpose, I draw on concepts such as *transmedia storytelling* and *storyworld*, as well as on the canonic work of Jenkins in *Convergence Culture*.[28] I explore character-inspired songs, offering examples from games like *Street Fighter* or *Free Fire*, and emphasize the effort to adapt these—more or less—independent music releases to a worldwide public.

This is followed by an epigraph that delves into game-inspired bands featuring game characters, which includes a thorough examination of Riot Games' *Pentakill*, *K/DA*, *True Damage*, and *HEARTSTEEL*, following the brand's impact in the industry. The reliance on K-pop in these and other cases places it at a central position in the discussion, and illustrates the success of the genre in gaming environments since the late 2010s. The conclusion underlines how character identities are built around background stories and features designed for each game, but also from personalized musical texts that move beyond strictly gamer audiences and competitive environments.

In Chapter 3, I focus on the music built around esports games and their promotion, appealing to the competitive ecosystem and the agents that conform and inform it. Following the previous chapter, I consider transmediality and convergence through different uses of popular music in games, including special events in games like *Fortnite*; promotional videos for competitions created by developers, which are frequently produced in collaboration with popular music artists, like in *Counter-Strike* or *PUBG*; external promotional videos by professional clubs, teams, or organizations, among which I analyze the LEC's *mediocre rap battle* series. I also open the discussion for fan-led music strategies that have been incorporated by official organizations and brands; and refer to streaming and influencer initiatives that have contributed to the popularization of esports from their close involvement with their fan communities and music artists.

With these categories, through which I trace a rudimentary map to study the convergence of esports and music on the international scene, I aim to reinforce the centrality of music in the current competitive panorama. Popular music has become a key marketing tool for the games but also for competitions, participating teams, and other agents. With this, I show how the continuous exchange between media has become a part of the identity-building process of the games' scenes, benefitting the growth of the esports scene and generating momentum around social media.

Chapter 4 approaches the phenomenon of in-game concerts as bidirectional promotional tools for esports games and popular music, with a point of departure on the work of authors like Rambarran[29] or Calleja,[30] who have discussed this topic in the frame of music and virtuality. The discussion has also gained some traction in media studies, as in-game concerts have created a mediatic point of attention for fans and brands alike, bridging competitive and non-competitive content.[31] This chapter underlines the potentialities and limitations of such virtual spaces, as well as their performative opportunities, as they entail a potential for global gatherings and democratic access to music, in contrast to a lack of space for spontaneous and transgressive behaviors. The potential of virtual spaces to hold virtual performances depends greatly on the marketing goals, on the connection of music and games industries, and on the capacity of developers and publishers to create their own music products or collaborate with external parties.

In the second part of this chapter, I review the concerts that took place in *Fortnite* between 2019 and 2024, from Marshmello's first intervention to the 2024 end-of-year performance starring Snoop Dogg, Eminem, and other artists. Epic Games' journey in implementing these events, from the DJ's intervention to their last hybrid productions, illustrates the impact of such virtual gatherings on a global scale, as well as the rapidly changing technologies that afford the expansion of the brand's universe. The conclusion underlines the implications of these concert formats at gaming and esports consumption levels in light of the existing discussions on *liveness* and virtuality, as they become intrinsically linked to digital socializing spaces.

In Chapter 5, I explore the musical forms of expression linked to live events in esports, including popular music and originally composed music, and discuss different collaboration formats that depend on the aims and needs of each title or developing brand. For this purpose, I delve into live shows and ceremonial openings in esports competitions, including the representation of virtual bands through popular music artists, and the featuring of regional personalities in geographically delimited events. I use two well-known MOBAs as case studies to illustrate this, *League of Legends* and *DotA 2*, as they offer two contrasting approaches to live performances in competitive contexts. Furthermore, I analyze how these events offer identity and community-building opportunities for attendees, and how some games have devised their productions to appeal to worldwide audiences.

The following epigraphs expand on the use of Computer-Generated Imagery (CGI) and the embodiment of virtual artists by popular music artists in live and recorded performances, as they become the real-life representatives of the brands with which they collaborate. I discuss how virtual artists are brought to life through their own avatars in products such as music videos and through social media, which becomes a primary channel to create an illusion of non-mediation between characters and fans. Lastly, I focus on the transmediation of characters into TV shows that serve a bidirectional promotion for the esports and music industries, along with the inclusion of real-life artists in the same fictional narratives. This chapter's conclusive remarks underline the growing presence of popular music on and around esports stages, and how performances and music products derived from the collaboration between industries align with the global music market.

Lastly, Chapter 6 focuses on music fandom in esports, and the role of fans in shaping the music scenes around their favorite titles. To discuss this, I find a basis in fandom theory and existing texts on esports fandom, such as Jarrett's contribution to the *Routledge Handbook of Esports.*[32] I review some early fan music initiatives around titles like *Counter-Strike* and *Starcraft*, and create a distinction between parody and original songs, not only in their composition but in their social purpose. I also address fan original or compilation playlists, and their cooptation by the esports industry; content creator strategies and contributions to the international esports scene; the contribution of transcriptions of arrangements through sheet music written by professional and amateur musicians; and the relevance of live music streaming on platforms like Twitch of YouTube as a form of dissemination of esports game content.

The last epigraphs of this chapter analyze the presence of esports music at video game conventions, with a special focus on BlizzCon, and the contribution of online visual art to extending the narratives around esports music products. I conclude by highlighting the continuous stream of contributions on social media and the internet in general and the growing encouragement of brands that understand fan engagement to be valuable assets, incorporating them into their marketing strategies. In sum, although User-Generated Content (UGC) initiatives are not directly involved with competitions, teams, or players, they contribute key pieces that support the esports industry.

I close this book with a short epilogue exploring possible developments around esports as part of the global entertainment industry, based on the current discussions on academic and informational media. The smaller amount of literature covering music in esports specifically, from a more-than-competition standpoint, is complemented by the qualitative research at the foundation of this book, which includes more than 30 in-depth interviews with active agents in music and gaming, including voices in the industry such as Toa Dunn, Eric Tan, or Mat Ombler. These pages provide tentative insight into the immediate future of the convergence of music and esports, allowing a sketch of potential directions for a growingly convergent global culture and, hopefully, for more researchers to follow.

NOTES

1 LoL Esports, "aAa vs fnatic – Grand Final Season 1 Championship", *Youtube*, 2011. Available at: https://www.youtube.com/watch?v=bMTI1kYG4h0&t=2420s. Accessed 29th December 2024.

2 The biggest prize pool for *League of Legends* was distributed in 2018, adding up to $6,450,000. Other events, such as *DotA 2*'s The International, gathered more than $40 million in 2021. See Esports Earnings, "Largest Overall Prize Pools in Esports", n.d. Available at: https://www.esportsearnings.com/tournaments. Accessed 7 January 2025.

3 Christina Gough, "Number of Viewers of League of Legends World Championship Finals from 2016 to 2023 (in Millions)", *Statista*, 2024. Available at: https://www.statista.com/statistics/518126/league-of-legends-championship-viewers/. Accessed 29 December 2024; Esports Charts, *League of Legends*, n.d. Available at: https://escharts.com/games/lol. Accessed 29 December 2024.

4 Seth E. Jenny, Nicholas Besombes, Tom Brock, Amanda C. Cote & Tobias M. Scholz (Eds.), *Routledge Handbook of Esports*, 6–17. Oxon: Routledge, 2024.
5 Karen Collins, *Game Sound: An Introduction to the History, Theory, and Practice of Video Game Music and Sound Design*. Cambridge, MA: MIT Press, 2008, 111.
6 Justin Hovey & Callie A. Bjurstorm, *Esports Industry Report*. Pillsbury Winthrop Shaw Pittman LLP, 2023. Available at: https://www.pillsburylaw.com/a/web/144736/Esports-Report-FINAL.pdf. Accessed 30 December 2024.
7 Mark Prensky, "Digital Natives, Digital Immigrants Part 1", *On the Horizon*, 2001, 9(5), 1–5; Mark Prensky, "Digital Natives, Digital Immigrants Part 2: Do They Really Think Differently?", *On the Horizon*, 2001, 9(6), 1–6.
8 Nepomuk Nothelfer, Seth E. Jenny & Nicolas Besombes, "Defining and Spelling Esports", in Seth E. Jenny, Nicholas Besombes, Tom Brock, Amanda C. Cote & Tobias M. Scholz (Eds.), *Routledge Handbook of Esports*, 6–17. Oxon: Routledge, 2024.
9 Juan Sebastián Díaz Gasca, "Music Beyond Gameplay: Motivators in the Consumption of Videogame Soundtracks" (Doctoral Thesis, Griffith University, 2015). Available at: https://research-repository.griffith.edu.au/bitstream/handle/10072/367483/Diaz%20Gasca_2015_02Thesis.pdf?sequence=1. Accessed 15 November 2023.
10 Campaign Experience Awards, "Arcane Netflix Global Experiential Launch", 2021. Available at: https://www.campaignexperienceawards.com/finalists/arcane-netflix-global-experiential-launch-d0004. Accessed 30 December 2024.
11 Eulalia Febrer-Coll, "'Everybody Wants to Be My Enemy': Música popular y transmedialidad en *Arcane*", *SeriArte. Revista científica de series televisivas y arte audiovisual*, 2023, 4, 68–86.
12 Yaewon Jin & Tae-Jin Yoon, "Convergence of Music and Esports", in Dal Yong Jin (ed.), *Global Esports: Transformation of Cultural Perceptions of Competitive Gaming*, 184–200. New York: Bloomsbury, 2021.
13 Andra Ivănescu, "Pop Music, Economics, and Marketing", in Melanie Fritsch & Tim Summers (Eds.), *The Cambridge Companion to Video Game Music*, 395–408. Cambridge: Cambridge University Press, 2021.
14 Jenny, Besombes, Brock, Cote & Scholz (Eds.), *Routledge Handbook of Esports*.
15 Nothelfer, Jenny & Besombes, "Defining and Spelling Esports."
16 Henry Jenkins, *Convergence Culture: Where Old and New Media Collide*. New York: New York University Press, 2006, 96.
17 Nicholas Besombes, "Esports Ecosystem and Landscape", *Medium*, 2019. Available at: https://medium.com/@nicolas.besombes/esports-ecosystem-and-landscape-3dbbd653dc2c. Accessed 30th December 2024.
18 José Agustín Carrillo Vera and Marcos Antón, "Esports Ecosystems and Stakeholders", in Seth E. Jenny, Nicholas Besombes, Tom Brock, Amanda C. Cote & Tobias M. Scholz (Eds.), *Routledge Handbook of Esports*, 30–40. Oxon: Routledge, 2024.
19 Henry Jenkins, *Fans, Bloggers, and Gamers: Exploring Participatory Culture*. New York: New York University Press, 1997.
20 Carlos Alberto Scolari, "Transmedia Storytelling: Implicit Consumers, Narrative Worlds, and Branding", *International Journal of Communication*, 2009, 3, 586–606.
21 Simon Frith, "The Popular Music Industry", in Simon Frith, Will Straw & John Street (Eds.), *The Cambridge Companion to Pop and Rock*, 26–52. New York: Cambridge University Press, 2001, 27.
22 Ian Cross, "Music in the Digital Age: Commodity, Community, Communion", *AI & Society*, 2023, 38, 2387–2400.
23 As understood by Jenkins in *Convergence Culture*.
24 Sensor Tower, *State of Mobile Gaming 2024: Market Milestones, Emerging Trends, and Exclusive Insights*, 2024. Available at: https://sensortower.com/state-of-mobile-gaming-2024. Accessed 5th January 2025.

25 Michiel Kamp, "Autoethnography, Phenomenology, and Hermeneutics", in Melanie Fritsch & Tim Summers (Eds.), *The Cambridge Companion to Video Game Music,* 159–175. Cambridge: Cambridge University Press, 2001, 168.
26 Karen Collins, *Game Sound: An Introduction to the History, Theory, and Practice of Video Game Music and Sound Design.* Cambridge, MA and London: MIT Press, 2008, 123.
27 Tim Summers, *Understanding Video Game Music.* Cambridge: Cambridge University Press, 2016, 88.
28 Henry Jenkins, *Convergence Culture.*
29 Shara Rambarran, ""Feel Good" with Gorillaz and "Reject False Icons": The Fantasy Worlds of the Virtual Group and Their Creators", in Sheila Whiteley & Shara Rambarran (Eds.), *The Oxford Handbook of Music and Virtuality,* 148–166. New York: Oxford University Press, 2016.
30 Gordon Calleja, "Immersion in Virtual Worlds", in Mark Grimshaw-Agaard (Ed.), *Oxford Handbook of Virtuality*, 222–236. New York: Oxford University Press, 2014.
31 Karina Moritzen, "Abrindo Moshpits Virtuais: Cenas Musicais e Shows ao vivo em Fortnite e Minecraft", *Journal of Sound and Music in Games,* 2022, 3(2–3), 115–140.
32 Jenkins, *Convergence Culture*; Henry Jenkins, *Textual Poachers: Television Fans & Participatory Culture.* New York: Routledge, 1992; Josh Jarrett, "Esports Fandom", in Seth E. Jenny, Nicolas Besombes, Tom Brock, Amanda C. Cote & Tobias M. Scholz (Eds.), *Routledge Handbook of Esports*, 426–435. Oxon: Routledge, 2024, 427.

REFERENCES

Besombes, Nicholas. "Esports Ecosystem and Landscape", *Medium*, 2019. Available at: https://medium.com/@nicolas.besombes/esports-ecosystem-and-landscape-3dbbd653dc2c. Accessed 30th December 2024.

Calleja, Gordon. "Immersion in Virtual Worlds", in Mark Grimshaw-Agaard (Ed.), *Oxford Handbook of Virtuality*, 222–236. New York: Oxford University Press, 2014.

Campaign Experience Awards. "Arcane Netflix Global Experiential Launch", 2021. Available at: https://www.campaignexperienceawards.com/finalists/arcane-netflix-global-experiential-launch-d0004. Accessed 30th December 2024.

Carrillo Vera, José Agustín & Antón, Marcos. "Esports Ecosystems and Stakeholders", in Seth E. Jenny, Nicholas Besombes, Tom Brock, Amanda C. Cote & Tobias M. Scholz (Eds.), *Routledge Handbook of Esports*, 30–40. Oxon: Routledge, 2024.

Collins, Karen. *Game Sound: An Introduction to the History, Theory, and Practice of Video Game Music and Sound Design.* Cambridge, MA: MIT Press, 2008.

Cross, Ian. "Music in the Digital Age: Commodity, Community, Communion", *AI & Society,* 2023, 38, 2387–2400.

Díaz Gasca, Juan Sebastián. "Music Beyond Gameplay: Motivators in the Consumption of Videogame Soundtracks" (Doctoral Thesis, Griffith University, 2015). Available at: https://research-repository.griffith.edu.au/bitstream/handle/10072/367483/Diaz%20Gasca_2015_02Thesis.pdf?sequence=1. Accessed 15th November 2023.

Esports Charts. *League of Legends*, n.d. Available at: https://escharts.com/games/lol. Accessed 29th December 2024.

Esports Earnings. "Largest Overall Prize Pools in Esports", n.d. Available at: https://www.esportsearnings.com/tournaments. Accessed 7th January 2025.

Febrer-Coll, Eulalia. "'Everybody Wants to Be My Enemy': Música popular y transmedialidad en *Arcane*", *SeriArte. Revista científica de series televisivas y arte audiovisual*, 2023, 4, 68–86.

Frith, Simon. "The Popular Music Industry", in Simon Frith, Will Straw & John Street (Eds.), *The Cambridge Companion to Pop and Rock*, 26–52. New York: Cambridge University Press, 2001.

Gough, Christina. "Number of Viewers of League of Legends World Championship Finals from 2016 to 2023 (in Millions)", *Statista*, 2024. Available at: https://www.statista.com/statistics/518126/league-of-legends-championship-viewers/. Accessed 29th December 2024.

Hovey, Justin & Bjurstorm, Callie A. *Esports Industry Report*. Pillsbury Winthrop Shaw Pittman LLP, 2023. Available at: https://www.pillsburylaw.com/a/web/144736/Esports-Report-FINAL.pdf. Accessed 30th December 2024.

Ivănescu, Andra. "Pop Music, Economics, and Marketing", in Melanie Fritsch & Tim Summers (Eds.), *The Cambridge Companion to Video Game Music*, 395–408. Cambridge: Cambridge University Press, 2021.

Jarrett, Josh. "Esports Fandom", in Seth E. Jenny, Nicolas Besombes, Tom Brock, Amanda C. Cote & Tobias M. Scholz (Eds.), *Routledge Handbook of Esports*, 426–435. Oxon: Routledge, 2024.

Jenkins, Henry. *Convergence Culture: Where Old and New Media Collide*. New York: New York University Press, 2006.

Jenkins, Henry. *Fans, Bloggers, and Gamers: Exploring Participatory Culture*. New York: New York University Press, 1997.

Jenny, Seth E., Besombes, Nicholas, Brock, Tom, Cote, Amanda C. & Scholz, Tobias M. (Eds.), *Routledge Handbook of Esports*. Oxon: Routledge.

Jin, Yaewon & Yoon, Tae-Jin. "Convergence of Music and Esports", in Dal Yong Jin (ed.), *Global Esports: Transformation of Cultural Perceptions of Competitive Gaming*, 184–200. New York: Bloomsbury, 2021.

Kamp, Michiel. "Autoethnography, Phenomenology, and Hermeneutics", in Melanie Fritsch & Tim Summers (Eds.), *The Cambridge Companion to Video Game Music*, 159–175. Cambridge: Cambridge University Press.

LoL Esports. "aAa vs fnatic – Grand Final Season 1 Championship", *Youtube*, 2011. Available at: https://www.youtube.com/watch?v=bMTI1kYG4h0&t=2420s. Accessed 29th December 2024.

Moritzen, Karina. "Abrindo Moshpits Virtuais: Cenas Musicais e Shows ao vivo em Fortnite e Minecraft", *Journal of Sound and Music in Games*, 2022, 3(2–3), 115–140.

Nothelfer, Nepomuk, Jenny, Seth E. & Besombes, Nicolas. "Defining and Spelling Esports", in Seth E. Jenny, Nicholas Besombes, Tom Brock, Amanda C. Cote & Tobias M. Scholz (Eds.), *Routledge Handbook of Esports*, 6–17. Oxon: Routledge, 2024.

Prensky, Mark. "Digital Natives, Digital Immigrants Part 1", *On the Horizon*, 2001, 9(5), 1–5.

Prensky, Mark. "Digital Natives, Digital Immigrants Part 2: Do They Really Think Differently?", On the Horizon, 2001, 9(6), 1–6.

Rambarran, Shara. ""Feel Good" with Gorillaz and "Reject False Icons": The Fantasy Worlds of the Virtual Group and Their Creators", in Sheila Whiteley & Shara Rambarran (Eds.), *The Oxford Handbook of Music and Virtuality*, 148–166. New York: Oxford University Press, 2016.

Scolari, Carlos Alberto. "Transmedia Storytelling: Implicit Consumers, Narrative Worlds, and Branding", *International Journal of Communication*, 2009, 3, 586–606.

Sensor Tower, *State of Mobile Gaming 2024: Market Milestones, Emerging Trends, and Exclusive Insights*, 2024. Available at: https://sensortower.com/state-of-mobile-gaming-2024. Accessed 5th January 2025.

Summers, Tim. *Understanding Video Game Music*. Cambridge: Cambridge University Press, 2016.

In-Game Music and Sound

1

The sonic identity of each game in the esports panorama is first established by the music present in the title itself, its intrinsic characteristics, and the ways in which the developers dialogue with the music industry. It is not the same talking about a shooter that does not count with a musical thread during the unfolding of a match, but includes brief musical inputs (like *Call of Duty*), as talking about a game that includes a variety of music packages to choose from (like *DotA 2*) to accompany each complete game. For this reason, it is only pertinent to make a first stop to discuss the music that plays in some of the main titles in the current esports landscape, as well as to briefly consider the ways in which each of these cases creates a reference for further intersection with the music industry in competitive contexts.

As ludomusicologists have discussed in the past, soundtracks in video games can be approached from different perspectives that include not only the strictly musical, but also sociocultural and economic aspects that determine their popularization. This has been noted regarding video game soundtrack consumption, and is worth underlining for a closer understanding of the layers that coexist and scaffold the success of music-related products in esports environments. In his doctoral thesis, Díaz Gasca[1] suggested a tripartite model for the analysis of video game soundtrack prevalence and usage that included these aspects—experiential, economic, and sociocultural—which are especially pertinent for the discussion at hand.

At an experiential level, music establishes an identification with different aspects of the game, ranging from character to franchise association, as it creates a connection between the game and real-life events. This is also linked to nostalgia or the evocation of memories of experiences, in which music again takes a central role. These aspects will be referred to in the esports industry to build a sense of identity and community among players, especially in staged events, creating a binding narrative for the game. An example of this can be found in the recurrent intervention of specific bands in events linked to particular titles, such as Imagine Dragons in *League of Legends*.

At an economic level, music is commodified into a product that extends beyond the game, in what may be one of the main connecting strains between the industries under discussion. An example of this can be observed in cases such as *Rocket League*, which according to ex-music director of Psyonix, Mike Ault, serves as a platform for the discovery of new artists.[2] In this sense, music is also closely linked to marketing and branding, as it connects the game industry to specific markets with elements that represent their identity. This is shown to be true, for example, through the participation of specific artists in different games, such as Justin Bieber in *Free Fire*.

 DOI: 10.1201/9781032625362-2

Lastly, at a sociocultural level, the personal experiences obtained in the connection of music and gaming are shared by a wider audience, and can function as consumption motivators. The singularity of the music related to each title affects the interaction of users and how they circulate their *cultural capital*.[3] This would be the case of online forums dedicated to the exchange of experiences and self-made products around specific games. In this environment, participants take the role of prosumers,[4] which is key to the success of originally branded content. Furthermore, fans—gamers and non-gamers—are bound by experiences happening in shared digital spaces that create socialization opportunities beyond face-to-face events, and allow the aforementioned dynamics to take motion.

These three dimensions are interconnected and will be the foundation of the discussion in this and other chapters. However, the level at which each point is present in specific esports will depend on their nature and on the strategy traced by developers and music teams in each case. In other words, the creative strategies may differ depending on the mechanics of the game itself and how specific companies conceptualize the sonic world presented through their products.

Although the connection between the video game and the esport—as in the *user-focused* versus *community* and *competition-focused* product—may present a distance music-wise, the search for continuity in their narrative implies the need for taking their original music into consideration. It will be key in understanding how the global scene functions and how the sonic identity formulated on-screen translates to off-screen contexts.

IN-GAME MUSIC FORMATS

There are different possibilities for including a soundtrack in video games, which are linked to the relationship established between the game and music. On a broad level, there are two main approaches to deciding how music is treated: as original soundtracks (OSTs) or as licensed contributions. However, these options need to be further nuanced as soon as specific cases come into discussion and according to each developer's vision for the role that music plays in relation to their product.

With regards to OSTs, we may underline existing work discussing in-game music, such as Collins' *Game Sound*[5] or Summer's *Understanding Video Game Music*,[6] which extensively detail the gears behind the implementation of music and sound. They do not only describe how music is used and inserted in video games, but also address examples from different moments in time, which provide a closer understanding of how music has been both technology-dependent and defining for the gaming industry.

The strategies defined in such volumes can be applied to video games in the realm of esports, specifically when discussing games that include music as a scaffolding element. However, to this day, it is not usual to find esports games that are completely oblivious to popular music influences, especially when they step into the competitive arena. Furthermore, the inclusion of OSTs does not necessarily imply that there is a single music narrative available to each game. Cases such as *DotA 2* are paradigmatic in this sense, as they allow players to select different originally composed *music packages* to accompany their matches.[7]

At the other end of the spectrum, titles that do not include OSTs but licensed music, usually resort to popular music artists to voice their products. A good example of this would be *FIFA* (now *EA Sports FC*), or other games outside of esports, such as *Tony Hawk's Pro Skater*. The introduction of external soundtracks implies a direct mediation of different agents, such as copyrighters, which can be seen as partly responsible for defining the trends and curating the sonic identities of specific games. This is not to say that originally produced soundtracks cannot be definitory at a game level, but that each case builds its own musical identity toward a unique *trade sound*.

Music licensing can also involve different approaches depending on the artist profiles chosen for a game, their variety, or the existence of intermediary companies—curators, talent managers, etc. That is, depending on the artists selected for participation in a game and their preexisting position in the music industry, the strategy followed by developers may imply different levels of contractual specificity. In this way, curating playlists for specific games also contributes to establishing the sonic image and identity of different titles.

Of course, these strategies are not new to the market. The inclusion of popular music artists in games has been discussed in the past by authors such as Gibbons in *Unlimited Replays*,[8] who also pinpoints how the use of pop songs presents challenges such as the need for adapting the songs to the dynamics of the non-linearity of video games. A similar idea regarding music selection applies to the choice of originally composed soundtracks, which are frequently reliant on budget and available technology. Outside of the esports environment, an example of this could be *Limbo*—an indie game mainly composed on electronic samples by Martin Stig Andersen—versus a triple-A such as *God of War*—which includes a full orchestral score and the intervention of film composer Bear McCreary.

Thus, all games are founded on a continuous dialogue between cultural, technological, and marketing agents, which helps establish gaming and music-listening experiences. As we move forward in the 21st century, transmediality is taking a growing role, creating more fluid connections among different markets. This starts with the inclusion of well-known musicians, composers, and performers on the credit lists of popular games. The interconnection between different media will be further discussed in upcoming chapters.

IN-GAME MUSIC PLACEMENT

Once the diverse ways of introducing soundtracks in games have been established, we may underline other sonic elements that are part of their soundscape and frequently connected to the music industry—more so than in other cases outside of esports. These events include *earcons*,[9] lobby music, radio stations, and other in-game diegetic sounds, character-associated in-game music and sounds, or dances.

While some of these elements align with a licensing approach—e.g., radio stations—others require trademarking for originally composed sounds—e.g., earcons. On the one hand, popular music can be introduced in video games to create a crossroads for promoting both the reproduced artist and the game itself. On the other hand, the growing dialogue between music and gaming, as well as with social media, opens spaces that afford marketing opportunities for non-music-related industries.

In line with such possibilities, regulations regarding music have extended toward *sound marks*, which have been delineated by entities such as the European Union Intellectual Property Office[10] or the United States Patent and Trademark Office.[11]

Earcons are the more obvious form of sound mark, as they associate a sound—usually a short, timed sound—with a product, in this case, virtual in origin. Such sounds, created exclusively for video games, serve a different purpose than background music or sync placements, and continue to allow users to identify them with the specific video games. Differently from auditory icons, which also represent signals for in-game events, earcons can be musical in origin. Medina-Gray specifies:

> The naturalistic sounds of auditory icons do not typically suggest themselves as musical, while the pitched and/or rhythmic content of earcons cast these sounds as at least semi-musical from the start; unlike auditory icons, earcons are poised to extend across the boundary into music, if a game's context allows them to do so.[12]

Character-associated music and sounds fall under a similar category, as they may be represented through these means rather than story-developing leitmotivs, which are usually inserted in the OST. These sounds range from the brief casting of character-specific spells—like in *Valorant*—to character selection—like in *Street Fighter*. That is, while taking into consideration possible added divergences from originally composed to licensed music.

Furthermore, character-associated sounds include those related to specific character performances in the games, like dance movements. Although *Fortnite* has been specially acknowledged for the use of this feature, games such as *League of Legends* also include dance movements that imply associated sounds. They imply them as there is no specific music attached to the gesture, but in their reminiscence of popular culture are made easily recognizable—e.g., character Twisted Fate's reproduction of *Gangnam Style* routine, by PSY.[13]

These dance cues are different from those in games that revolve around music, such as *Dance Dance Revolution* or *Beat Saber*. Although they are directly related to licensed music, their mechanics depend on choreographing or moving to popular songs, and as such, they constitute the sonic core of the title.

On another note, lobby music is found during character-selection or map-selection screens, as well as around waiting spaces before a match begins. Although we can, again, encounter both originally composed and licensed music, it is frequent for different titles to use their lobby spaces for the promotion of themes, artists, or events—e.g., *EA Sports FC*. In some instances, as in the aforementioned *Street Fighter*, these spaces may also coincide with the introduction of character-identifying music. Nevertheless, there are occasions in which in-game sound is specifically tailored for popular music marketing, and as such the selected tracks are not tradeable for originally composed scores. That would be the case of radio stations and other in-game diegetic sounds—e.g., public chants in sports games.

Radio stations are especially relevant, as they offer a diegetic resource that helps blur the fourth wall that separates what happens on-screen from the real life of each user, stepping into what Rambarran, quoting Baudrillard,[14] refers to as *hyperrealism*.[15] The introduction of artists through these broadcasting means may be approached from different standpoints that range from the inclusion of well-known music performers to emerging artists. An iconic case including radio stations is that of *Fortnite*, which during its partnership with Bandcamp offered a channel for the promotion of emerging artists on the music platform.[16]

Finally, it is worth noting how music may change according to the platform on which a game is played. For instance, mobile games are frequently tailored to include shorter pieces to develop with more agile matches and smaller screens. Although music placement may not change per se, platforms require adaptation for specific music introductions and may benefit from stepping aside from main titles. This is especially noticeable in the analysis of games that are present in different geographies, when linked both to territorial restrictions and user preference regarding artists—or even genres.[17] [18]

ESPORT GENRES AND THE MUSIC INDUSTRY

Although there is not only one way to study the wide spectrum of games included under the *esports* label, and as their different nature may require diverse approaches, I suggest a tentative categorization that allows an analysis of the specific strategies regarding music and sound treatment. These include—although are not restricted to—MOBAs, shooters, sports games, fighting games, and card games.[19] The classification is similar to that provided by Russell Hamer and Nicolas Besomes in the *Routledge Handbook of Esports*, which also considers additional groups like niche genres, and separates others into different categories—e.g., motion-based games are included as a niche category, and others are defined as strategy games.[20] Nevertheless, for the specific scope of this book, the categories have been rearranged as follows.

Multiplayer Online Battle Arena games (MOBAs) include games with multiple simultaneous players, who are usually grouped in teams that must face each other on a preset map. To this category belong games such as *League of Legends* or *DotA 2*.

Shooters cover games whose dynamics depend on eliminating enemies through the use of different weapons, especially firearms. These include tactical first-person shooters (FPS) such as *Counter-Strike,* as well as Battle Royale games such as *Fortnite* or *Free Fire*.

Sports games feature traditional sports such as football, basketball, or dancing, but are not limited to real-life simulators like *EA Sports FC* or *NB2K*, as they also encompass titles such as *Rocket League* or *Dance Dance Revolution*.

Fighting Games such as *Street Fighter* or *Tekken*, although sportive, count with specific dynamics that define them as their own genre. In these games, two characters face each other in several-round combats, during which they use special abilities.

Card Games are strategic games played on virtual boards, which present animations to represent each card's characteristics. These usually count with associated costs and parameters that need to be taken into consideration. Titles in this category include *Hearthstone* and *Legends of Runeterra*.

With this partition, the sound morphology of each group can be linked to Maldonado Parrales' *ring system*.[21] This system creates a comparative model for analyzing the sonic characteristics of different titles through concentric circles. In the center of these circumferences lies the "interaction based on the character's actions,"[22] which is surrounded by further layers that, in order, include listening intent, free interaction, spatial positioning, and sound particles from other players.

The author uses this model to contrast how music is placed in three different games, each belonging to one of the categories here established: *Call of Duty: Warzone* (shooter), *League of Legends* (MOBA), and *Fall Guys* (sports game). He then refers to the presence of the quoted concentric circles in each case, as follows:

These are, however, only a few examples. The strong dependence of the game genre to define its associated music was already noticed by Collins in 2008 when stating that "it helps to set the audience's expectations by providing a framework for understanding the rules of gameplay."[23] The author underlined the relevance of sound in early arcades, and how the model that was created was progressively extrapolated toward later games. We can still point this to be true as esports are, first and foremost, video games, and as such rely on the conventions established for each genre.

Thus, the idiosyncrasies passed on from early consoles have been defining for the music and sound design of competitive video games, despite their ecosystem moving beyond what happens on-screen to encompass transmedia scenarios. These afford the consumption and commercialization of title-related products beyond videoludic content, which extend the potential market apart from the gamer public. Although this can be said to be true for non-competitive video games too, OSTs in esports games are not usually built to create an hours-long narrative—e.g., in the case of adventure or horror games. As such, related products tend to fall beyond the game itself rather than in continuation of its specific soundtracks, making music a tool to scaffold game spaces. An example of non-esports video games that include music products and collaborations is the *Pokémon* saga, which exemplifies how the gaming and music industries are growing toward ubiquitous collaborations at a wider level—e.g., in the 25th-anniversary album, *Pokémon 25: The Album*, released in 2021, which features songs by Katy Perry, J Balvin, and other pop artists.[24]

The commodification of music and music-related products in video games creates alternative commercial routes for developers and publishers, as well as for record labels, to dialogue with their audiences. This is fundamentally sustained by the growing

Call of Duty: Warzone is described by its realistic aesthetic and, as such, interacts with sound at all concentric levels. The player is placed on a field that reproduces real-life environments, including no music narrative but ambiance sounds. The character can move freely in the preset map, interact with its materials and with other players. Thus, listening intent relates to free interaction and spatial positioning, as well as to the sound particles left by other players.

League of Legends does not count with a fully interactive environment, nor is it constructed to mimic real-life environments. Although the focus is put on spatial location on the map, play is not as dependent on sound particles emitted by other players. Each match is default accompanied by an originally composed soundtrack, and spatial positioning is mainly achieved through earcons.

Fall Guys can be assimilated into a sports game, as although it is not a simulation game it revolves around racing. In this case, each map is set with no free interaction or spatial positioning-related sounds, as these are not necessary to pursue the game's objective. Nevertheless, sound particles from other players are useful to gain sense of one's position along the race.

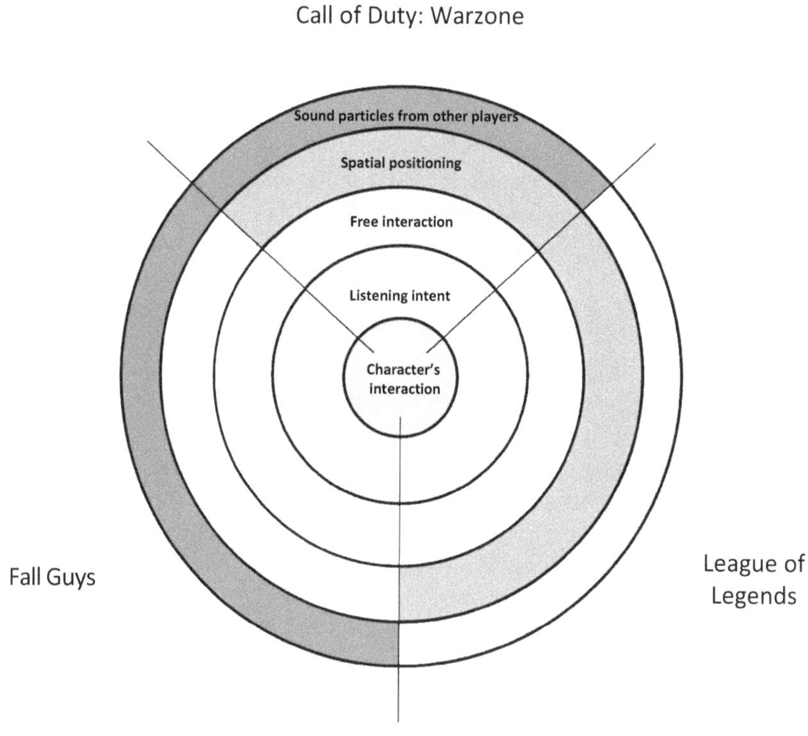

FIGURE 1.1 *Ring system* analysis, based on Maldonado Parrales (2020).

relevance of social media and its role in democratizing popular culture—or, at least, in giving the perception of user decision-making—which also serves the amplification of a potential public.

As highlighted by Díaz Gasca, "commercial tie-ins between video game publishers and the music industry are also a reflection of their practices and how the game will fit with the intended audience."[25] This has to do with the overlapping of the music industry networks described by Leyshon as a *value network*[26] with those of the video game industry.

According to Leyshon, there are four consecutive conglomerates that encompass the whole creation-to-consumption process in the music case: the network of creativity—where music is created and produced—the network of reproduction—in which licensing and the manufacturing of copies take place—the network of distribution—that serves as a link to the last point—and the network of consumption—referred to listening, reading, and overall purchasing. A similar network chain mirrors this building process in the video game industry, adding to the overlapping of stakeholders and co-occurring processes that Leyshon originally presented.

In this whole value chain, the music artist requires specific attention. Álvarez Vazquez[27] places this figure as a cornerstone of the traditional value chain in the music industry—that he constructs in reference to Leyshon.[28]

Although artists have played a crucial role in promoting their brands in the traditional chain, their growing presence on social media—and in the given illusion of non-mediation—makes it necessary to underline their key role in connecting with their audiences. This creates a three-way relationship that solidifies the pillars of the relationship among industries.

Nevertheless, the relationship between video game publishers and the music industry is foremost reliant on the genre and overall characteristics of each game, as previously discussed. Decisions taken in regard to the sonic identity of each title will be key to the agreements pursued for the benefit of both parties.

These relations do not occur in isolation to the dynamics of user social interaction, and thus the direct or indirect participation of the audience is essential in shaping a product to be successful. On the other hand, these stakeholders relate to the artists and their role in dynamizing live and virtual scenarios, not only at a product placement level

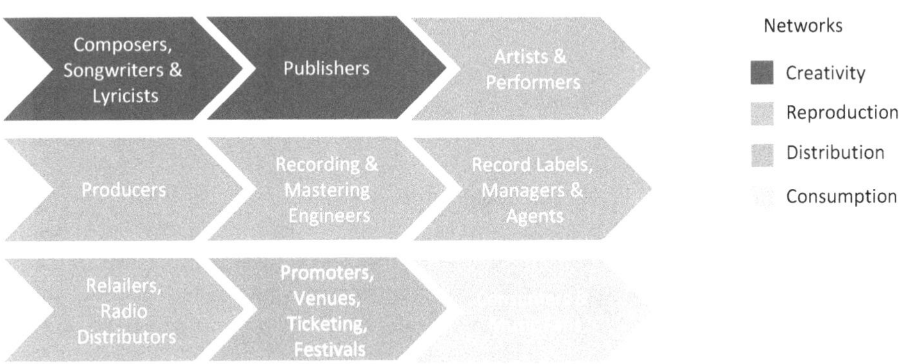

FIGURE 1.2 Chain value of the music industry, as proposed by Álvarez Vázquez (2017).

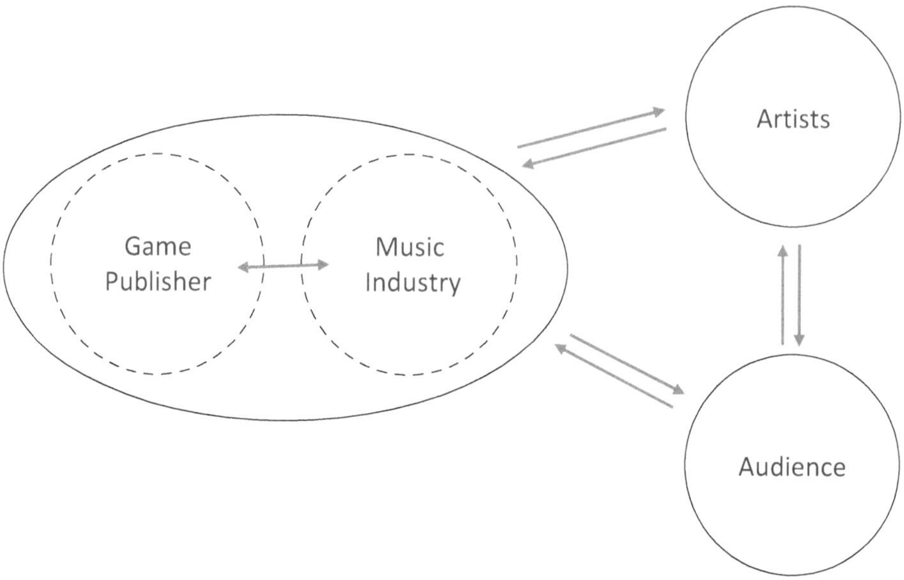

FIGURE 1.3 Industries—Artists—Audience Relationship.

but also in regard to their relation to fans. In this sense, we may find in popular artists a binding figure that articulates a three-way dialogue.

Specific examples must be used to analyze the embodiment of these associations, as the particular cases ground the suggested model.

MOBAs

MOBAs are especially known in the esports scene through two titles: *League of Legends* and *DotA 2*. Although both games are based on similar mechanics, as do other games such as *Vainglory*, their approach to the inclusion of music differs in several aspects, especially regarding user participation in the building of the music tracks included in the game. Nevertheless, both count with a default OST to go with their main maps.

From the very beginning, each map in *League of Legends* included its own OST, in pursuance of goals such as accompanying in-game action or setting the mood for its players. This is also true for lobbies and character selection, which count with their own themes, and can change in adaptation to new seasons and patches.

On *The Summoner's Rift*, the main map of the game, the music has been modified on different occasions to provide what can be read as an improved gaming experience, as the musical development evolves along the three main stages of each match. From 2015, the main track of the map has been presented through a tripartite adaptative structure that helps narrate match progress. That is, the piece counts with three main parts that are looped and transitioned depending on the obstacles being exceeded, through adaptative means.

These game stages include early, mid, and late-game music. When briefly analyzed, these seem to accompany the match and progressive accumulated tension: *Early-game* music, from the beginning of the game, plays from the start until the destruction of the first two turrets. When the track starts, the instruments that are going to define the sonority of the piece make an appearance, and the melodic lines that will carry the music narrative start unfolding. *Mid* or the middle of the game starts playing when two to seven turrets have been destroyed. During this stage, the meter increases, melodies are clearly delineated, and more layers of instrumentation are progressively included. Finally, when seven turrets or more have been destroyed, the music shifts toward *late-game*, or end of the game, melodies and drumming are taken to the foreground, and meter increases slightly. Lastly, when a team reaches victory or defeat, the player is shown a specific theme to go with the match's outcome.

Since its release, the game has included different maps and modes with their own music, some of which have been discontinued—e.g., *The Twister Treeline* or *Dominion*. Others, such as *The Howling Abyss*, are maintained and have a similarly produced OST, on which further transversal sounds, including character-specific music, are superimposed.

A complementary mode with growing popularity since its release in 2019 has been *Teamfight Tactics*: a game with a virtual board that mimics chess, which features the characters from *League of Legends*—with their respective abilities—as pieces. Although the mode included original music from the start, in 2023, the game showed its adaptability when featuring a special patch built around the musical products of Riot Games—namely their bands, such as K/DA or True Damage. The different compositions that can be created through the characters on the board, depending on their characteristics, adapted to different genres that mimicked the band or style that they referred to. For instance, when the player selected all character components of K/DA and placed them on the board, the soundtrack changed toward a K-pop style.

One of the features of the game, specifically on *The Summoners' Rift*, is brought precisely by different characters, which, when played, apply modifications to the base soundtrack—from character-specific earcons to the whole background. Nevertheless, each match follows a musical sequence that progressively increases in intensity, adapting to the progress of the game, superposing melodic and instrumental elements on a continuous underlying orchestral base, which sustains the entire track from beginning to end. With this strategy, the music in the game develops almost imperceptibly for the player, while—intendedly—contributing to the creation and maintenance of a state of mind that could be labeled as a state of flow.[29]

Furthermore, *League of Legends* incorporates an in-game feature which, as earlier mentioned, does not specifically *sound*: character dances. Each character or *champion* can perform a dance while a match is ongoing, which can be used for different purposes, from taunting to dawdling. These indirectly relate to music as some of the movements included for specific characters are clearly recognizable routines from popular music songs—i.e. Blitzcrank performs *La Macarena*, or Warwick dances to *Thriller*—which can be seen as early transmedia gestures in the connection with the music industry.

As stated, variations on the OST are possible, but most recurrent changes regarding music in the game occur around the lobby and character-selection screens. These pieces are composed by Riot Music Group team members such as Sebastien Najand or Brendon Williams, in a collaborative process that precisely portrays each new addition "to feel like a uniquely individual experience while also being part of a whole by deepening these characters and the world they live in."[30] This point reinforces the building of a relatable musical universe and sonic identity that players can easily associate to the game.

Furthermore, the mobile version of the game, *Wild Rift*, which constitutes a *mobile esport* in itself, counts with its own soundtracks to adapt to the hand-held device idiosyncrasies. Soon after its release in 2021, Game Director Brian Feeney underlined in an interview how the gameplay for the mobile format was intended to feel like *League of Legends* while also taking the opportunity to work on elements that were hard to understand by new players, regarding the PC game.[31] This transference, we may argue, also applies to music, as the OST is created to be reminiscent of that on *League*.

A different case is that of *DotA 2* which, although it has a main OST, includes the recurrent addition of *music packages* that the player can freely select. These options include both music recurrently uploaded by Valve and that contributed by external composers who wish to create their own version to accompany the game. The video game includes a series of guidelines on *Steam* for this very purpose,[32] although copyright issues and the difficulties in assessing the originality of contributed content by unknown artists make it challenging for the company to incorporate into the game.[33]

DotA 2 counts with distinct tracks for different positions and events in the game, adaptative to the players' position and actions. Besides menu and other lobby music, guidelines provided by Valve distinguish seven categories for in-game music, ranging from layered lane tracks to audio clips for each possible match outcome. Nevertheless, these can be classified into three groups: laning tracks, event tracks, and end-of-match tracks. Laning tracks encompass three superimposed musical layers, which correspond to the three main lanes of the game's map. The predominating layer appears adaptatively according to player position, although all three tracks always play simultaneously. These can also be interceded by other tracks belonging to specific events, such as battles or *kills*.

Some tracks come into play at specific times and are shorter in length. These include *Battle tracks*—which begin "when the game events drive the music intensity value higher than the Laning track values"[34]—*Roshan tracks*—which appears when the players are facing the monster Roshan—*Smoke tracks*—when a specific item is used in-game—*Gank Stringers*—when a hero is ambushed by enemies—and *Killed tracks*—when a player has died. Lastly, the tracks that end the game take different directions according to the outcome and the side of the player's team started, including four different short tracks: radiant win, radiant lose, dire win, and dire lose.

Like in *League of Legends*, game characters count with dances or similar movements to taunt enemies—or just have fun—although, in this case, they are illustrated sonically. These brief *emotes* include short sounds—e.g., Spirit Breaker's donkey sounds—as well as music fragments accompanied by dance movements—e.g., Jakiro with *The Blue Danube* by Richard Strauss, or Flopper with Tchaikovsky's *Nutcracker*.

Aside from main OSTs, the music included in both games features earcons and character-specific musical interventions that contribute to the soundscape of each title. These can act as character-identifying sounds that inform players about specific events from an auditory—and not only visual—perspective, and are non-modifiable. For instance, specific objects can cast easily recognizable sounds when activated, making it easier for both team's members react accordingly. Specific abilities from champions work similarly, as some can be heard all over the map when cast, aiding in the recognition of the actions taking place.

Along these, auditory signs serve the orientation of the player in the game, and contribute a complementary communication channel—for instance, tower alert or ping sounds. Many of these have also evolved communicatively to imply meanings other than those originally intended for the developers. For instance, in *League of Legends*, when using the *missing enemy from lane* question mark sign, the player is not always signaling that an enemy is really missing, but places it on another gamer to inquire about their behavior. All these sounds contribute to the establishment of a sonic identity for each game, as well as to an intersubjectively agreed language among players, that takes a crucial role when playing competitively.

Shooters

From an in-game perspective, shooters present a widely different relationship with music, as team communication needs and the spatial location of players is central to achieving a good performance. As described earlier, shooters are defined by reproducing real-life environments—e.g., *Call of Duty* or *Counter-Strike*—although these can refer to the spatiality of sound and not necessarily to the visual aspect of the game, which may be that of a fantastic world—e.g., *Fortnite* or *Free Fire*.

Shooters usually include preset maps in which the participants can move freely and with which they can interact to a high extent. In these, movement is not only horizontal—as taking place only on a lane—but can also be vertical—as players can jump, duck, enter buildings, etc. This implies that both teammates and enemies can appear from a wider range of angles that require close attention to one's environment. As Grimshaw stated in his thesis:

> The FPS game affords the player the perception of moving around the game world. This illusion is achieved by the game code creating the game's visual environment in real-time, by (re)positioning the game's visual objects (affording the illusion of parallax), by scaling visual objects differently (affording the illusion of visual depth) and by moving sound objects around the player as she issues movement commands.[35]

Therefore, listening intent is essential to the genre, as it relates to free interaction and spatial positioning, and the superimposition of a musical soundtrack could interfere with the ability of players to attend the aural aspect of the game. The sounds that can be found in these contexts are reproductions of real-life soundscapes, including the three categories described by R. Murray Schafer: natural—such as animals or meteorological factors—human—footsteps, voices—and artificial—weapons, radios.[36] However, other musical elements in shooters help define their sonic identity, which is not placed strictly on the *playgrounds*, such as lobby music or radio stations. To analyze this use of music in specific games, we can refer to two examples: one from a real-life simulating shooter and one from a fantasy-world shooter.

Counter-Strike sets a good example, as it presents a realistic world both at a visual and aural level. Its default music has adapted to the taste of a growing audience through consecutive updates, and specifically since stepping into the *esports* context. Differently from earlier versions, the OST released in 2023 for *Counter-Strike 2* includes electronic music on top of an orchestral base that defined previous versions, bringing a *sports* feel to the title, especially as associated with competitive settings. Mike Morasky, the main composer for the game, points out how "over time we also sort of invested more in Counter-Strike as an esport and less of a shooter. When I approached the new [*Counter-Strike*] we still wanted it to be aspirational, but the goal (...) was to really push the sports component."[37]

Nevertheless, since 2014, *Counter-Strike* has had music kits that can be installed to replace the OST of the game. These kits include music for specific moments in which in-game action is not central—i.e. main menu—or brief musical cues to signal specific events—i.e., won or lost round. Different artists have contributed to these soundtracks, although it is usual for players to disable all queues and only leave ambiance sounds—a fact of which composers are well aware (Table 1.1).

All music kits in the game must be purchased, which creates a complementary market and source of income for both the developers and the artists, as well as a form of engagement with the game for its audience. These packages have furthermore seen a change in their perspective since 2022, when Valve started working on the transition from *Counter-Strike: Global Offensive* to *Counter-Strike 2*. From the *Initiators Music Kit Box* forward, the strategy has leaned toward popular music artists more than video game composers in the creation of kits, as it had been in the past.[39]

Regarding less visually realistic FPS games, some popular titles include *Valorant*, by Riot Games, *Free Fire*, by Garena, or *Fortnite*, developed by Epic Games. These create alternative universes in which characters count with special abilities to complement their weaponry, or features, such as structure building for defensive and strategic purposes.

Fortnite has been celebrated for its music characteristics that comprehend from character dances to radio stations, and extend to modes such as *Fortnite Creative*—designed for a freer use of Epic's metaverse. Differently from *Counter-Strike*, this game launched once esports were already being positioned as a worldwide phenomenon and coexisted with transmedia strategies with the popular music industry since early on. That is not to say that the game does not count with OSTs to frame its own products, but that these closely coexist with licensed music.

If we take the game in its main *Battle Royale* mode and momentarily disregard complementary music products—e.g., in-game events or music videos—several points still need underlining. The player needs to hear their surroundings and obtain a good sense of orientation from sound alone to succeed in the game, whose goal is to be the last player standing.

Firstly, the main point for presenting the user with music is the game's lobby, which can be personalized, mainly through the obtention *battle passes*. This kind of passes were first presented in *DotA 2* in 2013, and the idea was later acquired by Epic Games and Valve,[40] among others, which have popularized them as players use them to display status in and outside of the game. In *Fortnite*, lobby music can be changed manually or put on shuffle, but it must first be purchased or acquired through in-game achievements. With each battle pass, the player can obtain different characters or *skins* as they level

TABLE 1.1 Counter-Strike: Global Offensive Music Kits[38]

YEAR OF RELEASE	*MUSIC KITS*	*TOTAL*
2014	Austin Wintory, *Desert Fire* Daniel Sadowski, *Crimson Assault* Dren, *Death's Head Demolition* Feed Me, *High Noon* Midnight Riders, *All I Want for Christmas* Noisia, *Sharpened* Robert Allaire, *Insurgency* Sasha, *LNOE* Sean Murray, *A*D*8* Skog, *Metal* Valve, *CS GO*	11
2015	AWOLNATION, *I Am* Beartooth, *Disgusting* Damjan Mravunac, *The Talos Principle* Daniel Sadowski, *Total Domination* Daniel Sadowski, *The 8-Bit Kit* Darude, *Moments CSGO* Ian Hultquist, *Lion's Mouth* Kelly Bailey, *Hazardous Environments* Ki:Theory, *MOLOTOV* Lennie Moore, *Java Havana Funkaloo* Mateo Messina, *For No Mankind* Matt Lange, *IsoRhythm* Michael Bross, *Invasion!* Mord Fustang, *Diamonds* New Beat Fund, *Sponge Fingerz* Proxy, *Battlepack* Skog, *II-Headshot* Troels Folmann, *Uber Blasto Phone* Various Artists, *Hotline Miami*	19
2016	StatTrak™ Radicals Box: Beartooth, *Aggressive* Blitz Kids, *The Good Youth* Hundredth, *FREE* Neck Deep, *Life's Not Out To Get You* Roam, *Backbone* Skog, *III-Arena* Twin Atlantic, *GLA*	7
2019	Halo, The Master *Chief Collection* Scarlxrd, King, *Scar* The Verkkars, *EZ4ENCE*	3

Continued

TABLE 1.1 Continued

YEAR OF RELEASE	*MUSIC KITS*	*TOTAL*
2020	Amon Tobin, *All for Dust* Darren Korb, *Hades Music Kit* Half-Life: Alyx, *Anti-Citizen* Masterminds Music Kit Box: Austin Wintory, *Bachram* Daniel Sadowski, *Eye of the Dragon* Dren, *Gunman Taco Truck* Matt Levine, *Drifter* Sam Marshall, *Bodacious* Tim Huling, Neo Noir Tree Adams and Ben Bromfield, *M.U.D.D. FORCE*	10
2021	Neck Deep, *The Lowlife Pack* Scarlxrd, *CHAIN$AW.LXADXUT.* bbno$, *u mad!* The Verkkars & nothing, *Flashbang Dance* Tacticians Music Kit Box: Austin Wintory, *Mocha Petal* Chipzel, *~Yellow Magic~* Freaky DNA, *Vici* Laura Shigihara, Work Hard, *Play Hard* Jesse Harlin, *Astro Bellum* Sarah Schachner, *KOLIBRI*	10
2022	Music Kit/Perfect World, *花脸 Hua Lian (Painted Face)* Initiators Music Kit Box: 3kliksphilip, *Heading for the Source* Humanity's Last Breath, *Void* Juelz, *Shooters* Knock2, *dashstar** Meechy Darko, *Gothic Luxury* Sullivan King, *Lock Me Up*	7
2023	Denzel Curry, *ULTIMATE*	1
2024	NIGTHMODE TWERL and Ekko & Sidetrack, *Under Bright Lights* Rad Cat, *Reason* Dryden, *Feel the Power* Kill Script, *All Night* ISOxo, *inhuman* Knock2, *Make U SWEAT!*	6
Total		**74**

up, which may come with associated music and other cosmetic objects to be equipped. At the end of 2023, there were nearly 200 songs that had been made available for the game's lobby, most of them including urban styles—from hip-hop to rock or EDM. Since these are not directly linked to specific artists, they constitute originally composed soundtracks for the game. Where the music—and overall audiovisual—industry

TABLE 1.2 Radio Stations in Fortnite

RADIO STATION	*GENRE*	*YEAR*
Beat Box	Rap, reggaeton, and R&B	2020
Icon Radio	Various genres, classics	2022
Party Royale	Fortnite originals	2020
Power Play	Pop	2020
Radio Underground	Alternative and grunge	
Radio Yonder	EDM and dubstep	2021
Rock & Royale	Rock	2020

came to intersect with the game through licensing was, firstly, through the celebrated in-game dances.

Fortnite dances are considered *emotes*, as they constitute short actions that can be performed by a character for communicative and recreative purposes, although they are purely cosmetic items. They were first introduced in September 2017, and have been a distinctive feature since. Many of them take reference in popular culture and, more precisely, from choreographed popular music songs—i.e. *Blinding Lights* by The Weekend, or *Never Gonna Give You Up* by Rick Astley—while others propose imagined movements to world music—such as the *Capoeira* or *Gwan Yu's Sword Dance* emotes—to quote a few examples. These work similarly to the priorly mentioned dances, including music accompanying them, making them brief *earcons* of sorts. Further auditory signs are introduced in the game, to the imaginary environment in which the player is placed, such as trunks. These emit a specific sound when the user approaches them, making them easily accessible and retrieving objects to gain advantages in the game.

More essentially for the topic at hand, radio stations established a cornerstone for the collaborations between Epic and the wider music industry. Radio stations were introduced in the game in 2020, bringing a new element to the game as they allowed players to listen to a multitude of tracks while playing, specifically when driving different vehicles around the island. Each radio station features a unique playlist with a mix of songs from different genres (Table 1.2).

These stations have been key to the intersection with platforms such as Bandcamp, the independent online music platform and record store, which was acquired by Epic Games in 2022.[41] While teamed up, Radio Underground was used as a channel to broadcast and promote smaller artists in a wide range of genres, creating an innovative point for unveiling non-mainstream music. As initially described by Bandcamp's CEO, Ethan Diamond:

> In Epic, we've found a partner who believes as deeply as we do that the future of music, and art itself, depends on the creation of equitable and inclusive communities like the one our fans and artists have helped to build. We're excited to work alongside the Epic team to accelerate the realization of our mission and pursue our shared goal of empowering more creators in a fair and open way.[42]

Although the music platform was later sold to Songtradr in 2023 to "make it easier for independent artists to connect with creators and developers looking to license their music and enable Epic to focus on its core metaverse, games, and tools efforts,"[43] their collaboration created a reference for engaging with smaller artists.

Other joint efforts regarding *Fortnite* radio stations have come hand in hand with Monstercat, who oversaw the playlist for Radio Yonder, which features EDM artists such as Dion Timmer, Slushii, or Pegboard Nerds. These collaborations have continued to grow with the inclusion of new play modes in the game, based on *LEGO*, *Rocket League*, and *Rock Band*. All three modes step aside from the shooter genre, although *LEGO Fortnite* is the closest to *Battle Royale* in its soundscape and use of music, as it introduces an open-world building and survival mode similar to that of *Minecraft*, which situates music on specific loading screens and not in-game.

On the one hand, *Rocket Racing*, developed by *Rocket League*'s studio Psyonix, presents an engine and other sounds aimed at bringing a realistic feel to the soundscape, which is superimposed to electronic music tracks to accompany play. The mode includes an EDM piece for the game's main lobby as well, to add on other music packages in the main game. On the other hand, *Fortnite Festival* was developed in collaboration with Harmonix, following up the success of *Rock Band*. This mode is based on the rhythm-game mechanics of its predecessors and features songs from different artists and genres, thus making it strictly reliant on licensing. The presence of the mode in the *Fortnite* universe, however, does not end up there: the *jam system* mode allows players to lay down different elements of a track inside of a circle when close together, creating a jam with other characters in which music acts adaptatively. This feature is also available in the game's whole ecosystem, such as in *Battle Royale*.[44]

Although some of these alternative modes include rankings for players as well, it is yet to be seen how they will be incorporated into competitive settings. They do, nevertheless, contribute to the expanding musical universe that Epic Games is creating around *Fortnite* and display diverse routes through which the game developers dialogue with the music industry to create a joint experience for its users.

Sports Games

Sports games form a wide category, encompassing traditional sports simulators to fantastic sports-based scenarios, including disciplines from car racing to dancing. Depending on the nature of the games and the approach to reproducing reality intended by their developers, music can take a different role and be placed in different spaces.[45] Nevertheless, it can be argued that this category is the closest in its dependence on licensing among the ones described here.

Some authors have approached sports games regarding their use of—usually licensed—music to illustrate them and create their sonic identity.[46] Nevertheless, the participation of these games in the esports international panorama is not always as notorious. For instance, games such as *Dance Dance Revolution*, although counting with world championships and regular participatory events, have not received as much attention as other titles in the Western media. On the contrary, Eastern countries like Japan have incorporated it in competitions such as the *BEMANI Pro League*[47] that also feature other games such as *Beatmania IIDX* and *Sound Voltex*.

Díaz Gasca pointed out the similarity in the development of *Dance Dance Revolution* with other titles such as *Rock Band* or *Sing Star*, as they have been "heavily influenced by their licensing agreements, and the marketing of these games also revolves around the music itself and the artists involved."[48] These agreements have, furthermore, contributed to the bidirectional promotion of the products involved: the music industry perceives royalties for the licensing of their recordings, while the gaming industry increases sales through the promotion afforded by the recordings included in their games. This is especially relevant in titles that depend on the reproduction of popular music for their main objectives, but can be nuanced for other games which do not count with this same premise.

To illustrate two different approaches to sports games, it comes in handy to use two examples based on soccer, each one belonging to either end of the realistic-to-fantastic spectrum: *EA Sports FC* and *Rocket League*.

EA Sports FC, previously known as *FIFA*, is a soccer simulator developed by Electronic Arts Sports (EA Sports), which was first launched in 1993 and began betting on competitive events as early as 2001.[49] The title's approach to music has changed over the years to become progressively more intermingled with the mechanics of the music industry, so much so that the music selection in each year's release has become one of the most anticipated elements of the game.

Since the game is presented as a real-life simulator, the matches do not count with music per se, but rather cast commentary simulating real-life events. Although the inclusion of chants from the virtual public may be seen as a musical feature, the intersection with the music industry is mainly developed around menu-screen music. The playlists curated for this purpose have grown in number of tracks since the first editions of the game—which included one song by Blur, four songs by The Crystal Method and one by Electric Skychurch—and have come to be a referent for shaping and bringing forward musical trends (Table 1.3).

In 2011, Electronic Arts Music Group's director Steve Schnur already described their *modus operandi* as being based on listening and discovering new songs and artists, paying attention to the development of the music industry at a global scale: "If a song is currently on the radio or on top of the charts, it's already past its peak for us. Everything

TABLE 1.3 First Playlist in *FIFA*

FIFA INTERNATIONAL SOCCER	
ARTISTS	*SONG*
Blur	*Song 2*
Electric Skychurch	*Hugga Bear*
The Crystal Method	*Keep Hope Alive*
The Crystal Method	*More*
The Crystal Method	*Now Is the Time*
The Crystal Method	*Busy Child*

Source: FIFA International Soccer (1998).

we do, particularly any sports games with a year in the title, must move music forward for the entire year to come."[50]

This process has been further reinforced in recent years through the preselection of potential tracks by collaborating companies such as BMG. During the first half of the year, this company opens a pitching window for tracks to be released around October that would like to be featured in the game. They preselect the contributions that they feel can work with the sonic identity of *EA Sports FC* and forward them to EA, in charge of making the final decision of which tracks make the cut.[51] This implies that although the potential contributions are high, the artists must adjust to what the companies envision and reckon will be most successful on the market.

At the other end of the sports-games spectrum, *Rocket League* by Psyonix made it into the market in 2015. The game is based on a fantastic environment in which cars are the soccer players—thus, creating a sort of intersection between racing and soccer. Differently from the previous case, *Rocket League* includes music during the matches as a means to complement the ludic experience, as well as on other spaces in the game. Likewise, due to its later release, it has been inserted into the esports ecosystem since almost its beginning.

The relationship with the music industry in this game has had at least two differentiated stages: the first, in which former Psyonix audio director Mike Ault composed and directed the original tracks, and the second, which developed during the collaboration with EDM record label Monstercat.

The OST of the game was composed by Ault, who combined his original work with that of Hollywood Principle, a band that he shared with two other members within the electronic music genre. These early compositions contributed to setting the EDM sonic identity of the game, which was later perpetuated by featured artists. The songs that formed the first OST for the game were released in two albums: one in 2015, and a second one a year later—which also featured tracks by *Gears of War* composer Kevin Riepl and producer Adam B. Metal. The success of the product led these records to a third release in 2016, under the title *Rocket League: The Vinyl Collection*.[52]

With the publication of complementary downloadable content (DLCs), the music team started experimenting with the inclusion of indie artists in the game, such as TheFatRat or Drunk Girl. This step toward the incorporation of licensed music shows an increased interest in finding an intersection with the music industry, which would consolidate with the incorporation of Monstercat as a partner. Moreover, the developers took a conscious direction to make the game a "platform for the discovery of new artists" of sorts, as they continued to bet on less-known musicians to illustrate the game.[53]

Psyonix's collaboration with Montsercat was initiated in 2017 and has since followed this same direction, which has afforded some of the artists of the label to notably increase their popularity (Table 1.4):

> [*Rocket League*]'s helped Monstercat become one of the most influential brands in gaming and also endemic in gaming, to where the brand's synonymous with music in gaming, and *Rocket League* and *Fortnite* have definitely been instrumental to that for Monstercat. It's great crosspolinization of fanbases, great crosspoliniztion of brand, for the artist, and to bring longevity to the records. The records clearly have a longer tail when they're integrated into engaging or facing activations.[54]

TABLE 1.4 Artists and Songs Featured in *Rocket League* × *Monstercat Vol. 1*

SONG TITLE	*ARTIST*
Rock It	Tokyo Machine
Fury	Rogue
Luv U Need U	Slushii
Bone Dry	Tristam
Weapon" (featuring Baum)	Grant
Outbreak" (featuring Mylk)	Feint
Apex	Vicetone
Collisions	Droeloe
Call Me	Subtact
Break Me" (featuring Karra)	Trivecta
Drift Away	Wrld
Wake Up, You're Dreaming	Notaker
All Me	Conro
Skyforth	Ephixa
Play to Win" (featuring Holly Drummond)	Rameses B
Drop It	Aero Chord
0202	Eminence
Twilight	Zero Hero

This phenomenon was already noted by Collins in *From Pac-Man to Pop Music*, when stating that "it would appear that the shared demographics between video games and consumers of popular music make for a comfortable relationship where benefit flows in both directions."[55] Monstercat's director of Sync, Gavin Johnson, reaffirmed this intersection between the music and gaming industries, while underlining the essential role of both involved artists and public to the equation, in stating that:

> It's really our core roster that the *Rocket League* community became fans of during the years, even to the point when Throttel has his own creator garage, or he has his own car, cosmetics… and that's something that typically would be reserved for triple-A artists.[56]

The mobile version of the game, *Rocket League Sideswipe*, which works similarly to its homonymous game for non-portable hardware, extends these strategies by curating additional playlists featuring musicians from the same label. This not only affords a sense of continuity and shared sonic identity between the games but also creates new opportunities for the commercialization of Psyonix and Monstercat products.

Fighting Games, Card Games, and Others

Fighting games can be seen as their own niche within the esports international panorama, and along with sports and card games, represent a relatively small portion of the overall esports ecosystem competitively.[57] The intersection with the music industry for titles such as *Street Fighter* or *Tekken* has been accordingly smaller, although other titles such as *Super Smash Bros* have benefitted from Nintendo's related products—despite the disconnection of the company from the competitive scene. The music in fighting games has likewise been tangentially discussed outside of the esports context, besides specific analysis that affords a wider comprehension of the genre's mechanics.[58]

Fighting games first became popular in arcades, as they were "a perfect gameplay type for two friends that wanted to play against each other,"[59] but decreased their popularity in later decades. Their music and sound were initially strongly dependent on the technology available,[60] but the first releases of well-known franchises already included melodies to represent their different characters. For instance, in *Street Fighter 2* specific themes were added to represent character geographical origins, as composer Yoko Shimomura describes:

> When it was decided that I'd be doing *Street Fighter 2*, it was mostly the planner who explained what kind of songs they wanted. He gave me a kind of list. There were different scenes from different countries. We discussed the idea of, rather than character theme songs, maybe making background music with the feeling of each country instead.[61]

These first efforts evolved along with rapidly changing technology, which made a stronger musical presence in games possible. Today, music in fighting games is mostly present in their different menus, champion selection screens, and fighting arenas—besides cinematics of story modes—although specifics depend on each title and its own style of gameplay. They, however, seem to have continued to follow Shimomura's original vision of sound structure.

If we take *Street Fighter 6* as an example, we can see the growing need for connecting the game to a globalized audience that seeks products that transcend gameplay and that take competitive contexts into account. This has a direct impact on the music that is devised for the new titles, as well as on their promotion. In this vein, composer Yoshiya Terayama stated that:

> When aiming for a new sound that might sound modern, what everyone has to keep in mind is that the game you're currently working on comes out a few years later. So if you only focus on chasing after the current trends, there's a chance that it might not be reflective of what the modern sounds are at the time of the release. (…) As a new approach, we are aiming for new elements and genres of music that we haven't seen in the past in *Street Fighter* titles, while simultaneously incorporating strong musical elements from the past titles and mixing that to come up with something that we haven't seen before.[62]

The connection of the series to the music industry—when excluding by-products of the game—is thus mainly present in a more "traditional" sense than other titles. Nevertheless, in recent years, we have seen the popularity of adjacent collaborative products, such as the celebratory album dedicated to the 50th anniversary of the hip-hop genre, released by Capcom in collaboration with NERDS Clothing and producers Steel Sessions, through MNRK Music Group.[63] The album, which featured well-known hip-hop artists, was, however, only made available in the United States (Table 1.5).

Fighting games have also developed a specific focus on *earcons* (and sonic icons), since each character can be recognized from the sounds that accompany their vocal

TABLE 1.5 "Street Fighter 6 × NERDS Clothing presents Steel Sessions"

SONG TITLE	*ARTIST(S)*
Intro	HipHopGamer
Street Fighting	Dave East
Perfect	Black Soprano Family (Benny the Butcher, Heerm & Rick Hyde)
Blood On Me	D-Block
Evil Ryu	Charlie Clips
Already Up	Royce da 5'9" & Courtney Bell
I Got Next	Nino Man
Final Boss	Smoke DZA
GG	Real.Novus
Prada Purna	Prada Mama
No E.Honda's	Nym Lo
Violent Ken	DNA
Toe Tag	Al-Doe
Wrong One's	Oswin Benjamin, Iman Nunez & Aaron Green
Southpaw	Papoose
Power	Grafh
Sonic Boom	Mega Ran & Dezzy Yates

queues and fighting abilities. These have transcended the games themselves, and been introduced into a wider popular cultural context—e.g., *Street Fighter*'s *hadouken* attack, cast by characters Ryu or Ken, is rapidly associated with the saga,[64] and even created its own internet *meme* during the first decade of the current century.[65]

The genre gained popularity during the past few years with the announcement of initiatives such as Riot Game's *Project L*,[66] which was first presented as a new product in 2021 and features characters from other games in the same company. Although at the time of writing the game has not been released yet, Riot Games' investment in music assets makes it plausible to speculate that a reinforced focus on the sonic aspects of the game could affect the way in which other fighting games are presented.

In card games, Riot Games has had a similar impact on popularizing the format with *Legends of Runeterra*, despite the genre's reduced popularity compared to MOBAs or shooters. However, it was *Hearthstone,* developed by Blizzard Entertainment that created a significant turning point for the genre in 2014.

Card games generally mimic real-life board games, but offer a twist to their dynamics from an audiovisual perspective. The cards, with their characters, objects, and items, are animated to bring an added appeal to the strategic nature of a traditional card match. This implies that music and sound are present to illustrate each movement that takes place on the board, as well as to give voice to the characters, the spells that are cast, and any movement from the player. Music is present mainly in three environments: menu screens, boards, and in battle. To these situations, earcons and other sounds belonging to specific cards illustrate the movements and mechanics of the game—including the narrations of characters in tutorials, among other interventions.

If we take a specific example, such as *World of Warcraft*'s spin-off *Hearthstone*, the underlined categories are given continuity through the establishment of a transversal sonic aesthetic that completes the Celtic visuals of the title. This is afforded through different elements, such as the use of specific instruments—e.g., the harp—modal scales, or rhythms that are reminiscent of modal patterns. As composer Peter McConnell pointed out, when describing how he came up with the presentation theme for the title:

> I started riffing around with a triplet guitar groove, and "Bad Reputation" was what I came up with. The piece has a Celtic flavor, especially in the instrumentation with the guitar, fiddle, and harp, but the Celtic triplet rhythm is transformed into more of a steady blues groove. The wind instruments, especially contrabassoon, give an ancient flavor, and the piece also has a lot of space, so that you have time to feel the mood without being overloaded by melody as you play the game. When bits of original Warcraft themes do appear, they are meant to work like little cheers, as if they are from the player's faction, or taunts from the faction the player is facing. "Bad Reputation" really set the precedent for the whole score, including the game's title music.[67]

The game, which is available for desktop and mobile, counts with intro music, main menu music, secondary menu pieces—for battlefield selection, diary, store, etc.—and arena music according to set selection. To these, short pieces are added when "legendary" cards are played, which make them stand out as "rare." Furthermore, decks can be extended through purchasable card sets that can also be obtained as in-game rewards free of charge. To each corresponds a sonic aesthetic that is tailored by the composers to complement the visual and overall feel of the sets. It is especially relevant in our field to highlight the *Festival of Legends* set, which is built around music alter egos for different characters, and features "harmonic spells," "instrument weapons," as well as other cards.[68]

Unlike other titles, *Hearthstone* has not presented music industry collaborations beyond the publication of OSTs or promotional music videos. *Legends of Runeterra*, on the other hand, has followed the dynamics of its developing company and its intersection with popular music artists, who have collaborated on character incorporations, announcements for competitive events, etc. Both games, however, are articulated independently from the companies' esports departments.

Lastly, different games follow under the esports umbrella that are difficult to assign to one of the established categories, which count with different relationships with the music industry. Some of these are labeled by Hamer and Besombes as *niche genres*, while others are relocated as *strategy games*.[69] An example of this is *Brawl Stars,* a mobile real-time strategy game developed by Supercell, which besides its in-game preset music and sound features, which illustrate the different menus, battle arenas, and characters, has been in the spotlight through collaborations with music industry agents. For instance, their 2022 introduction of K-pop band BTS skins in the game came with thematic music associated to characters.[70]

Another well-known case is that of *Pokémon*, owned by Nintendo, which in its worldwide transmedia presence reached esports early in the 21st century. Besides proposals such as the *Trading Card Game*, titles that are present in the current panorama include *Pokémon Unite*, and others in non-specific categories such as *Pokémon GO.*

These are part of the official tournament circuit, the Video Game Championship, which comprehends several "disciplines" under the same name.[71]

Pokémon GO, which first became popular in 2021, has contributed to the settlement of the saga into the esports scene. The competition pits two players against each other, mimicking the Pokémon trainer fashion displayed in the original series, but excludes other dynamics present in the mobile game, such as world-searching for new creatures to add to one's collection. Thus, the description of the overall use of music in the game differs from the competitive section that is used sportingly.

In what regards to the direct intersection of the game with the music industry, *Pokémon GO* has featured artists such as Ed Sheeran, although he was not present directly in the battle environments that are included in the competitive scene. This collaboration included the display of the artist's song "Overpass Graffiti" at the same time every day for an entire week, as well as an in-game performance featuring popular songs by the artist.[72] However, *Pokémon*'s saga as a whole has reached far beyond these interventions marketing-wise and promotionally. It is especially worth highlighting the game's 25th-anniversary celebration, in 2021, for which Nintendo partnered with Universal Studios, producing multiple music videos and events, such as Post Malone's virtual concert in streaming, or collaborations with Katy Perry and J Balvin, among others.[73]

Despite this, the complexity of this universe's saga, and its wide interest from a musicological perspective, falls outside of the scope of this text. For further reference, authors who have addressed this matter include Daniel Muriel and Garry Crowford's work in *Video Games as Culture*,[74] or contributions to the *Journal of Sound and Music in Games* such as Jame Ellis'.[75]

CONCLUSION

As shown through the overview of case studies in each of the suggested categories, the approach of esports video games toward the music industry is strongly dependent on the vision and possibilities of the music team behind each specific title. Cases such as *DotA 2* or *Counter-Strike* allow the external input of music creativity through their packages, while others present opportunities for indie artists to be featured alongside big names in the music industry, like on *Fortnite*'s radios or *Rocket League* playlists. On the other hand, games such as *League of Legends*, which have created a point of reference for its music innovation besides *The Summoner's Rift*, do now show a strong engagement with the industry at an *in-game* level.

Therefore, even though the spaces in which different game genres include music may share similarities because of their particularities, the ways in which each case approaches the original or licensed composition of their soundtracks may differ notably. Because of this, it is essential to disclose the specifics of each case focusing on their music and sound-related goals, especially when tackling the work of multinational companies with rising agreements with other niches.

One of the main limitations for the analysis of games inserted within a largely technologically mediated society, and more so regarding titles whose mechanics are strongly intermingled with competitive settings, is that the definition of a line between in-game and *around-game* music becomes complex. As Summers states, "to consider game music only within the bounds of the game text is to only see part of the story,"[76] not allowing a wider vision of its permeation at a wider sociocultural level. Video games extend beyond themselves and "into a network of paratextual and intertextual machinations"[77] which are closely intermingled and act as part of the music industry.

These statements, although true in the discussion of video games and music at a broad level, find specific significance in the growing ecosystem of electronic esports, which is closely connected to the affordances of social media. The chain value of the traditional music industry or that of video games becomes thus subject to alterations through the participation of artists in the distribution stages, which adds to their purely artistic role. Users also acquire a more transversal role, as they become an essential part in shaping the aesthetic and goals of each brand, but also work as indirect distributors of the titles that they consume. That is, music products associated with the games and featured in the games themselves benefit from the consumers' voices to gain market presence through different platforms.

This directly correlates with the economic dimension regarding the popularization of video games, as described at the beginning of this chapter. Although some titles' OSTs are not as susceptible to commodification as others, those that include popular music artists present a clear opportunity to extend the presence and influence of the product beyond a gaming audience. The sonic identity tailored for each game becomes essential to appeal to the objective public and their preferences—even if, as stated, this works bidirectionally in attracting new gamers with similar music likings.

At an experiential level, the creation of connections between games and real-life events can be approached from perspectives ranging from the reproduction of real environments in simulators—like in *Counter-Strike*—to the lowering of the fourth wall through the introduction of popular music and culture in the games—like in *League of Legends*. The inclusion of radios or cameos of popular music artists (and cultural artifacts) in games such as *Fortnite* aids in blurring the limits of the real and the virtual—an idea that will be further extended once extra-ludic elements are added to the equation. These phenomena are socioculturally developed, as they develop in shared environments which, referencing Bourdieu,[78] contribute to the building of what we may call its participants' *cultural capital*.

In sum, despite the dependence of each game genre in formulating their music plan, the current affordances of the music industry in its intersection with *esports as video games* imply a need for a delimited case analysis that will certainly show within a range of possibilities. The comparative overview of different games highlights how the baseline OSTs of each title is linked to the growing engagement of the gaming industry with its music homonymous. This does not only allow a shared construction of a musical identity, but also of paramusical fields of connotation that extend beyond the games, allowing communities all around the globe to feel connected to themselves, and to the products that they consume.

NOTES

1 Juan Sebastián Díaz Gasca, "Music Beyond Gameplay: Motivators in the Consumption of Videogame Soundtracks" (Doctoral Thesis, Griffith University, 2015). Available at: https://research-repository.griffith.edu.au/bitstream/handle/10072/367483/Diaz%20Gasca_2015_02Thesis.pdf?sequence=1. Accessed 15 November 2023.
2 Mike Ault, former Audio Director at Psyonix. Interview by Eulalia Febrer-Coll. 10 November 2023.
3 Pierre Bourdieu, "The Forms of Capital", in John G. Richardson (Ed.), *Handbook of Theory and Research for the Sociology of Education,* 241–258. New York: Greenwood Press, 1986.
4 Stephen Kline, Nick Dyer-Withford & Grieg de Peuter, *Digital Play: The Interaction of Technology, Culture and Marketing.* Quebec City: McGill-Queen's University Press, 2003.
5 Karen Collins, *Game Sound: An Introduction to the History, Theory, and Practice of Video Game Music and Sound Design.* Cambridge and London: MIT Press, 2008, 123.
6 Tim Summers, *Understanding Video Game Music.* Cambridge: Cambridge University Press, 2016, 88.
7 Steam Support, "Dota 2 Workshop – Music Packs", *Steam*, n.d. Available at: https://help.steampowered.com/en/faqs/view/1D61-78DF-01D7-603B. Accessed 15 November 2023.
8 William Gibbons, *Unlimited Replays: Video Games and Classical Music.* New York: Oxford University Press, 2018. Also see Karen Collins, "Grand Theft Audio? Popular Music and Intellectual Property in Video Games", *Music and the Moving Image*, 2018, 1(1), 35–48.
9 *Earcons* are abstract synthetic tones that are used in games to communicate an action or in-game event. See Elisabeth Medina-Gray, "Interacting with Soundscapes: Music, Sound Effects and Dialogue in Video Games", in Melanie Fritsch and Tim Summers (Eds.), *The Cambridge Companion to Video Game Music,* 176–192. Cambridge: Cambridge University Press, 2021.
10 United States Patent and Trademark Office. "Trademark Sound Mark Examples." U.S. Patent and Trademark Office. Available at: https://www.uspto.gov/trademarks/sound-marks/trademark-sound-mark-examples. Accessed 18 November 2023.
11 European Union Intellectual Property Office. "Common Communication CP11." European Union Intellectual Property Office. Available at: https://euipo.europa.eu/tunnel-web/secure/webdav/guest/document_library/contentPdfs/EUIPN/CP11/common_communication_cp11_en.pdf. Accessed 18 November 2023.
12 Medina-Gray, "Interacting with Soundscapes", 188.
13 Park Jae-Sang, "Gangnam Style." *PSY 6 (Six Rules).* YG, Universal Republic & School Boy, 2016.
14 Shara Rambarran, "'Feel Good' with Gorillaz and 'Reject False Icons': The Fantasy Worlds of the Virtual Group and Their Creators", In Sheila Whiteley & Shara Rambarran (Eds.), *The Oxford Handbook of Music and Virtuality*, 148–169. New York: Oxford University Press, 2016.
15 See *Chapter 5. Artists on Esports Stages: Out-of-Game.*
16 Murray Stassen, "After Buying Bandcamp, Epic Games Pushes Indie Artists to Millions of Fortnite Players in Curated Radio Station", *Music Business Worldwide*, 2023. Available at: https://www.musicbusinessworldwide.com/a-year-after-buying-bandcamp-epic-games-pushes-indie-artists-to-millions-of-fortnite-players-in-curated-radio-station/. Accessed 19 December 2023.

17 Wilhelm Voutilainen, Sr. Chief Game Analyst at GameRefinery. Interview by Eulalia Febrer-Coll. 31st October 2023.
18 Mike Ault. Interview by Eulalia Febrer-Coll. 10 November 2023.
19 A similar categorization was suggested by William Collis in *The Book of Esports*. New York: Rosetta Books, 2020.
20 Russell Hamer & Nicolas Besombes, "Esports Genres and Games", in Seth E. Jenny et al. (Eds.), *Routledge Handbook of Esports,* 42–52. Oxon: Routledge, 2024.
21 See Figure 1.1. Based on Fernando Maldonado Parrales, "Active Listening, Interaction and Immersion: An Analytical Proposal on the Creation and Reception of Soundscapes in Video Games", *Journal of Sound, Silence, Image and Technology*, 2020, 3, 21.
22 Parrales, "Active Listening, Interaction and Immersion", 18.
23 Collins, *Game Sound*, 123.
24 Various Artists. *Pokemon 25: The Album.* Capitol Records & Universal Music Records, 2021.
25 Díaz Gasca, "Music Beyond Gameplay", 39.
26 Andrew Leyshon, "Time-Space (and Digital) Compression: Software Formats, Musical Networks, and the Reorganisation of the Music Industry", *Environment and Planning A*, 2001, 33(1), 49–77.
27 Ricardo R. Álvarez Vázquez, *The Music Industry in the Dawn of the 21st Century: Networking for a Thriving Music Industry.* Elverum: sKunnskapsverket, 2017.
28 Leyshon, "Time-Space (and Digital) Compression."
29 Mihaly Csikszentmihalyi, *Flow: The Psychology of Optimal Experience.* New York: Harper Collins Publ., 2008.
30 Riot Games, "The Making of a League of Legends Champion Theme", *Riot Games*, 2023. Available at: https://www.riotgames.com/en/news/creating-champion-themes-riot-games-music. Accessed 15 December 2023.
31 Brian Feeney, Game Director at Riot Games. Interview by Travis Gafford, "How WILD RIFT Is Designed ESPORT FIRST, Bringing League to Mobile, and Rammus Lessons", *Youtube,* 2021. Available at: https://www.youtube.com/watch?v=rE2pHMuBOE4&list=PLqjghJYJg3XeF_LfK_mAVHXvbqq2HsxT2. Accessed 15 December 2023.
32 Steam Support, "Dota 2 Workshop – Music Packs."
33 Mike Morasky, Composer at Valve. Interview by Eulalia Febrer-Coll. 14 December 2023.
34 Steam Support, "Dota 2 Workshop – Music Packs."
35 Mark N. Grimshaw, "The Acoustic Ecology of the First-Person Shooter" (PhD Thesis). University of Waikato, 2007, 20.
36 R. Murray Schafer, *The Soundscape: Our Sonic Environment and the Turning of the World.* Rochester, VT: Destiny Books, 1977.
37 Mike Morasky. Interview by Eulalia Febrer-Coll. 14 December 2023.
38 CounterStrike Wiki, "Music Kit", *CounterStrike Wiki*, n.d. Available at: https://counterstrike.fandom.com/wiki/Music_Kit. Accessed 9 December 2023.
39 Mike Morasky. Interview by Eulalia Febrer-Coll. 14 December 2023.
40 Sergiy Galyonkin, "Battle Pass Fundamentals", *Medium*, 2023. Available at: https://galyonk.in/battle-pass-fundamentals-309efd9975a8#:~:text=Fortnite%27s%20Battle%20Pass%20was%20inspired,against%20the%20philosophy%20of%20Fortnite. Accessed 10 December 2023.
41 Epic Games, "Epic Games just bought Bandcamp – so what does that mean?", *Epic Games*, 2022. Available at: https://cdm.link/epic-games-just-bought-bandcamp-so-what-does-that-mean/. Accessed 10 December 2023.
42 Epic Games, "Epic Games just bought Bandcamp", n.p.

43 Christian Eede, "Epic Games Sells Bandcamp to Songtradr", *The Quietus*, 2023. Available at: https://thequietus.com/articles/33440-epic-games-sells-bandcamp-to-songtradr#:~:text=Steve%20Allison%2C%20vice%20president%20and,%2C%20games%20and%20tools%20efforts.%22. Accessed 10 December 2023.
44 Andrew Webster, "Fortnite Festival Is Rock Band without the Plastic Instruments", *The Verge*, 2023. Available at: https://www.theverge.com/2023/12/9/23992574/fortnite-festival-harmonix-guitar-hero-rock-band. Accessed 10 December 2023.
45 Summers, *Understanding Video Game Music*.
46 Andra Ivănescu, "Pop Music, Economics and Marketing", in Melanie Fritsch and Tim Summers (Eds.), *The Cambridge Companion to Video Game Music*, 395–408. Cambridge: Cambridge University Press, 2021.
47 BEMANI Pro League, *Konami*, n.d. Available at: https://p.eagate.573.jp/game/bpl/season2/. Accessed 20 December 2023.
48 Díaz Gasca, "Music Beyond Gameplay", 27.
49 Trey Walker, "Intel to sponsor CPL World Championship", *Gamespot*, 2001. Available at: https://www.gamespot.com/app.php/articles/intel-to-sponsor-cpl-world-championship/1100-2806357/. Accessed 20th December 2023.
50 Dale Kawashima, "Interview with Steve Schnur, Worldwide President of Music at Electronic Arts (EA) Video Games", *Songwritter Universe*, n.d. Available at: https://www.songwriteruniverse.com/steve-schnur-123.htm. Accessed 20 December 2023.
51 Mariana Migliore, Director and Creative Synch at BMG. Interview by Eulalia Febrer-Coll. 17 September 2023.
52 Mike Ault, "Vinyl Collection Available for Pre-Order", *Rocket League*, 2016. Available at: https://www.rocketleague.com/news/vinyl-collection-available-for-pre-order/. Accessed 14 December 2023.
53 Mike Ault. Interview by Eulalia Febrer-Coll. 10 November 2023.
54 Gavin Johnson, Director of Sync and Partnerships at Monstercat. Interview by Eulalia Febrer-Coll, 13 December 2023.
55 Karen Collins, *From Pac-Man to Pop Music: InteractiveAudio in Games and New Media*. Hampshire: Ashgate, 2008.
56 Gavin Johnson. Interview by Eulalia Febrer-Coll, 13th December 2023.
57 Esports Charts, "Street Fighter", n.d. Available at: https://escharts.com/games/sfv. Accessed 14 December 2023.
58 See Lidia López, "Vega's Musical Spanishness in Street Fighter", paper presented at *VIII Workshop do CYSMUS. Prácticas Mediáticas em Rede*, Research Cluster in Sound and Music in Digital and Audiovisual Meida, Universidade Nova de Lisboa, 2023.
59 Alyssa Aska, *Introduction to the Study of Video Game Music*. Self-pub, 2017, 103.
60 Collins, *Game Sound*.
61 Telemaster, "Yoko Shimomura Interview - Street Fighter II Soundtrack OST", *Youtube*, 2017. Available at: https://www.youtube.com/watch?v=HOxN8Dzv2sw. Accessed 1 February 2023.
62 Yoshiya Terayama. Interview by Jon Weigell. 27 August 2022. Available at Rolling Stone, "Street Fighter 6 Producer Shuhei Matsumoto & Composer Yoshiya Terayama Discuss the Game's Music", *Youtube*, 2022. Available at: https://www.youtube.com/watch?v=6P_bj5R-jLUY. Accessed 5 February 2024.
63 Media Alert, "50th Anniversary of Hip Hop Celebration Continues with Today's Release of Original Street Fighter™ Soundtrack", *Plaion*, 2023. Available at: https://press.kochmedia.com/nl/50-th-Anniversary-of-Hip-Hop-Celebration-Continues-with-Todays-Release. Accessed 5th February 2024.
64 Riot Games, "Project L", *Riot Games*, n.d. Available at: https://project-l.riotgames.com/en-us/. Accessed 5 February 2024.

65 Jacob Osterhout, "Latest Internet Meme Is Hadouken, Where People Imitate Midair Fight Movies from Video Game Street Fighter", *Daily News*, 2013. Available at: https://www.nydailynews.com/2013/04/07/latest-internet-meme-is-hadouken-where-people-imitate-midair-fight-movies-from-video-game-street-fighter/. Accessed 5 February 2024.
66 Xiaoquan, "Evolution of Ryu's Hadoken 1987–2022", *Youtube*, 2023. Available at: https://www.youtube.com/watch?v=3ihrSG0j6l0. Accessed 5 February 2024.
67 Jayson Napolitano, "Enjoy These Hearthstone: Heroes of Warcraft Music Samples", *Destructoid*, 2013. Available at: https://www.destructoid.com/enjoy-these-hearthstone-heroes-of-warcraft-music-samples/. Accessed 5 February 2024.
68 Blizzard, "Festival of Legends: The Stage is Set", *Hearthstone*, n.d. Available at: https://hearthstone.blizzard.com/en-us/expansions-adventures/festival-of-legends. Accessed 5 February 2024.
69 Hamer and Besombes, "Esports Genres and Games."
70 US BTS ARMY, "Brawl Stars x BT21", 2022. Available at: https://www.usbtsarmy.com/bts-endorsements/brawlstars-x-bt21. Accessed 6 February 2024.
71 Pokémon, "Pokemon Video Game Championship Series", n.d. Available at: https://www.pokemon.com/us/play-pokemon/pokemon-events/pokemon-tournaments/video-game. Accessed 6 February 2024.
72 Pokémon GO, "A Brand-New Collaboration Event with Ed Sheeran!", 2021. Available at: https://pokemongolive.com/post/ed-sheeran-collab/?hl=en. Accessed 6 February 2024.
73 Samantha Hissong, "J Balvin Joins Katy Perry and Post Malone on Pokémon Compilation Album", *Rolling Stone*, 2021. Available at: https://www.rollingstone.com/music/music-news/pokemon-p25-album-universal-katy-perry-j-balvin-post-malone-1133408/. Accessed 6 February 2024.
74 Daniel Muriel and Garry Crowford, "Chapter 2. The Emergence and Consolidation of Video Games as Culture", in *Video Games as Culture: Considering the Role and Importance of Video Games in Contemporary Society*, 16–59. New York: Routledge, 2018.
75 Jame Ellis, "On the Trail of a Nostalgic Adventure: Identifying and Analyzing the Nostalgic Potential of Video Game Music in the Context of the Pokémon Franchise", *Journal of Sound and Music in Games*, 2022, 3(2–3), 77–114.
76 Summers, *Understanding Video Game Music*, 393.
77 Ivănescu, "Pop Music, Economics and Marketing", 406.
78 Pierre Bourdieu, "The Forms of Capital", 241–258.

REFERENCES

Álvarez Vázquez, Ricardo R. *The Music Industry in the Dawn of the 21st Century: Networking for a Thriving Music Industry*. Elverum: sKunnskapsverket, 2017.

Aska, Alyssa. *Introduction to the Study of Video Game Music*. Self-pub, 2017.

Ault, Mike. "Vinyl Collection Available for Pre-Order", *Rocket League*, 2016. Available at: https://www.rocketleague.com/news/vinyl-collection-available-for-pre-order/. Accessed 14th December 2023.

BEMANI Pro League. *Konami*, n.d. Available at: https://p.eagate.573.jp/game/bpl/season2/. Accessed 20th December 2023.

Blizzard. "Festival of Legends: The Stage Is Set", *Hearthstone*, n.d. Available at: https://hearthstone.blizzard.com/en-us/expansions-adventures/festival-of-legends. Accessed 5th February 2024.

Bourdieu, Pierre. "The Forms of Capital", in John G. Richardson (Ed.), *Handbook of Theory and Research for the Sociology of Education*, 241–258. New York: Greenwood Press, 1986.

Collins, Karen. *From Pac-Man to Pop Music: InteractiveAudio in Games and New Media.* Hampshire: Ashgate, 2008.

Collins, Karen. *Game Sound: An Introduction to the History, Theory, and Practice of Video Game Music and Sound Design.* Cambridge, MA and London: MIT Press, 2008.

Collins, Karen. "Grand Theft Audio? Popular Music and Intellectual Property in Video Games", *Music and the Moving Image,* 2018, 1(1), 35–48.

Collis, William. *The Book of Esports.* New York: Rosetta Books, 2020.

CounterStrike Wiki. "Music Kit", *CounterStrike Wiki,* n.d. Available at: https://counterstrike.fandom.com/wiki/Music_Kit. Accessed 9th December 2023.

Csikszentmihalyi, Mihaly. *Flow: The Psychology of Optimal Experience.* New York: Harper Collins Publ., 2008.

Díaz Gasca, Juan Sebastián. "Music Beyond Gameplay: Motivators in the Consumption of Videogame Soundtracks" (Doctoral Thesis). Griffith University, 2015. Available at: https://research-repository.griffith.edu.au/bitstream/handle/10072/367483/Diaz%20Gasca_2015_02Thesis.pdf?sequence=1. Accessed 15th November 2023.

Eede, Christian. "Epic Games Sells Bandcamp to Songtradr", *The Quietus,* 2023. Available at: https://thequietus.com/articles/33440-epic-games-sells-bandcamp-to-songtradr#:~:text=Steve%20Allison%2C%20vice%20president%20and,%2C%20games%20and%20tools%20efforts.%22. Accessed 10th December 2023.

Ellis, Jame. "On the Trail of a Nostalgic Adventure: Identifying and Analyzing the Nostalgic Potential of Video Game Music in the Context of the Pokémon Franchise", *Journal of Sound and Music in Games,* 2022, 3(2–3), 77–114.

Epic Games. "Epic Games just bought Bandcamp – so what does that mean?", *Epic Games,* 2022. Available at: https://cdm.link/epic-games-just-bought-bandcamp-so-what-does-that-mean/. Accessed 10th December 2023.

Esports Charts. "Street Fighter", n.d. Available at: https://escharts.com/games/sfv. Accessed 14th December 2023.

European Union Intellectual Property Office. "Common Communication CP11", European Union Intellectual Property Office. Available at: https://euipo.europa.eu/tunnel-web/secure/webdav/guest/document_library/contentPdfs/EUIPN/CP11/common_communication_cp11_en.pdf. Accessed 18th November 2023.

Gafford, Travis. "How WILD RIFT Is Designed ESPORT FIRST, Bringing League to Mobile, and Rammus Lessons", *Youtube*, 2021. Available at: https://www.youtube.com/watch?v=rE2pHMuBOE4&list=PLqjghJYJg3XeF_LfK_mAVHXvbqq2HsxT2. Accessed 15th December 2023.

Galyonkin, Sergiy. "Battle Pass Fundamentals", *Medium*, 2023. Available at: https://galyonk.in/battle-pass-fundamentals-309efd9975a8#:~:text=Fortnite%27s%20Battle%20Pass%20was%20inspired,against%20the%20philosophy%20of%20Fortnite. Accessed 10th December 2023.

Gibbons, William. *Unlimited Replays: Video Games and Classical Music.* New York: Oxford University Press, 2018.

Grimshaw, Mark N. "The Acoustic Ecology of the First-Person Shooter" (PhD Thesis). University of Waikato, 2007.

Hamer, Russell & Besombes, Nicolas. "Esports Genres and Games", in Seth E. Jenny et al. (Eds.), *Routledge Handbook of Esports*, 42–52. Oxon: Routledge, 2024.

Hissong, Samantha. "J Balvin Joins Katy Perry and Post Malone on Pokémon Compilation Album", *Rolling Stone*, 2021. Available at: https://www.rollingstone.com/music/music-news/pokemon-p25-album-universal-katy-perry-j-balvin-post-malone-1133408/. Accessed 6th February 2024.

Ivănescu, Andra. "Pop Music, Economics and Marketing", in Melanie Fritsch and Tim Summers (Eds.), *The Cambridge Companion to Video Game Music*, 395–408. Cambridge: Cambridge University Press, 2021.

Kawashima, Dale. "Interview with Steve Schnur, Worldwide President of Music at Electronic Arts (EA) Video Games", *Songwritter Universe*, n.d. Available at: https://www.songwriteruniverse.com/steve-schnur-123.htm. Accessed 20th December 2023.

Kline, Stephen, Dyer-Withford, Nick & de Peuter, Grieg. *Digital Play: The Interaction of Technology, Culture and Marketing*. Quebec City: McGill-Queen's University Press, 2003.
Leyshon, Andrew. "Time-Space (and Digital) Compression: Software Formats, Musical Networks, and the Reorganisation of the Music Industry", *Environment and Planning A,* 2001, 33(1), 49–77.
López, Lidia. "Vega's Musical Spanishness in Street Fighter", paper presented at *VIII Workshop do CYSMUS. Prácticas Mediáticas em Rede*, Research Cluster in Sound and Music in Digital and Audiovisual Meida, Universidade Nova de Lisboa, 2023.
Maldonado Parrales, Fernando. "Active Listening, Interaction and Immersion: An Analytical Proposal on the Creation and Reception of Soundscapes in Video Games", *Journal of Sound, Silence, Image and Technology,* 2020, 3, 8–24.
Media Alert. "50th Anniversary of Hip Hop Celebration Continues with Today's Release of Original Street Fighter™ Soundtrack", *Plaion,* 2023. Available at: https://press.kochmedia.com/nl/50-th-Anniversary-of-Hip-Hop-Celebration-Continues-with-Todays-Release. Accessed 5th February 2024.
Medina-Gray, Elisabeth. "Interacting with Soundscapes: Music, Sound Effects and Dialogue in Video Games", in Melanie Fritsch & Tim Summers (Eds.), *The Cambridge Companion to Video Game Music*, 176–192. Cambridge: Cambridge University Press, 2021.
Muriel, Daniel & Crowford, Garry. "Chapter 2. The Emergence and Consolidation of Video Games as Culture", in Daniel Muriel & Garry Crowford (Eds.), *Video Games as Culture: Considering the Role and Importance of Video Games in Contemporary Society*, 16–59. New York: Routledge, 2018.
Napolitano, Jayson. "Enjoy These Hearthstone: Heroes of Warcraft Music Samples", *Destructoid,* 2013. Available at: https://www.destructoid.com/enjoy-these-hearthstone-heroes-of-warcraft-music-samples/. Accessed 5th February 2024.
Osterhout, Jacob. "Latest Internet Meme Is Hadouken, Where People Imitate Midair Fight Movies from Video Game Street Fighter", *Daily News*, 2013. Available at: https://www.nydailynews.com/2013/04/07/latest-internet-meme-is-hadouken-where-people-imitate-midair-fight-movies-from-video-game-street-fighter/. Accessed 5th February 2024.
Pokémon. "Pokemon Video Game Championship Series", n.d. Available at: https://www.pokemon.com/us/play-pokemon/pokemon-events/pokemon-tournaments/video-game. Accessed 6th February 2024.
Pokémon GO. "A Brand-New Collaboration Event with Ed Sheeran!", 2021. Available at: https://pokemongolive.com/post/ed-sheeran-collab/?hl=en. Accessed 6th February 2024.
Rambarran, Shara. "'Feel Good' with Gorillaz and 'Reject False Icons': The Fantasy Worlds of the Virtual Group and Their Creators", in Sheila Whiteley & Shara Rambarran (Eds.), *The Oxford Handbook of Music and Virtuality,* 148–169. New York: Oxford University Press, 2016.
Riot Games. "Project L", *Riot Games*, n.d. Available at: https://project-l.riotgames.com/en-us/. Accessed 5th February 2024.
Riot Games. "The Making of a League of Legends Champion Theme", *Riot Games*, 2023. Available at: https://www.riotgames.com/en/news/creating-champion-themes-riot-games-music. Accessed 15th December 2023.
Rolling Stone. "Street Fighter 6 Producer Shuhei Matsumoto & Composer Yoshiya Terayama Discuss the Game's Music", *Youtube*, 2022. Available at: https://www.youtube.com/watch?v=6P_bj5RjLUY. Accessed 5th February 2024.
Schafer, R. Murray. *The Soundscape: Our Sonic Environment and the Turning of the World.* Rochester, VT: Destiny Books, 1977.
Stassen, Murray. "After Buying Bandcamp, Epic Games Pushes Indie Artists to Millions of Fortnite Players in Curated Radio Station", *Music Business Worldwide*, 2023. Available at https://www.musicbusinessworldwide.com/a-year-after-buying-bandcamp-epic-games-pushes-indie-artists-to-millions-of-fortnite-players-in-curated-radio-station/. Accessed 19th December 2023.

Steam Support. "Dota 2 Workshop – Music Packs", *Steam*, n.d. https://help.steampowered.com/en/faqs/view/1D61-78DF-01D7-603B. Accessed 15th November 2023.

Summers, Tim. *Understanding Video Game Music*. Cambridge: Cambridge University Press, 2016.

Telemaster. "Yoko Shimomura Interview - Street Fighter II Soundtrack OST", *Youtube*, 2017. https://www.youtube.com/watch?v=HOxN8Dzv2sw. Accessed 1st February 2023.

United States Patent and Trademark Office. "Trademark Sound Mark Examples", *U.S. Patent and Trademark Office*. https://www.uspto.gov/trademarks/soundmarks/trademark-sound-mark-examples. Accessed 18th November 2023.

US BTS ARMY. "Brawl Stars x BT21", 2022. Available at: https://www.usbtsarmy.com/bts-endorsements/brawlstars-x-bt21. Accessed 6th February 2024.

Various Artists. *Pokemon 25: The Album*. Capitol Records & Universal Music Records, 2021.

Webster, Andrew. "Fortnite Festival Is Rock Band without the Plastic Instruments", *The Verge*, 2023. Available at: https://www.theverge.com/2023/12/9/23992574/fortnite-festival-harmonix-guitar-hero-rock-band. Accessed 10th December 2023.

Walker, Trey. "Intel to Sponsor CPL World Championship", *Gamespot,* 2001. Available at: https://www.gamespot.com/app.php/articles/intel-to-sponsor-cpl-world-championship/1100-2806357/. Accessed 20th December 2023.

Xiaoquan. "Evolution of Ryu's Hadoken 1987–2022", *Youtube*, 2023. Available at: https://www.youtube.com/watch?v=3ihrSG0j6l0. Accessed 5th February 2024.

Narrative and Music Identity of Esports Characters

2

In 2013, Riot Games released a music video to present *League of Legends* character Jinx, in collaboration with singer Agnete Kjølsrud, and animation by studio Fortiche Productions—which would later become a concurrent partner. The song, which helped form the personality and image of the character, became pivotal for the development of the music department at the company, and was a cornerstone for the growing intersection between the video game brand and the music industry.[1] It can further be argued that *Get Jinxed* was decisive in developing the interest among esports agents to invest in popular music, and that the case served Riot as a reference for the musical definition of their later transmedia explorations.

At a global level, esports characters have become relevant in and outside of games that count with well-developed background stories, which offer iconic references for fans and help articulate the games' imagined *lore*.[2] In these universes, the role of playable characters surpasses that of in-game peons, as they become socializers for the brands, the card of presentation of the titles in which they are featured. This is reinforced through the association of specific music with particular characters, objects, and environments.

The background stories that agglutinate the direct and indirect products of video games, as well as the games themselves, need coherent narratives to rely on that provide a sense of plausibility for fans, a coherence in the events of each imagined world. This also applies to characters, consequently inserted in the plot of each game. In this equation, music is key to creating continuity and affording a sense of belongingness. However, to discuss this further, the links between narrativity and video games need to be first clarified, since the mechanics and overall conceptualization of each game are key to understanding how character identities are constructed.

When addressing the ludo-narrative complexity of video games, Martínez Núñez and Navarro Remesal[3] outline the existing ludology-narratology debate from a methodological standpoint that contrasts Game Studies with other traditional forms of audiovisual analysis. Films can be seen, for instance, as one of the referents for the development of video games, especially those that aim to (co-)build a story through

DOI: 10.1201/9781032625362-3

gameplay. This perspective, which has been similarly adopted by other authors,[4] posits a fundamental issue for games under the category that attains us. The titles that are usually selected when discussing narrative are delimited in nature—this includes adventure games, horror, etc.—as they have marked beginnings and endings. However, through the current multimediated market in which esports are placed, there is little room for beginning-to-end stories that are not open to continuous (transmedia) exploitation.

Lucia Škripcová argues that the convergence of these transmedia narratives is necessary for such games to survive, stating that "game convergence can be seen as whether such content can survive without the player knowing about the original game from which the content converged, and whether such content will be successful and its tendency replicable to other domains."[5] This makes it reasonable to differentiate the games per se as separate products from the competitive contexts, although they become part of a continuum.

In their analysis of *Overwatch*, Raine Koskimaa and colleagues argue that two parallel worlds coexist: "one focused on fictional world-building and another on actual esports."[6] This coexistence is strongly linked to transmediality and the continuous dialogues between complementary industries, as the ones discussed here. In this way, the authors suggest that *Overwatch* must be explored from two different areas, which are closely related and often intermingle:

> One can be called the Jenkisian transmedia storytelling approach, which emphasizes the fictional worlds and stories set in them, and is focused on the game itself. The other one, focused on Overwatch esports, emphasizes the spectacle: matches and tournaments bounded by time and place, as well as stories and media content used to build this spectacle.[7]

This idea can be applied to other titles that also distinguish their main videoludic content from related events in esports, despite their necessary continuity. Similarly, music is not only present as a scaffolding element for in-game action, but it provides consistency between the fictional world on-screen and other products that can be presented in other contexts, such as real-life events. This applies to the construction of characters, which are musically devised in the games' universes: in-game and around-game story-building narratives may occur separately, but music provides a point of continuity that addresses any potential dissonances.[8] Furthermore, this is usually a bidirectional link, as the music identity given to characters in a game can inform their presentation on live stages, while the re-imagination of characters on live stages can later be incorporated into specific games.

It is not uncommon for video game companies to see their creative outcomes through this partition, and consider separate teams for *video game* and *competition* organization. Because of this, composers for in-game music are frequently not responsible for events, while these rather rely on complementary or external teams,[9] including marketing.

Nevertheless, as stated in Chapter 1, it is essential to consider not only the genre of the game but also the specifics of each title. In addition to the traditional challenges related to video game music narratives, competitive video games rely on the sonic environments that have been preestablished for them and that serve to unify each brand's storytelling.

VIDEO GAME NARRATIVES

Although it is not the goal of this chapter to discuss narrativity in depth, some concepts like *narrative memorability* are illustrative for the comprehension of character-associated music. Díaz Gasca[10] places this concept in the context of traditional video game soundtrack analysis, pointing out that "the musical representation of places, players, settings, stories, and the involvement that the player has in the forging and metamorphosis of musical meaning is what gives stories the power to transcend the game."[11] The ability of music to create memorable references for players, which associate them with characters as well as to their own experiences, is key to the mediatic success of the games.

In this sense, it is not only the detail in the construction of the sonic identity of a character that makes them stand out, but also the appropriation of the discourse by its objective audience. As López-Cano states, narrativity can be considered "a specific form of discourse, a linguistic artifact, an epistemological category, a cognitive strategy that gives coherence and a particular meaning to certain aspects of people's lives, and a specific thinking mode."[12] Thus, we may argue that it also presents a reference for music marketing, as it provides a tool to connect with targeted audiences.

The construction of character identities across platforms makes these narratives become inexorably linked to *transmedia storytelling*, described by Jenkins as unfolding "across multiple media platforms, with each new text making a distinctive and valuable contribution to the whole."[13] Following this, Ryan nuanced the concept in suggesting the coexistence of two major forms—or poles—in transmedia storytelling: the "snowball effect," and franchising.[14] The first refers to a story that becomes popular to the extent that it generates other same-medium or cross-media products spontaneously, while the second implies the original conception of a story from different media platforms. Each of these constitutes a different approach to the gaming and music industries, as the articulation of agents and the control held by each company depends on the nature of their generated products.

Ryan also emphasizes the *storyworld* as the concept "that holds together the various texts of the system"[15] and defines it through two components: one static and one

"Snowball effect"
Prequels, sequels, fan fiction, and adaptations
E.g. *The Lord of the Rings*

Franchising
Storyworlds become commercial franchises
E.g. *The Matrix*

FIGURE 2.1 Forms of transmedia storytelling, based on M-L. Ryan (2013).

dynamic. The first includes the lore of the story—it considers the species, objects, institutions, topography, folklore, social rules, and values of the imagined world, etc.—while the second refers to any events that develop the lore. These can be physical or psychological in origin and can involve anything from social changes to plot twists.

Multiple video game companies have followed this path, embedding music both diegetically and extra-diegetically into their stories, benefitting from the growing interest of their public in consuming their products through diverse platforms—from Nintendo to Activision. It can be argued that this strategy differentiates competitive and non-competitive games to an extent, as the first is frequently reliant on continuous change and development—rather than consecutive releases—to maintain their position in the market. This, indeed, includes storyworld-developing music products.

To give an example, we can take the case that opened this chapter and analyze it within its wider context.

League of Legends counts with a static story component that includes music as part of its imaginary world. In Runeterra, where the game is framed, some items specifically appeal to the imagined world's sonic environment. For instance, the area of Frelijord includes a tribe called *the Notai,* which is "known for their mastery of songs and their knowledge of ancient legends."[16] The complete ideation of this and other locations, history, wildlife, culture, etc., makes it essential to contemplate sonic elements that can later be translated into the game and other products.[17]

In Jinx's case, she is contextualized in the city of Zaun, which was depicted in detail on the TV show *Arcane*. The series aided in constructing the character and the city's sonic identities, and served as a dynamic component to unfold the game's narrative. Furthermore, it featured the original song through which the character was presented in 2013 diegetically, in a scene,[18] providing continuity to the (transmedia) narrative. The game later included a *skin* for the character themed around the show, incorporating the brand's extra-ludic elements back into its main product.

However, the strategy followed by Riot Games did not end there, as the character was also featured in other games such as *Fortnite*, in a collaboration with Epic Games.[19] In *Fortnite*'s multiverse, the character appeared as one of the identities that the player can take—or win with a *battle pass*—and included a theme song from *Arcane* to play in the lobby. Although this last point does not add to the development of the narrative in *League of Legends*, the sum of elements shows how character identities are built—even across brands—and how franchising has become essential to the marketing of video games, specifically, esports. This is not to say that the "snowball effect" is not contemplated by Riot Games, as plenty of fan-made music circulates on a daily basis around the internet.[20]

A different matter is that of introducing real-life artists to a game's narrative, since it implies rethinking how transfictional identities[21] are created, as they move in a continuum between real life and fiction, traveling between worlds and stories. This applies to our case study through the participation of band Imagine Dragons in *League of Legends*' storyworld as additional characters—including *Arcane*. Their participation in the series contributed to tearing the fourth wall and afforded an extension of the story to wider audiences.[22]

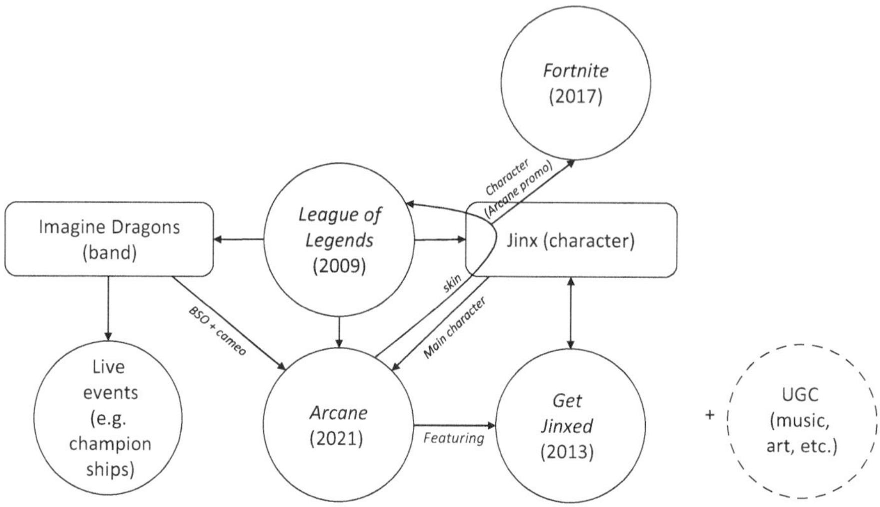

FIGURE 2.2 *League of Legend's* Jinx transmedia storytelling.

Another example is *Free Fire* by Garena, which has also developed its storyworld and lore through various channels—from comic books to animated videos—including music as a key component. These contribute to profiling each character, their personalities, and the situations in which they are involved.

As one of their in-game shows, in 2022 *Free Fire* featured Justin Bieber in a participative music video. They did not only create an avatar for players to use in the game, as they have done on other occasions—e.g., with Alok or Dmitri—and included Bieber as a new character under the name *J Biebs*, who counted with his own background story,[23] becoming embedded into the preexisting narrative. In this scenario, following Ryan's model, the static component of the game's world was dynamized through the introduction of the character that interacted with the environment and contributed to expanding its lore.

Other games such as *Fortnite* have steadily developed a plot that gives similar incorporations—and patches—meaning.[24] As the existence of a multiverse is a part of the game's logic, the presence of characters such as Jinx is seamlessly included as part of the possibilities that this offers. In all instances, a great part of what is created musically at a *not-in-game* level relies on the existence of a lore that affords overall coherence and articulates it, making it challenging for video game and esports teams to row in the same direction. However, it is precisely in the context of these very stories where characters are given their unique identities.

A SONG FOR EACH CHARACTER

In her chapter *Game Narrative and Storyworld in League of Legends*,[25] Emily J. Bembeneck addresses some of the issues previously discussed and specifically highlights the construction of the game's *champion* identities. These identities are strongly reliant on sound and music to be fully developed, like in other games such as *DotA 2*, which also conceptualize new incorporations from a holistic perspective.

Although many esports games count with closely tailored characters to fit their storyworlds, not many of them have gravitated toward creating character-specific music products. For this, it is first essential to distinguish between *avatars* and *characters* to set a point of departure for the discussion at hand.

Avatars are in-game representations of the player that can usually be customized and are not directly inserted into the story. Their body features, gender, clothing, as well as other elements, can be chosen by the player. Characters, on the other hand, "imply a connection with the game and narrative story."[26] Although these can be personalized to an extent with available *skins*, they do not change the nature of or their role in the plot. This extends to the music associated with each, since avatars do not have an impact or direct relation to the music in—or around—the game, while characters are usually linked to specific music that is part of their unique identity and the brands that they represent. Therefore, video game audiences can draw character associations based on music, but not usually on avatars—especially in non-esports adventure sagas such as *The Legend of Zelda* or *Final Fantasy*, that rely on *leitmotivs* to afford narrative continuity and aural guidance for the players (Table 2.1).[27]

As underlined, competitive video games have tended to include music to develop the background stories of their characters and make them approachable—and marketable—for fans. This has translated into the progressive approach of the esports and music industries, as the first has come to involve game by-products that attain extra-ludic agents. In any case, this does not mean that the characters and their sonic representations are oblivious to amateur and professional gamers from a performative perspective. As Koskimaa and colleagues argue, in the specific case of *Overwatch*,[28] characters are relevant both for players beyond their technical features:

> In *Overwatch* esports, the characters are present first and foremost in connection with professional players. Most players are known for playing particular characters, and audiences strengthen this connection through different practices such as creating fan art about the players as playable heroes of the game. These depictions of players as game characters are occasionally integrated into official marketing materials, which blur the lines between the fictional world of *Overwatch* and the nonfictional world of *Overwatch* esports.

TABLE 2.1 Avatars *versus* Characters

AVATARS	*CHARACTERS*
Customizable	Not customizable
Not inserted in the storyworld	Inserted in the storyworld
Not narratively relevant	Contribute to narrative development
No specific music attached	Specific music that illustrates their personality, background story, etc.
No transmedia presence	Transmedially present
E.g.: *Rocket League, EA Sports FC, NBA2K.*	E.g.: *DotA 2, League of Legends, Overwatch.*

This statement can be extended to other titles, which follow a similar strategy in including esports content back into the games. An example is that of *League of Legends*, which includes character *skins* for each year's World Championship winners,[29] or *Rocket League*, which features *decals* (personalizable items) for players to show support for their favorite Championship Series teams during each season.[30] These are not as relevant from a musical standpoint as other incorporations, such as skins for esports-band members, but they still contribute to the overall lore of the title.[31]

The inclusion of music-related skins for characters is, in any case, a different matter than that of *music-based* characters, which are included in a strict relation to a preexisting musical figure—e.g., *J Biebs* in *FreeFire*. In other words, music associated with these characters, we may argue, stands on different grounds than those created from scratch, which do not count with an *a priori* sonic identity.

Some games with self-tailored characters have made clear their effort to construct well-rounded identities that consider all the dimensions of their new additions. Sebastien Najand, principal composer at Riot Games, points out how:

> Knowing everything about [the characters] is so important, the story behind them. You want to have as much information, before you start composing, so having an idea of who they are, about where they are from in the world of *League of Legends* (...) Also the way they play in game, so we'll watch game footage, we'll play the game ourselves in beta to see what the character feels like. That also might influence how we approach the music. And of course, the art I think is super important. I might see a lot of the descriptions, verbal descriptions (...) but once I get the art that's usually when I start having some ideas or more concrete ideas in my head.[32]

Although many games choose to present new characters along specific soundtracks that showcase their characteristics and personalities, in the sense described by Najand, few have produced songs as popular music products in collaboration with well-known artists.

On a broad level, three categories can be outlined as frequently used to shape character identities, using music as a mediator:

Firstly, new characters are commonly released along music tracks that appeal to their presence in their storyworld and to their unique abilities. In these cases, music works as an Original Soundtrack that is produced symphonically, electronically, or else, depending on the intent and resources of each company. For example, *League of Legends* releases a soundtrack for each of its characters, which is also used as the login screen theme during their introduction period to the game. These serve the consolidation of the sonic identity of the champions and imply paramusical fields of connotation[33] that contribute to the imagery built around them. Furthermore, these themes have the potential to be quoted in competitive settings to appeal to the knowledge of the audience, in continuity of their individual experiences with the games.

To quote an example, Tahm Kench is a wels catfish, described as a demon that "travels the waterways of Runeterra, feeding his insatiable appetite with the misery of others."[34] It was introduced with a theme that features a deep bass humming voice tracing a pentatonic-Aeolian melody, accompanied by an acoustic slide guitar and sound effects that recall the conventions of horror films—such as the use of clicking and other unidentified sounds on a low bourdon. The use of this mode, the humming, and added

FIGURE 2.3 Tahm Kench's theme humming melody.

effects, along with the visual image created for the character, afford a connection of the character with dark water environments and its lonely-wolf nature.

Similarly, characters in *Street Fighter* have been associated with specific themes throughout different franchise editions, as pointed out by Lidia López in her review of the character Vega.[35] In this case, the fighter's *Spanishness* is depicted through the inclusion of Andalusian music cadences and instrumentation along with physical features such as clothing that frame the character into its respective storyworld.

A second category is that of cinematic presentations of characters, which have become increasingly popular as narrative tools in the development of each game's lore. This may be attributed to progressive technological improvements,[36] as well as to the growing interest in the esports industry to create transmedia products that expand into *audio-and-visual* products. In this sense, we must differentiate between cinematic clips destined for the promotion of game-related products, such as competitive event announcements, and lore-related clips, focused on the story and characters—considering the lack of practical precision of this theoretical division.

If we retake Tahm Kench's case, we will find that its profile was further nuanced in a presentation trailer that included the character's music, along with a brief narration. In this story, a lone traveler is lured by the champion's song—the humming melody—and offered a demonic deal, that unfolds catastrophically for the first, as the catfish ends up eating his bride as a recollection of his earlier favor.[37] The aesthetics of the music video contribute to defining the personality and ambiance in which the character is inserted, and to the continuous development and extension of the game's story.

Another good example of this is that of *Free Fire*, as it also counts with presentation trailers, that resemble short films and serves the unfolding of the dynamic dimension of the corresponding storyworld. Characters such as Alvaro have been introduced through short films that offer profound insight into their personality, traits, and backstories.[38] In this case, the video is mostly accompanied by incidental music, but Alvaro's identity is given a more accurate definition during the end credits, which feature his own theme, produced in collaboration with rapper Saint Josh. Differently, other characters like Skyler have been showcased in closer relation to the music chosen for their sonic definition—e.g., electronic. In either case, music is key in providing the narrative with a part of its content, as it scaffolds the discourse and helps insert featured characters in the plot according to their own traits.

In other games, anecdotally, some characters have also been introduced through music videos or CGI during live events, which allows companies to play with the live reaction and inclusion of the assistant public. For instance, *DotA 2* character

Pangolier was introduced during The International (2017), accompanied by a symphonic orchestra.[39] These occasions offer an opportunity for fans to approach the characters communally, and create expectation through the impact generated by the live event, which can be argued adds to the overall lore of the game from which the community participates.

Lastly, and more significatively, popular music songs for specific characters have also been released by companies such as Riot Games, as described in Jinx's case. These songs have appeared sporadically in collaboration with music industry agents, usually in substitution to ambiance music tracks such as the ones included in the first category. Two further examples are characters Rell—released in December 2020—and Zeri—during January 2022.

Zeri's theme was produced in collaboration with singer and YouTube personality Lauren Babic, who is also the front singer for the progressive metal band *Red Handed Denial*.[40] The song was originally accompanied by a video showing the design of the character, which scaffolded the construction of its identity. She, "the Spark of Zaun," is placed in the fictional environment depicted in *Arcane*, and as such brand fans can more accurately place her in a specific context.[41] Her cheerful personality and sense of loyalty are captured through a D major tonality and a playful rhythm of the drums, which contrasts with the decadent environment of the city that surrounds her in the lore—and music video.

Similarly, Rell's song was created along with singer Ecca Vandal, following the character's description as "The Iron Maiden"[42]—which can be maybe read as a quote to the band. This piece featured a heavy metal sound aesthetic to go along with the character's look, and was rapidly associated with Riot Games' band Pentakill through its aesthetic.[43]

This strategy has been followed by other gaming companies in their progressive approach to the music industry. *Free Fire* case, with Saint Josh's collaboration to create Alvaro's theme,[44] also was released as a separate music video. It is especially worth noting the effort made by the company to release music translations featuring regional artists for the engagement of their international communities, for instance in the production of a homonymous song along Mexican freestyler Zticma, aimed at the game's Latin-American community (Table 2.2).

Overall, the range of music genres and styles proposed by these and other companies has been essential in creating a diverse environment to which fanbases from all over the world can relate. The diversity of characters, their backstories, and their overall lores—of which fans are part of—offer a way of self- and community exploration[45] and an opportunity to temporarily inhabit the games' imagined worlds.

TABLE 2.2 Alvaro's Theme Song Lyrics in English and Spanish Excerpts

ENGLISH (FEAT. SAINT JOHN)	*SPANISH (FEAT. ZTICMA)*
That's right, man, the victory is mine Red hair like no other you will find So much style of everyone of a kind, I throw bombs so you better run and hide	Así es, la victoria mía será, El rojo carmín arrasará, Yo soy Alvaro, el hombre sin igual, Y lanzo bombas, mi estilo es fatal.

The marketing of different games through the exploitation of their characters, hand in hand with the music industry, has become a key component in the continuous collaboration among both parties. Characters are then not only necessarily defined by an Original Soundtrack exclusively, which illustrates their place within the storyworld, but with the incorporation of real-life music artists, producers, and record labels they can transcend their ludic realms and expand their reach toward complementary audiences.

This partnership between industries has been expressed to its maximum extent with the creation of video game-specific music bands, which, as will be shown, are afforded a special role in competitive settings, such as live championships.

BANDS AND POP MUSIC ARTISTS

One of the most celebrated intersections of the music and esports industries are game-inspired bands that feature game characters, which serve to promote their products and the attraction of audiences with diverse interests. Furthermore, they support the expansion of the backstory of specific characters and allow fans to feel reflected and identified.

Riot Music Group at Riot Games has pioneered the creation of game-character bands and established music as the central element dynamizing the overall competitive gaming ecosystem. Some scholars have described their contributions as relevant to the international music scene,[46] although the literature on the topic is still scarce.

Most game-originated bands are eminently virtual, and as such find a clear precedent in existing groups such as Alvin and the Chipmunks, created by Ross Badasarian, who released their first track in 1958, *Witch Doctor*;[47] or Gorillaz, who in 2005 broke the screen barrier with a live performance for the European Music Awards. Video game bands work similarly to these, as they introduce artists that exist digitally, but offer a link with the games when reimagining existing characters as popular music performers. In this sense, they represent another form of transmediality that contributes to the definition of their unique identities, as previously argued.

However, these are not new or exclusive to esports: Old Gods of Asgard in *Alan Wake,* Midnight Riders in *Left 4 Dead*, Off the Hook in *Splatoon 2*, or Love Fist in the *Grand Theft Auto* saga, are only a few of many examples. A difference between these and the bands that will be discussed in the following, is that the latter are inserted into audiovisual and social media as independent products, that constitute their own separate content—i.e. they are not strictly DLC, but a separate commodity from the game. To give an example, one might know who the band K/DA is and consume its music, but not know or have not played *League of Legends*. More significantly, these bands become part of the overall lore of the games and an icon for building a sense of community among fans. However, in the first instance, they represent marketing assets for the companies that create them, rather than complements to their storyworlds.[48]

How these bands are linked to different games depends first and foremost on the strategy devised by each company, for which they range from real-life bands that are put together to be part of a specific title—like Midnight Riders in *Left 4 Dead*—real bands that take a fictional identity in specific titles—such as Refused in *Cyberpunk 2077*, in which they take the name "Samurai"—[49]to game characters embodied by real-flesh popular artists, who maintain game-character identity—e.g., True Damage by Riot Games. In esports, these categories are usually explored as a way of expanding a game's impact among non-gamer audiences, as well as to engage existing fans with new commodities.[50] They also contribute to the link between games and esports, as they are susceptible to being showcased in competitive contexts.

An example of this is the Bad Randoms, a punk-rock band created by Supercell—in collaboration with rhythm-game *Beatstar*—and featured in *Brawl Stars,* whose members are re-imagined characters of the game. As described by Supercell Community Manager Daniel Medeiros,[51] the band was created organically when a previous artist in the team sketched some random skins for characters, and came up with a punk version of Stu—a crash-test-robot Brawler in the game. From that, they created two more punk skins, the band was assembled, and later introduced through a promotional song: *We Won't Cooperate.*[52]

> Their style dictated the genre of the music, but the lyrics and themes were around things the community hates, but relates with –which is, playing with bad teammates (so bad randoms). (...) All the skins performed super well and better than average, but more importantly, is that the Bad Randoms became a new talking point in our community and marketing tool we can use when the time is right. By also being a really good song, it also reached outside our bubble and we've seen that our musical videos are the best ones to get the attention of new users organically.[53]

The band was also introduced in *Brawl Stars* itself to promote the title and construct a bidirectional connection between the game and its related products. For this purpose, it was featured in the game, playing on a small in-game stage, and later brought to life—on a real stage—during the 2022 World Championship.

FIGURE 2.4 The Bad Randoms by *Supercell.*

TABLE 2.3 T.R.A.P. Composition

MEMBER	*ROLE*	*REPRESENTED BY*	*VERSES IN*
Miguel as *DJ Miguel*	Rapper / Singer	Krawk	English / Portuguese
Kelly as *Killa K*	Rapper / Singer	Awich	English / Japanese
Antonio as *A to the O*	Main Rapper	Faruz Feet	English / Spanish
Mocco As *M.C Mocco*	Lead singer	BJRNCK	English

The ensemble found continuity in the extension of its narrative in an alternative timeline, which included a parallel band called the Good Randoms. This did not only provide a marketing opportunity for new skins, but an overall new look for the characters accompanied by songs, now showcased as a boy band reminiscent of 1990s pop—[54] that also made it on stage in 2023. Looking forward, and according to Medeiros, it is also likely that other genres will be explored in the future, to provide further continuity to the ensemble and the marketing opportunities that it affords.

Another case worth quoting here is that of *Free Fire's* band T.R.A.P., also featuring characters from the game. The virtual band has served to dynamize the title's gaming communities around the globe along with continuous collaborations with regional artists such as Anitta in Brazil or Kill Chori in India. The band was originally developed after the success of Riot Game's K/DA, although it was constructed around a genre more appealing to *Free Fire's* audience. The creative department found a compromise halfway between trap, hip-hop, and pop music, to accommodate the band's repertoire to their listeners. This is exemplified in their first release, *I'm on Fire*, launched in 2020, which also includes lyrics in different languages.

The members of T.R.A.P. are presented as alter egos of the characters in the game but are not as strictly linked to its lore as other games, which is mainly due to how the title is marketed and who it is marketed toward. The featured characters are represented by real-life artists, as shown in Table 2.3, who serve to connect with the main audiences of the game.

Later solo pieces for each character did contribute to delineating more specific personalities for each—*The Last One* for Miguel, *Force* for Kelly, *Be the Hero* for Antonio, and *I Am Power* for Mocco. However, these did not entirely match the interventions of the band members in *I'm of Fire*, as they were produced entirely by *Free Fire*, bringing a degree of inconsistency to the individual profiles.

A CASE STUDY: POP MUSIC BANDS IN *LEAGUE OF LEGENDS*

Among these somewhat isolated efforts, Riot Games stands out for its commitment to the musical universe that accompanies its games' lore—especially in *League of*

Legends. The team at Riot Music Group has been pivotal in providing the company with a rich, creative environment that wraps gaming products and extends them toward other marketable items. A clear indicator of the company's interest in exploring this path further is found in its partnerships with Universal Studios or BMG,[55] which afford a direct relation with the music industry and new ways of engaging with the brand's community.

The bands created by the brand are mostly given names that refer to the game and directly appeal to the knowledge of players and existing fans: a *Pentakill* happens when a player eliminates five team opponents in a row; the initials *K/DA* refer to the player's counter on kills, deaths, and assists; *true damage* is a marker for the damage inflicted on opponents that bypasses existing armor; and *heartsteel* is an object in the game that allows the player to increase their health points.

More relevantly, the bands are built around genres that appeal to the features and background stories of their characters, but also to the preferences of fans—so much so that band HEARTSTEEL was fan-art inspired. Maria Egan, Head of Music at Riot Music Group underlined in an interview:

> For HEARTSTEEL, the concept started with players' fan art that inspired the music team to develop a new virtual artist. When we chose the champions, we considered factors like personality, member chemistry, and genre fit. The Champions in HEARTSTEEL are also some of our players' favorite characters and they've been speculating about versions of this lineup for years. For example, Ezreal was a perfect fit as the lead vocalist for HEARTSTEEL. For years our fans have loved his hotshot attitude, but he's also an innovative visionary with never-ending curiosity. It felt authentic and fun to apply that DNA to his lead singer role in HEARTSTEEL. We also thought about role diversity in the game. It was important to have champions with diverse play styles so the band would resonate with players both in their music identity and gameplay.[56]

In this vein, the members of the existing virtual ensembles find a correlation in their aesthetic and background stories to the genre of each group—e.g., metal for Pentakill, or K-pop for K/DA (Table 2.4).

If each band is analyzed separately, the dynamics built around them not only offer greater insight into the creative process and the will of exploring the personality of individual characters, but also a progressive immersion into the music industry and attention to fan engagement.

TABLE 2.4 Bands and Member-Characters by Riot Games

BAND	*MEMBER-CHARACTERS*	*GENRE*	*YEAR OF DEBUT*
Pentakill	Kayle, Karthus, Olaf, Sona, Yorick, Viego*	Heavy Metal	2014
K/DA	Akali, Ahri, Evelynn, Kai'Sa, Seraphine*	K-pop	2018
True Damage	Ekko, Senna, Qiyana, Yasuo, Akali	Pop, hip-hop	2019
HEARTSTEEL	Ezreal, Kayn, Yone, K'Sante, Sett	Pop, K-pop	2023

* Characters that have participated but are not part of the band.

Pentakill

The first group assembled by the brand, Pentakill, was first launched in 2014 as the result of a particular project of some team workers who "decided to start recording a metal album on their own time over the weekends."[57] They imagined the band as a real group, and the favorable reception of fans turned it into the first virtual ensemble of the company. The character members of the band were given background lore that fit their musical traits, contributing to slowly profiling the game's intricate storyworld. For instance, Karthus ("The Deathsinger") is the band's lead singer, inserted in the lore as "an undying spirit whose haunting songs are a prelude to the horror of his nightmarish appearance;"[58] or Sona ("Maven of the Strings"), one of the explicitly musical characters in the game, takes the role of keyboard player in the band.[59] Although other character members did not count with such peculiar profiles, their belongingness to specific areas of the imagined world of Runeterra and given features can be seen as fitting to complete the ensemble.

To land the project, Riot Games hired Norwegian singer Jørn Lande to voice Karthus, who also participated live as the character's alter ego in competitive events such as the *League of Legends* Brazilian Championship in 2015 and 2017. Kayle was likewise embodied by a Norwegian metal singer, Noora Louhimo, while Viego was represented by Telle Smith,[60] all adding their own takes to the fictional personae they were assigned. With this, the vocalists and instrumentalists included in the project not only helped shape it, but contributed a more detailed sonic and visual identity to the game characters.

After their first album release, *Smite and Ignite* (2014), they reappeared with *II: Grasp of the Undying* (2017) and *III: Lost Chapter* (2021). This last recording was coordinated for launching a 45-minute online live event in the context of the pandemic, which showed the company's interest in expanding its products and creating approachable content for fans through adapted means. Furthermore, it was relevant character-wise as it featured a new addition in *League of Legends*, Viego "The Ruined King," who served as an attraction for attendees.

The event, titled *Pentakill III: The Lost Chapter,*[61] was built as a virtual computer-generated concert with the collaboration of startup Wave, in which the participants were given the opportunity to support one of the three Gods of Metal—the Deep One, the Mad One, or the Immortal One.[62] The deities were introduced on social media as an attendance claim, and were interactively endorsed during the concert by fans, who were asked to follow simple keyboard instructions to *win* the event for their God's team—which was tracked by a leaderboard on-screen. The cinematics for the concert depicted the band members embodying their metal alter egos, and showcased live comments and images of fans to closely include them in the fictional battle. Furthermore, the brand showed the attention to its content creators when directly interpelling YouTuber Tobias Fate—"the old gods are dead, do you hear that, Tobias Fate?"—[63] known for playing band member and character Gangplank on *League of Legends*, in what can be interpreted as a nod to his new incorporation to the title.

The event was presented with a narrative that allowed continuity to the band and its characters, creating a coherent event within the brand's universe, and providing an opportunity for fans to come together mid-pandemic. It likewise served the development of the stories of characters who had not been approached since the release of new virtual bands, and the promotion of Viego as a new piece on the game's board. It is important to take in mind that, differently from other bands, *Pentakill* was assembled from an early initiative during the first developments of the Music department at Riot Games, and how its growth showcases the dedication to affording a storyworld in which characters can be inserted independently of the moment of their inclusion in the game.

K/DA

After this, the bands created by Riot stepped into urban and pop styles, prioritizing the taste of fans at a worldwide level and the inclusion of the diverse cultures that constitute the main consumers for the brand. This implied the inclusion of K-pop as one of their cornerstones, not only for its growing popularity all over the globe, but also to the developer's relation with east-Asian countries. In this sense, K-pop afforded an ideal point of connection between Eastern and Western markets, as it grew 44.8% in Korea during 2021, positioning itself as the fastest-growing major market of the year.[64]

Hallyu, the Korean wave,[65] continued its growth in the following years, along with the success of bands such as Blackpink or BTS, drawing from "a cultivated combination of cultural adaptability, innovative production, and market-driven strategies that have ensured its place in the global music industry."[66] The cultural hybridity of the genre has made it appealing to a worldwide audience and, as such, fit for gaming—and especially esports—audiences. Nevertheless, authors such as Millie Firgaard[67] or Sim and colleagues have argued that the aesthetics of K-pop present an appropriation of hip-hop culture that is translated into a hybrid genre. This is, in any case, not exempt from conflict:

> The fact that the K-pop aesthetic generally includes wearing flashy and experimental clothes and make-up regardless of gender, means that a lot of hip-hop traditionalists automatically excluding idols from claiming affiliations with hip-hop culture, simply based on this seeming conflict with the hyper-masculine image that the culture originated with. On top of this, K-pop also conflicts with Korean hip-hop culture as it's very common for K-pop songs to use English in rap verses, which conflicts with the Korean ideal of linguistic authenticity.

Regardless of its success and mediatically transgressive proposals, the genre has shown to be well-incorporated into the music industry machinery, which makes it a fit option for collaborations with video games. This can be seen through bands K/DA and HEARTSTEEL, which are formed respectively as girl and boy bands featuring characters from the games.

K/DA was first launched in 2018, during the opening ceremony of the *League of Legends* World Championship, with the song *POP/STARS*. The band members, who are characters from *League of Legends*, have preexisting backstories and aesthetics which were later incorporated as features for the band members. The creative lead for this first video, Patrick Morales, pointed out how

> by bending the expectations of what players would expect from these characters while still remaining true to the core of who they are as champions, we were able to surprise players with something that felt fresh while also doing something that felt authentic to a broader audience as a flashy and fun music video.[68]

TABLE 2.5 K/DA Composition[69]

MEMBER	*ROLE*	*CHARACTERISTICS*	*REPRESENTED BY*
Ahri	Main vocalist	Leader of the band. Confident, charming. Calmed, encourages self-expression. Looks for new talent to shape them toward their full potential.	Miyeon (member of (G) I-dle); Nayeon (member of Twice); Sana (member of Twice); Jiyho (member of Twice); Bekuh Boom
Akali	Main rapper	Street punk style. Daring and dangerous. Values creative independence and does not compromise her art. Always looking for new projects.	Soyeon (member of (G) I-dle); Chaeyoung (member of Twice); Annika Wells
Evelynn	Lead vocalist	Hypnotic stage presence. Carefully crafted image. Willing to take creative risks.	Madison Beer; Bea Miller; Kim Petras
Kai'sa	Main dancer	Perfectionist. Intense and quiet focus, attention to detail. Cosmopolitan approach to life. Finds inspiration in every environment.	Jaira Burns; Wolftyla; Aluna Francis; Bekuh Boom

Following this, each character was given a role in the band that fit their profile and assigned a real-life singer to represent them, who could work as an alter ego on stage. This implies that the singer behind each character does not need to be the same every time but can vary according to the needs of every occasion (Table 2.5).

The following releases by the band, such as *The Baddest* and *More*, were also featured as promotional themes for *League of Legends*' World Championships, which allowed the inclusion of an opening performance that preluded the matches. These songs—and their respective music videos—were mainly produced by Riot Music Group, which acted as the main label for the band despite their collaboration with the South Korean music distribution company Stone Music Entertainment. If we follow the chain value presented in the previous chapter, we can see how Riot Games was intermingled with different agents from the music industry to produce *More*.

Although other agents were involved in the distribution and promotion of the song, Figure 2.5 shows how Riot Games retains control over the whole process, as it becomes not only the conceptualizer but also the executor of the piece. To this, other agents could be added such as sponsors—e.g., Ducati designed a motorbike for one of the characters in the video—choreographers, studio musicians, etc.

To appeal to the larger global audiences of the game,[70] songs by K/DA include lyrics in different languages and artists from diverse geographies—a strategy followed also in other bands such as True Damage.[71] More significatively, Korean-English bilingualism is connected to the K-pop genre and its audience, as it allows self and group identification among participants, who share common beliefs and values, helping consolidate the

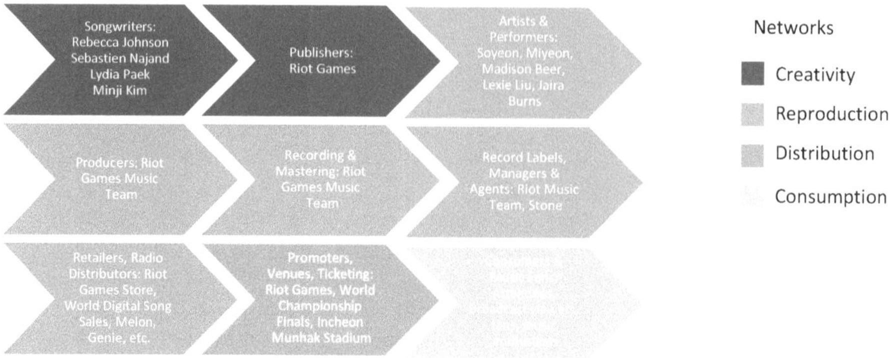

FIGURE 2.5 Chain value of *More* by K/DA (based on Álvarez Vázquez, 2017).

brand's fan community. Furthermore, this contributes to a more effective identification between the characters and the viewers, who can find a form of expression that appeals to them individually in their virtual idols. Additionally, the song was given different versions in various languages (French, Polish, Russian, Spanish, and Swedish) in collaboration with artists to represent each region, which contributes to the sense of identity here underlined.

More also served the presentation of a new game character, Seraphine, who was built with a music-centric backstory.[72] This featured member worked toward the consolidation of the concept behind the band, and in the line of the creation of well-defined identities for the game's *champions*:

> The album overall was meant to be an exploration of individual styles and identity, and how that comes together to make a greater whole. Sera was always going to be a feature that allowed us to explore a storytelling approach to a music release, showing the ascent of a popstar through a different/more personal lens.[73]

HEARTSTEEL

The dynamics in the band HEARTSTEEL, introduced in 2023, are similar to its feminine predecessor, as it consists of diverse *League of Legends* characters that form a K-pop boy band. The character members of the group were chosen for their profiles to fit the different roles to be assigned: Ezreal is the main vocalist of the band (voiced by Baekhyun, from the Korean-Chinese boy band EXO); K'Sante is the band's coleader and vocalist (voiced by Nigerian-American singer and songwriter Toby Lou); Kayn is the rapper and instrumentalist (voiced by American rapper Carl Scruby); Sett is a coleader and rapper (voiced by Taiwanese American singer-songwriter and producer ØZI); and Yone acts as the producer.

Their first release, *Paranoia* (2023), strongly impacted social and more traditional media due to the collaboration of the listed artists and, especially, due to the presence of Baekhyun, a well-known Korean pop star, as lead singer.[74] This popularity also contributed to the creation of a dedicated K-pop fandom under the name *Heartbeats*—a suggestion led, in the first instance, by Riot Games.[75] The Heartbeats mimic other K-pop fan groups such as BTS Army, which serves the connection of BTS fans, their group- and self-identification.[76] Nevertheless, organized K-pop fanbases constitute primarily fan-made environments that offer participation in art and music creation, as already suggested by Jenkins in *Fans, Bloggers, and Gamers* regarding video game environments.[77] This complementary or reinforcing industry can be seen as an effort by Riot Games to expand its reach and embed HEARTSTEEL within the current multimediated gaming panorama.

These videos extend characters' identities through alternative versions of themselves while still retaining their personalities and backgrounds. However, their treatment as actual pop artists contributes to their perception as more than virtual beings. Band-related products such as bloopers videos work in this very sense,[78] as they show the characters in everyday environments where they can express themselves freely. Although music is not a baseline element in these occasions, it is the mediator for the expression of their personalities.

True Damage

Lastly, up to 2024, True Damage is the last band left to discuss. It was presented in 2019 between the launches of K/DA and HEARTSTEEL, to be the main show on the World Finals of *League of Legends* in Paris.[79] The company opted for a pop style that featured rapped sections in the group's presentation song, *Giants*, although the promotional theme for the event was *Phoenix*, starring singers Cailin Russo and Chrissy Costanza. The characters featured in the band included members from previous bands as well as new incorporations. For this purpose, the ensemble's narrative was inserted into the preexisting storytelling to create a continuum.

Furthermore, the attention to character development was, from the beginning, central to the band. As former Executive Producer for *League of Legends* described in a press conference preceding the event:

> We really liked the idea of Akali. Like, when we looked at her history and kind of how the fanbase connected with her a lot, we wanted to see and explore what her career would develop into if she had complete creative control. We worked off of that, and after a lot of discussion in development we were like: Ok, if Akali had her way, she would just go hard into hip-hop, and have her choice of what her dream cast would be. That's actually how True Damage was born: it is a hip-hop collective of Akali's choosing. It's very much born from her roots and her beginning, and what she is inspired by.[80]

Like in other occasions, each True Damage member was embodied by a real-life artist, who also represented them on stage for the quoted Championship: Akali was personified by Soyeon, in continuation to K/DA; Qiyana was illustrated by Becky G; Ekko was embodied by rappers Thutmose and Duckwrth; Senna's vocals were in charge of Keke Palmer; and Yasuo, as the band's DJ, did not have a direct representative. The song that they introduced in the 2019 event was *Giants*, which was launched along with an animated music video featuring the characters and their abilities. Although it stylistically differs from the previous bands, it features similar elements such as the inclusion of languages alluding to the game's biggest audiences, or well-known artists in their respective communities.

The relevance of each of these bands surpasses their anecdotical presence in performative stages or their momentary popularization among players since, as argued, they have explored a two-way connection with *League of Legends*. Each consecutive ensemble has worked to position Riot Games as a referent in the esports industry, as they have contributed to the brand's popularity beyond its gaming audience, maintaining the title as one of the most popular competitive games in the world.[81] Furthermore, with the exploitation of these and other audiovisual products, they have extended their influence on the music industry which, as shown here, has taken an increased interest in the sector.

With this in mind, popular music does not only work as a "particular kind of cultural artifact that provides people with different elements they utilize in their processes of identification"[82] through the creation of lead musical identities embodied by game characters. Popular music is also provided through self-tailored virtual personae that act as mediators for companies, which are not musical agents per se, allowing them to expand their reach and permeate multiple cultural layers.

CONCLUSION

This chapter has shown how character identities are built not only around the background stories and features designed in each game but also from personalized musical texts that extend beyond the games into competitive arenas and beyond strictly gamer audiences. In this sense, game characters have become relevant outside of their digital grounds in esports, as much as others in the overall videogame industry—from Pikachu to Cloud Strife—and become iconic references for fans in competitive settings.

In the cases discussed, identities are frequently built in continuation of more extensive lores, which are the constitutive basis of the games' storyworlds. Thanks to the multimedia strategies followed by developers and producers, many characters find a presence in their gaming communities that surpasses their in-game roles, and allows them to break into popular culture more widely—e.g., as pop-star alter egos. To create a sense of plausibility among derived products, music is key in providing continuity and creating marketing opportunities, bound by transmedia storytelling strategies.

Therefore, music does not only work as a scaffolding element for in-game action but it provides constancy and consistency for the games' fictional worlds when they extend beyond the screen. This is also reinforced by the bidirectionality suggested by the introduction of real-life characters, objects, or events in and outside of the game—like competitions.

The shaping of character identities can be outlined through different categories, which are frequently used also considering multimedia consumption by the games' objective publics. These include specific music tracks to go with the release of new characters, which tend to be composed following their presence in the storyworld and unique characteristics; cinematic presentations of characters, and cinematic shorts that include them, building on the same elements; and popular music songs, which are frequently brought to life with the collaboration of regional artists. Nevertheless, these categories are not only present, nor need to be the only ones taken into consideration to explore the musical presence of game characters.

Popular music is provided as a means to connect with current audiences and reach beyond preexisting publics, especially with the attention to regionality shown by companies such as Garena. This is useful to the extent that real or virtual personae, including game bands, can act as mediators for the companies that they represent, which frequently do not include specific record labels.

In this context, Riot Games supposes an exceptional case which, as jokingly defined by the company, has become "a music company that make[s] games."[83] This frequent statement shows their effort and artistic interest in exploring the market beyond their most successful titles, as does the creation of their own label under the name Riot Games Music. Furthermore, they have established a precedent that has been taken by other companies and, undoubtedly, will continue to expand the collaborations between the gaming and music industries.

Music scaffolds the creation of well-rounded and relatable music identities through the stories given to shape each character, as well as to the genres explored to present them to fans and not-fans alike. In this way, characters' identities can be built musically while they contribute to the identity-creation of the fans that receive and consume them, in referring to genres that are already part of their daily experiences. As suggested by McKinlay and McVittie, "even for groups or communities that are not primarily organized around musical preferences, music talk can provide central elements of collective identities."[84] This idea will become crucial in providing memorable experiences in competitive contexts, as they become able to appeal to physical and virtual attendees through different media.

NOTES

1 Toa Dunn, former Head of Music at Riot Games. Interview by Eulalia Febrer-Coll. 4 September 2020.

2 The term *lore* refers to the "knowledge and information related to a particular subject, especially when this is not written down; the stories and traditions of a particular group of people" (see Oxford Learner's Dictionary, "Lore". Available at: https://www.oxfordlearnersdictionaries.com/definition/english/lore, n.d. Accessed 14 April 2023. In the fantasy contexts that are pinpointed here, it refers to the story built to give depth to the narrativity of the imagined world.

3 Marta Martínez Núñez & Víctor Navarro Remesal, "La complejidad ludonarrativa en el videojuego: un doble boomerang", *L'Atalante*, 2021, 31 , 7–32.

4 See José García Hernández, "La teoría narrativa del videojuego: Intertextualidad, Hipertexto y videojuego", *Revista Laboratorio,* 2018, 18. Available at: https://revistalaboratorio.udp.cl/index.php/laboratorio/article/view/28. Accessed 28 December 2023.
5 Lucia Škripcová, "Convergence in Digital Games: A Case Study of League of Legends", *Acta Ludologica*, 2022, 5(2), 87–103.
6 Raine Koskimaa, Tanja Välisalo, Maria Routsalainen & Veli-Matti Karhulahti, "Esports Transmedia Universes: The Case of *Overwatch*", in Dal Yong Jin (Ed.), *Global Esports: Transformation of cultural Perceptions of Competitive Gaming*, 162. New York: Bloomsbury, 2021.
7 Koskimaa et al., "Esports Transmedia Universes", 161.
8 Emily Joy Bembeneck, "Game Narrative and Storyworld in *League of Legends*", in Matthew Wilhelm Kapell (Ed.), *The Play Versus Story Divide in Game Studies: Critical Essays*, 41–56. Jefferson, MO: McFarland & Company, 2016.
9 Mike Morasky, Composer at Valve. Interview by Eulalia Febrer-Coll. 14 December 2023.
10 Juan Sebastián Díaz Gasca, "Music Beyond Gameplay: Motivators in the Consumption of Videogame Soundtracks" (Doctoral Thesis). Griffith University, 2015.
11 Díaz Gasca, "Music Beyond Gameplay", 77.
12 Translated in Pablo Vila, "Narrative Identities and Popular Music: Linguistic Discourses and Social Practices", in Pablo Vila (ed.), *Music and Youth Culture in Latin America: Identity Construction Processes from New York to Buenos Aires.* New York: Oxford University Press, 2014, 18.
13 Henry Jenkins, *Convergence Culture: Where Old and New Media Meet.* New York: New York University Press, 2006, 95–96. The author credits the origin of the term in the public domain around 1999, and links it to the release of independent film *The Blair Witch Project* (Haxan Films). Also see Carlos Alberto Scolari, *Narrativas Transmedia.* Barcelona: Deusto, 2013.
14 Marie-Lauren Ryan, "Transmedial Storytelling and Transfictionality", *Poetics Today*, 34 (2013), 361–387.
15 Ryan, "Transmedial Storytelling and Transfictionality", 363.
16 League of Legends Wiki, "Notai", *League of Legends Fandom*, n.d. Available at: https://leagueoflegends.fandom.com/wiki/Notai?so=search. Accessed 9 January 2024. The adventure game *Song of Nunu*, released by Riot Games in 2023, is precisely set in this imaginary geography.
17 The attention to detail in the creation of each area on the world of Runeterra can be found on *League of Legends*' website, at https://map.leagueoflegends.com/en_US, n.d. Accessed 29 December 2023.
18 *Arcane*, sason 1, episode 4, "Episode 4: Ghosts of the Past". Fortiche Productions, 2021.
19 The Fortnite Team, "From League of Legends and Arcane, Jinx Brings her Aura of Anarchy to Fortnite", *Fortnite*, 2021. Available at: https://www.fortnite.com/news/from-league-of-legends-and-arcane-jinx-brings-her-aura-of-anarchy-to-fortnite?lang=en-US. Accessed 10 January 2024.
20 See Chapter 6.
21 Ryan defines transfictionality as "the migration of fictional entities across different texts, but these texts may belong to the same medium, usually written narrative fiction. Transmedial storytelling can be regarded as a special case of transfictionality—a transfictionality that operates across many different media." In "Transmedial Storytelling and Transfictionality", 365–366.
22 See Chapter 5.
23 The character was only temporarily available on the platform. See FreeFire, "J. Biebs", n.d. Available at: https://ff.garena.com/es/chars/550. Accessed 11 January 2024.

24 Fortnite Wiki, "The Storyline (Battle Royale)", *Fortnite Archive*, n.d. Available at: https://fortnite-archive.fandom.com/wiki/The_Storyline_(Battle_Royale). Accessed 11 January 2024.
25 Bembeneck, "Game Narrative and Storyworld in *League of Legends*", 41–55.
26 Díaz Gasca, "Music Beyond Gameplay", 64.
27 Richard Anatone, "Leitmotivic Strategies in Nobuo Uematsu's Final Fantasy Soundtracks", *Music Theory Spectrum*, 2023, 45(2), 257–283.
28 Koskimaa et al., "Esports Transmedia Universes", 156.
29 Fahim Shahriar, "T1 Confirms Skin Selections for Future World 2023 Skins", *GameRiv,* 2023. Available at: https://gameriv.com/t1-skin-selections-lol-worlds-2023-skins/. Accessed 25 January 2024.
30 Scout Seshimo, "New Esports Shop Items for 2022-2023 Season", *Rocket League,* 2022. Available at: https://www.rocketleague.com/en/news/new-esports-shop-items-for-202223-season. Accessed 25 January 2024.
31 Not in-game exclusive. By *overall lore*, I refer to the ecosystem-comprising storyworld that is built around the game which includes practices and occurrences relevant to the game's community.
32 Sebastien Najand. Inteviewed by Jacob Westberg, 18 December 2020. Available at Mount West Music, "Sebastien Najand: Interview with a Principal Composer at Riot Games", *Youtube*, 2020. Available at: https://www.youtube.com/watch?v=CUoCPIql4Cw. Accessed 1 February 2024.
33 Philipp Tagg, "Intersubjectivity", in *Music's Meanings: A Modern Musicology for Non-Musos.* New York & Huddersfield: The Mass Media Music Scholars' Press, 2012.
34 Riot Games, "Tahm Kench: The River King", *Riot Games Universe*, n.d. Available at: https://www.leagueoflegends.com/en-pl/champions/tahm-kench/. Accessed 31 January 2024.
35 Lidia López, "Vega's Musical Spanishness in Street Fighter", paper presented at *VIII Workshop do CYSMUS. Prácticas Mediáticas em Rede*, Research Cluster in Sound and Music in Digital and Audiovisual Meida, Universidade Nova de Lisboa, 2023.
36 Toa Dunn. Interview by Eulalia Febrer-Coll. 4 September 2020.
37 League of Legends, "Tahm Kench: The River King | New Champion Teaser - League of Legends", *Youtube,* 2016. Available at: https://www.youtube.com/watch?v=u9RM4HwwoKs&t=57s. Accessed 31 January 2023.
38 Garena Free Fire Global, "Full Animation | Alvaro: Reignition | Free Fire Tales", *Youtube*, 2023. Available at: https://www.youtube.com/watch?v=pNhxrczcH8g&t=58s. Accessed 31 January 2024.
39 Emma Avemour, "TI7 Crowd Reaction to Dueling Fates Update Reveal", *Youtube*, 2017. Available at: https://www.youtube.com/watch?v=JSm2drzQWFk. Accessed 31 January 2024.
40 Lauren Babic, *Youtube*, n.d. Available at: https://www.youtube.com/@laurenbabic, n.d. Accessed 31 January 2024.
41 League of Legends, "Zeri, The Spark of Zaun | Champion Theme (ft. Lauren Babic) - League of Legends", *Youtube*, 2022. Available at: https://www.youtube.com/watch?v=jDXCgs5SRfw. Accessed 31 January 2024.
42 Riot Games, "Rell: The Iron Maiden", *Riot Games Universe*, n.d. Available at: https://universe.leagueoflegends.com/en_GB/story/champion/rell/. Accessed 31 January 2024.
43 League of Legends, "Rell, The Iron Maiden | Champion Theme (ft. Ecca Vandal) - League of Legends", *Youtube*, 2021. Available at: https://www.youtube.com/watch?v=ETaX9DZBSEk. Accessed 31 January 2024. See following epigraph.
44 Garena Free Fire Global, "EXPLOSIVE SURPRISE Lyric Video | "Alvaro: Reignition" Theme Song", *Youtube*, 2023. Available at: https://www.youtube.com/watch?v=cBHB3rn0XBY. Accessed 31 January 2024.

45 Simon Frith, "Towards an Aesthetic of Popular Music", in Richard Leppert & Susan McClary (Eds.), *The Politics of Composition, Performance and Reception*, 133–172. Cambridge: Cambridge University Press.

46 Karina Moritzen, "Abrindo Moshpits Virtuais: Cenas Musicais e Shows ao vivo em Fortnite e Minecraft", *XXX Encontro Anual Da Compós*, 2021, 1–24; Yaewon Jin & Tae-Jin Yoon, "Convergence of Music and Esports", in Dal Yong Jin (Ed.), *Global Esports: Transformation of Cultural Perceptions of Competitive Gaming*, 184–200. New York: Bloomsbury, 2021.

47 Alicia Stark, "Gender, Ethnicity, and Identity in Virtual Bands and Vocaloid" (Doctoral Thesis). Cardiff University, School of Music, 2018.

48 Ian Cross, "Music in the Digital Age: Commodity, Community, Communion", *AI & Society*, 38, 2023, 2387–2400.

49 Cyberpunk Fandom, "Refused", *Cyberpunk Wiki*, n.d. Available at: https://cyberpunk.fandom.com/wiki/Refused. Accessed 5 February 2024.

50 Eulalia Febrer-Coll, "Everybody Wants to Be My Enemy: Popular Music and Transmediality in Aracane", *SeriARTE*, 2023, 4, 68–86.

51 Daniel Medeiros, Community Manager at Supercell, written personal communication. 1 March 2024.

52 Brawl Stars, "Brawl Stars Music Video: Bad Randoms - We Won't Cooperate!", *Youtube*, 2021. Available at: https://www.youtube.com/watch?v=zQRgLZDp5Ds. Accessed 10 February 2024.

53 Daniel Medeiros, written personal communication. 1 March 2024.

54 Brawl Stars, "Brawl Stars Music Video: Good Randoms – The One", *Youtube*, 2023. Available at: https://www.youtube.com/watch?v=PEfSpxi8wag. Accessed 10 February 2024.

55 Murray Stassen, "Riot Games and BMG Strike Strategic Partnership, Extend Global Publishing Admin Deal", *MusicBusiness Worldwide*, 2023. Available at: https://www.musicbusinessworldwide.com/riot-games-and-bmg-strike-strategic-partnership-extend-global-publishing-admin-deal/. Accessed 10 February 2024.

56 Kay Sesoko, "'There's a Special Connection between the "League of Legends" & K-Pop Fandoms,' Maria Egan of Riot Games On Gaming & Music | Exclusive Interview", *Kpopmap*, 2023. Available at: https://www.kpopmap.com/theres-a-special-connection-between-the-league-of-legends-kpop-fandoms-maria-egan-of-riot-games-on-gaming-music-exclusive-interview/. Accessed 10 February 2023.

57 Words by Christopher, "Toa Dunn, Head of Riot Games Music, on the Future of Virtual Music Groups", *Virtual Humans*, 2022. Available at: https://www.virtualhumans.org/article/toa-dunn-head-of-riot-games-music-on-the-future-of-virtual-music-groups. Accessed 10 February 2024.

58 Riot Games, "Karthus: The Deathsinger", *Riot Games Universe*, n.d. Available at: https://universe.leagueoflegends.com/en_PL/story/champion/karthus/. Accessed 12 February 2024.

59 Riot Games, "Sona: Maven of the Strings", *Games Universe*, n.d. Available at: https://universe.leagueoflegends.com/en_PL/story/champion/sona/. Accessed 12 February 2024.

60 Ethan Millman, "Wave and Riot Games are Teaming up on a concert for a Fictional Metal Band", *Rolling Stone*, 2021. Available at: https://www.rollingstone.com/pro/news/riot-games-wave-concert-pentakill-1219232/. Accessed 15 December 2024.

61 Riot Games Music, "Pentakill III: Lost Chapter - An Interactive Album Experience", *Youtube*, 2021. Available at: https://www.youtube.com/watch?v=vnwp6PHn9Kk&t=35s. Accessed 15 December 2024.

62 Riot Games Music, "Metal Is Born | Pentakill III: Lost Chapter | Riot Games Music", *Youtube*, 2021. Available at: https://www.youtube.com/watch?v=SX0LCItDxgM. Accessed 15 December 2024.
63 Based Amumu, "Tobias Fate Reacts to Being Mentioned in 'The Battle of the Pentakill'!!!", *Youtube*, 2021. Available at: https://www.youtube.com/watch?v=mEpDQmbu8ug. Accessed 15 December 2024.
64 IFPI, *Global Music Report 2021*, 2021, https://www.ifpi.org/wp-content/uploads/2020/03/GMR2021_STATE_OF_THE_INDUSTRY.pdf. Accessed 12 February 2024.
65 Hee-chul Sim, Soel-ah Kim & Byung-min Lee, "K-pop Strategy Seen from the Viewpoint of Cultural Hybridity and the Tradition of the *Gwangdae*", *Kritika Kultura*, 2017, 29, 292–317.
66 Isabella Chen, "Expansion of K-pop in the Global Market", *American Journal of Student Research*, 2023, 1(1), 1–5, https://ajosr.org/wp-content/uploads/journal/published_paper/volume-1/issue-1/ajsr3_f8QwTxMu.pdf.
67 Sim, Kim & Lee, "K-pop Strategy Seen from the Viewpoint of Cultural Hybridity".
68 Donghyun "Wony" Won & Yudae "Akiin" Oak, "Interview with Patrick Morales, Janelle Jimenez, and Toa Dunn; the Creators of the Global Sensation, K/DA-POP/STARS", *INVEN Global*, 2018. Available at: https://www.invenglobal.com/articles/6859/interview-with-patrick-morales-janelle-jimenez-and-toa-dunn-the-creators-of-the-global-sensation-kda-pop-stars. Accessed 12 February 2024.
69 Riot Games, "K/DA Official Fan Club", n.d. Available at: https://www.leagueoflegends.com/en-gb/event/kda-official-fan-club/. Accessed 12 February 2024.
70 Samuel Tan, "Charting the Global Landscape of Esports Viewership", *YouGov*, 2023. Available at: https://business.yougov.com/content/46705-charting-the-global-landscape-of-esports-viewership-may-2023?redirect_from=%2Fcontent%2F8333-charting-the-global-landscape-of-esports-viewership-may-2023. Accessed 16th February 2024.
71 Eulalia Febrer-Coll, "Living Like Giants: 'League of Legends' from the Screen to the Stage", *Journal of Sound, Silence, Image and Technology*, 2020, 3, 71–88.
72 Riot Games, "Seraphine: The Starry-Eyed Songstress", *Riot Games Universe*, n.d. Available at: https://universe.leagueoflegends.com/en_US/story/champion/seraphine/. Accessed 16 February 2024.
73 Riot_Westbroke, "[AMA] We're the Riot Games Music Team, Here to Answer All of Your Music Questions. Ask Us Anything!", *Reddit*, 2021. Available at: https://www.reddit.com/r/leagueoflegends/comments/rh98m9/comment/hoqik9r/. Accessed 16th February 2024.
74 For example, Hazeeq Sukri, "Baekhyun of K-pop Group EXO Joins 'League of Legends' New Virtual Boy Group", *CNA Lifestyle*, 2023. Available at: https://cnalifestyle.channelnewsasia.com/entertainment/baekhyun-joins-league-legends-group-heartsteel-373246. Accessed 16 February 2024.
75 Riot Games Music, "Wait, Before We Go/Official Fandom Name = HEARTBEATS/Because You Keep Us Going", *X*, 24th October 2023. Available at: https://twitter.com/riotgamesmusic/status/1716562155586437509. Accessed 18 February 2024.
76 Jin Ha Lee & Anh Thuy Nguyen, "How Music Fans Shape Commercial Music Servies: A Case Study of BTS and ARMY", *Proceedings of the 21st ISMIR Conference*, Montréal, 11–16 October 2020.
77 Henry Jenkins, *Fans, Bloggers, and Gamers: Exploring Participatory Culture*. New York: New York University Press, 2006.
78 League of Legends, "HEARTSTEEL - PARANOIA Music Video Bloopers", *Youtube*, 2023. Available at: https://www.youtube.com/watch?v=rUPocq8frr4. Accessed 18 February 2024.
79 Febrer-Coll, "Living Like Giants: *League of Legends* from the Screen to the Stage", 71–88.

80 Tom Matthiesen, "[Worlds 2019] Pre-Finals Press Conference: Riot Games Executives Talk True Damage and Louis Vuitton x LoL", *INVEN Global*, 2019. Available at: https://www.invenglobal.com/articles/9571/worlds-2019-pre-finals-press-conference-riot-games-executives-talk-true-damage-and-louis-vuitton-x-lol. Accessed 16 December 2024.

81 Esports Charts, "All-Time Popular Esports by Viewership", n.d. Available at: https://escharts.com/top-games?order=peak&year=all-time. Accessed 18 February 2024.

82 Vila, "Narrative Identities and Popular Music: Lingüistics Discourses and Social Practices", 17–80.

83 Riot Games Music, "Hey, We're RGM. The Music Company That Makes Gam-- Wait, We Mean, the Games Company That Makes Mus-- Shoot, That's Not Right Either. We Really Should Have Prepared More for This. Just uh, Just Follow Us Here for All Things Music", *X*, 2nd July 2021. Available at: https://twitter.com/riotgamesmusic/status/1410963889110491136?ref_src=twsrc%5Etfw%7Ctwcamp%5Etweetembed%7Ctwterm%5E1410963889110491136%7Ctwgr%5E10d7fdf49014160a75b63d8096fcce7e037fcaa2%7Ctwcon%5Es1_&ref_url=https%3A%2F%2Fwww.virtualhumans.org%2Farticle%2Friot-games-launches-virtual-record-label-riot-games-music. Accessed 18 February 2024.

84 Andy McKinlay and Chris McVittie, "'Will the Real Slim Shady Please Stand Up? Identity in Popular Music", in Raymond Macdonald, David J. Hargreaves & Dorothy Miell (Eds.), *Handbook of Musical Identities*, 137–151. New York: Oxford University Press.

REFERENCES

Anatone, Richard. "Leitmotivic Strategies in Nobuo Uematsu's Final Fantasy Soundtracks", *Music Theory Spectrum,* 2023, 45(2), 257–283.

Avemour, Emma. "TI7 Crowd Reaction to Dueling Fates Update Reveal", *Youtube,* 2017. Available at: https://www.youtube.com/watch?v=JSm2drzQWFk. Accessed 31st January 2024.

Babic, Lauren. *Youtube*, n.d. Available at: https://www.youtube.com/@laurenbabic. Accessed 31st January 2024.

Based Amumu. "Tobias Fate Reacts to Being Mentioned in 'The Battle of the Pentakill'!!!", *Youtube*, 2021. Available at: https://www.youtube.com/watch?v=mEpDQmbu8ug. Accessed 15th December 2024.

Bembeneck, Emily Joy. "Game Narrative and Storyworld in *League of Legends*", in Matthew Wilhelm Kapell (Ed.), *The Play versus Story Divide in Game Studies: Critical Essays,* 41–56. Jefferson: McFarland & Company, 2016.

Brawl Stars. "Brawl Stars Music Video: Bad Randoms - We Won't Cooperate!", *Youtube,* 2021. Available at: https://www.youtube.com/watch?v=zQRgLZDp5Ds. Accessed 10th February 2024.

Brawl Stars. "Brawl Stars Music Video: Good Randoms - The One", *Youtube*, 2023. Available at: https://www.youtube.com/watch?v=PEfSpxi8wag. Accessed 10th February 2024.

Chen, Isabella. "Expansion of K-pop in the Global Market", *American Journal of Student Research*, 2023, 1(1), 1–5, https://ajosr.org/wp-content/uploads/journal/published_paper/volume-1/issue-1/ajsr3_f8QwTxMu.pdf.

Cross, Ian. "Music in the Digital Age: Commodity, Community, Communion", *AI & Society,* 2023, 38, 2387–2400.

Cyberpunk Fandom. "Refused", *Cyberpunk Wiki*, n.d. Available at: https://cyberpunk.fandom.com/wiki/Refused. Accessed 5th February 2024.

Díaz Gasca, Juan Sebastián. "Music Beyond Gameplay: Motivators in the Consumption of Videogame Soundtracks" (Doctoral Thesis). Griffith University, 2015.

Esports Charts. "All-Time Popular Esports by Viewership", n.d. Available at: https://escharts.com/top-games?order=peak&year=all-time. Accessed 18th February 2024.

Febrer-Coll, Eulalia. "Everybody Wants to Be My Enemy: Popular Music and Transmediality in Aracane", *SeriARTE,* 2023, 4, 68–86.

Febrer-Coll, Eulalia. "Living Like Giants: 'League of Legends' from the Screen to the Stage", *Journal of Sound, Silence, Image and Technology,* 2020, 3, 71–88.

Fortnite Wiki. "The Storyline (Battle Royale)", *Fortnite Archive*, n.d. Available at: https://fortnite-archive.fandom.com/wiki/The_Storyline_(Battle_Royale). Accessed 11th January 2024.

FreeFire. "J. Biebs", n.d. Available at: https://ff.garena.com/es/chars/550. Accessed 11th January 2024.

Frith, Simon. "Towards an Aesthetic of Popular Music", in Richard Leppert & Susan McClary (eds.), *The Politics of Composition, Performance and Reception,* 133–172. Cambridge: Cambridge University Press.

García Hernández, José. "La teoría narrativa del videojuego: Intertextualidad, Hipertexto y videojuego", *Revista Laboratorio*, 2018, 18. Available at: https://revistalaboratorio.udp.cl/index.php/laboratorio/article/view/28. Accessed 28th December 2023.

Garena Free Fire Global. "EXPLOSIVE SURPRISE Lyric Video | "Alvaro: Reignition" Theme Song", *Youtube,* 2023. Available at: https://www.youtube.com/watch?v=cBHB3rn0XBY. Accessed 31st January 2024.

Garena Free Fire Global. "Full Animation | Alvaro: Reignition | Free Fire Tales", *Youtube*, 2023. Available at: https://www.youtube.com/watch?v=pNhxrczcH8g&t=58s. Accessed 31st January 2024.

IFPI. *Global Music Report 2021*, 2021, https://www.ifpi.org/wp-content/uploads/2020/03/GMR2021_STATE_OF_THE_INDUSTRY.pdf. Accessed 12th February 2024.

Jenkins, Henry. *Convergence Culture: Where Old and New Media Meet.* New York: New York University Press, 2006.

Jenkins, Henry. *Fans, Bloggers, and Gamers: Exploring Participatory Culture*. New York: New York University Press, 2006.

Jin, Yaewon & Yoon, Tae-Jin. "Convergence of Music and Esports", in Dal Yong Jin (ed.), *Global Esports: Transformation of Cultural Perceptions of Competitive Gaming*, 184–200. New York: Bloomsbury, 2021.

Koskimaa, Raine, Välisalo, Tanja, Routsalainen, Maria & Karhulahti, Veli-Matti. "Esports Transmedia Universes: The Case of *Overwatch*", in Dal Yong Jin (Ed.), *Global Esports: Transformation of cultural Perceptions of Competitive Gaming,* 162. New York: Bloomsbury, 2021.

League of Legends Wiki. "Notai", *League of Legends Fandom*, n.d. Available at: https://leagueoflegends.fandom.com/wiki/Notai?so=search. Accessed 9th January 2024.

League of Legends. "HEARTSTEEL - PARANOIA Music Video Bloopers", *Youtube,* 2023. Available at: https://www.youtube.com/watch?v=rUPocq8frr4. Accessed 18th February 2024.

League of Legends. "Rell, The Iron Maiden | Champion Theme (ft. Ecca Vandal) - League of Legends", *Youtube*, 2021. Available at: https://www.youtube.com/watch?v=ETaX9DZBSEk. Accessed 31st January 2024.

League of Legends. "Tahm Kench: The River King | New Champion Teaser - League of Legends", *Youtube,* 2016. Available at: https://www.youtube.com/watch?v=u9RM4HwwoKs&t=57s. Accessed 31st January 2023.

League of Legends. "Zeri, The Spark of Zaun | Champion Theme (ft. Lauren Babic) - League of Legends", *Youtube*, 2022. Available at: https://www.youtube.com/watch?v=jDXCgs5SRfw. Accessed 31st January 2024.

Lee, Jin Ha & Nguyen, Anh Thuy. "How Music Fans Shape Commercial Music Servies: A Case Study of BTS and ARMY", *Proceedings of the 21st ISMIR Conference*, Montréal, 11–16th October 2020.

López, Lidia. "Vega's Musical Spanishness in Street Fighter", paper presented at *VIII Workshop do CYSMUS. Prácticas Mediáticas em Rede*, Research Cluster in Sound and Music in Digital and Audiovisual Meida, Universidade Nova de Lisboa, 2023.

Martínez Núñez, Marta & Navarro Remesal, Víctor. "La complejidad ludonarrativa en el videojuego: un doble boomerang", *L'Atalante*, 2021, 31, 7–32.

Matthiesen, Tom. "[Worlds 2019] Pre-Finals Press Conference: Riot Games Executives Talk True Damage and Louis Vuitton x LoL", *INVEN Global*, 2019. Available at: https://www.invenglobal.com/articles/9571/worlds-2019-pre-finals-press-conference-riot-games-executives-talk-true-damage-and-louis-vuitton-x-lol. Accessed 16th December 2024.

McKinlay, Andy & McVittie, Chris. "'Will the Real Slim Shady Please Stand Up? Identity in Popular Music", in Raymond Macdonald, David J. Hargreaves & Dorothy Miell (Eds.), *Handbook of Musical Identities,* 137–151. New York: Oxford University Press.

Millman, Ethan. "Wave and Riot Games Are Teaming Up on a Concert for a Fictional Metal Band", *Rolling Stone*, 2021. Available at: https://www.rollingstone.com/pro/news/riot-games-wave-concert-pentakill-1219232/. Accessed 15th December 2024.

Moritzen, Karina. "Abrindo Moshpits Virtuais: Cenas Musicais e Shows ao vivo em Fortnite e Minecraft", *XXX Encontro Anual Da Compós*, 2021, 1–24.

Mount West Music. "Sebastien Najand: Interview with a Principal Composer at Riot Games", *Youtube,* 2020. Available at: https://www.youtube.com/watch?v=CUoCPIql4Cw. Accessed 1st February 2024.

Oxford Learner's Dictionary. "Lore", n.d. Available at: https://www.oxfordlearnersdictionaries.com/definition/english/lore. Accessed 14th April 2023.

Riot Games. "Karthus: The Deathsinger", *Riot Games Universe*, n.d. Available at: https://universe.leagueoflegends.com/en_PL/story/champion/karthus/. Accessed 12th February 2024.

Riot Games. "K/DA Official Fan Club", n.d. Available at: https://www.leagueoflegends.com/en-gb/event/kda-official-fan-club/. Accessed 12th February 2024.

Riot Games. "Rell: The Iron Maiden", *Riot Games Universe*, n.d. Available at: https://universe.leagueoflegends.com/en_GB/story/champion/rell/. Accessed 31st January 2024.

Riot Games. "Seraphine: The Starry-Eyed Songstress", *Riot Games Universe*, n.d. Available at: https://universe.leagueoflegends.com/en_US/story/champion/seraphine/. Accessed 16th February 2024.

Riot Games. "Sona: Maven of the Strings", *Games Universe*, n.d. Available at: https://universe.leagueoflegends.com/en_PL/story/champion/sona/. Accessed 12th February 2024.

Riot Games. "Tahm Kench: The River King", *Riot Games Universe*, n.d. Available at: https://www.leagueoflegends.com/en-gb/champions/tahmkench/. Accessed 31st January 2024.

Riot Games Music. "Hey, We're RGM. The Music Company That Makes Gam-- Wait, We Mean, the Games Company That Makes Mus-- Shoot, That's Not Right Either. We Really Should Have Prepared More for This. Just uh, Just Follow Us Here for All Things Music", *X*, 2nd July 2021. Available at: https://twitter.com/riotgamesmusic/status/1410963889110491136?ref_src=twsrc%5Etfw%7Ctwcamp%5Etweetembed%7Ctwterm%5E1410963889110491136%7Ctwgr%5E10d7fdf49014160a75b63d8096fcce7e037fcaa2%7Ctwcon%5Es1_&ref_url=https%3A%2F%2Fwww.virtualhumans.org%2Farticle%2Friot-games-launches-virtual-record-label-riot-games-music. Accessed 18th February 2024.

Riot Games Music. "Metal Is Born | Pentakill III: Lost Chapter | Riot Games Music", *Youtube,* 2021. Available at: https://www.youtube.com/watch?v=SX0LCItDxgM. Accessed 15th December 2024.

Riot Games Music. "Pentakill III: Lost Chapter - An Interactive Album Experience", *Youtube,* 2021. Available at: https://www.youtube.com/watch?v=vnwp6PHn9Kk&t=35s. Accessed 15th December 2024.

Riot Games Music. "Wait, Before We Go / Official Fandom Name = HEARTBEATS/Because You Keep Us Going", *X*, 24th October 2023. Available at: https://twitter.com/riotgamesmusic/status/1716562155586437509. Accessed 18th February 2024.

Riot_Westbroke. "[AMA] We're the Riot Games Music Team, Here to Answer All of Your Music Questions. Ask Us Anything!", *Reddit,* 2021. Available at: https://www.reddit.com/r/leagueoflegends/comments/rh98m9/comment/hoqik9r/. Accessed 16th February 2024.

Ryan, Marie-Lauren. "Transmedial Storytelling and Transfictionality", *Poetics Today,* 201334, 361–387.

Scolari, Carlos Alberto. *Narrativas Transmedia.* Barcelona: Deusto, 2013.

Seshimo, Scout. "New Esports Shop Items for 2022-2023 Season", *Rocket League*, 2022. Available at: https://www.rocketleague.com/en/news/new-esports-shop-items-for-202223-season. Accessed 25th January 2024.

Sesoko, Kay. "'There's A Special Connection Between the "League of Legends" & K-Pop Fandoms,' Maria Egan of Riot Games On Gaming & Music | Exclusive Interview", *Kpopmap,* 2023. Available at: https://www.kpopmap.com/theres-a-special-connection-between-the-league-of-legends-kpop-fandoms-maria-egan-of-riot-games-on-gaming-music-exclusive-interview/. Accessed 10th February 2023.

Shahriar, Fahim. "T1 Confirms Skin Selections for Future World 2023 Skins", *GameRiv,* 2023. Available at: https://gameriv.com/t1-skin-selections-lol-worlds-2023-skins/. Accessed 25th January 2024.

Sim, Hee-chul, Kim, Soel-ah & Lee, Byung-min. "K-pop Strategy Seen from the Viewpoint of Cultural Hybridity and the Tradition of the *Gwangdae*", *Kritika Kultura*, 2017, 29, 292–317.

Škripcová, Lucia. "Convergence in Digital Games: A Case Study of League of Legends", *Acta Ludologica,* 2022, 5(2), 87–103.

Stark, Alicia. "Gender, Ethnicity, and Identity in Virtual Bands and Vocaloid" (Doctoral Thesis). Cardiff University, School of Music, 2018.

Stassen, Murray. "Riot Games and BMG Strike Strategic Partnership, Extend Global Publishing Admin Deal", *MusicBusiness Worldwide*, 2023. Available at: https://www.musicbusinessworldwide.com/riot-games-and-bmg-strike-strategic-partnership-extend-global-publishing-admin-deal/. Accessed 10th February 2024.

Sukri, Hazeeq. "Baekhyun of K-Pop Group EXO Joins 'League of Legends' New Virtual Boy Group", *CNA Lifestyle,* 2023. Available at: https://cnalifestyle.channelnewsasia.com/entertainment/baekhyun-joins-league-legends-group-heartsteel-373246. Accessed 16th February 2024.

Tagg, Philip. "Intersubjectivity", in Tagg Philip (Ed.), *Music's Meanings: A Modern Musicology for Non-Musos*. New York & Huddersfield: The Mass Media Music Scholars' Press, 2012.

Tan, Samuel. "Charting the Global Landscape of Esports Viewership", *YouGov,* 2023. Available at: https://business.yougov.com/content/46705-charting-the-global-landscape-of-esports-viewership-may-2023?redirect_from=%2Fcontent%2F8333-charting-the-global-landscape-of-esports-viewership-may-2023. Accessed 16th February 2024.

The Fortnite Team. "From League of Legends and Arcane, Jinx Brings her Aura of Anarchy to Fortnite", *Fortnite*, 2021. Available at: https://www.fortnite.com/news/from-league-of-legends-and-arcane-jinx-brings-her-aura-of-anarchy-to-fortnite?lang=en-US. Accessed 10th January 2024.

Vila, Pablo. "Narrative Identities and Popular Music: Linguistic Discourses and Social Practices", in Pablo Vila (Ed.), *Music and Youth Culture in Latin America: Identity Construction Processes from New York to Buenos Aires,* 18. New York: Oxford University Press, 2014.

Won, Donghyun "Wony" & Oak, Yudae "Akiin". "Interview with Patrick Morales, Janelle Jimenez, and Toa Dunn; the Creators of the Global Sensation, K/DA-POP/STARS", *INVEN Global*, 2018. Available at: https://www.invenglobal.com/articles/6859/interview-with-patrick-morales-janelle-jimenez-and-toa-dunn-the-creators-of-the-global-sensation-kda-popstars. Accessed 12th February 2024.

Words by Christopher. "Toa Dunn, Head of Riot Games Music, on the Future of Virtual Music Groups", *Virtual Humans,* 2022. Available at: https://www.virtualhumans.org/article/toa-dunn-head-of-riot-games-music-on-the-future-of-virtual-music-groups. Accessed 10th February 2024.

3 Music around the Games and Esports Promotion

The previous chapters have offered a glimpse into the multimediated environment in which the current esports panorama is articulated, which means that a great number of music products derived from games' content are developed around—not *as part of*—the gaming experience. In other words, a great part of the content that intersects with the music industry is not inherent to the games as such—at least, as a primary focus. This does not only apply to products such as story-developing music videos, like special in-game events, but also to promotional songs for competitive encounters, and fan-led initiatives that permeate into professional organizations.

These elements, which mostly work for the promotion of the titles that they represent, have different purposes and uses. They are commonly presented as marketing opportunities as well as socializers for the esports scene, since they are starred or promoted by agents with high visibility on social media, such as influencers, brands, and professional players. Although popular music artists may be involved in the promotion of such products, they are not necessarily the ones to carry the weight of their dissemination. In this sense, and to frame the contexts that will follow, it is worth underlining a few concepts before moving forward.

Firstly, the transmedia presence of participants in the global esports scene needs special attention, as the embeddedness of external agents in the lore of the games contributes to expanding its relevance beyond fiction. The presence of players, coaches, casters, hosts, and influencers, among others, plays a central part in popularizing the competitive scene.

Convergence is also a key concept to keep in mind. As argued by Jenkins, it ensures that "every important story gets told, every brand gets sold, and every consumer gets courted across multiple media platforms."[1] This allows music to be presented through a wide variety of media, with different purposes, while maintaining a connection and continuity between what could otherwise be seen as divergent products. Convergence is thus closely linked to transmediality and, more essentially, to the active participation of fans to keep all products connected and in circulation. This idea has been further discussed by authors such as Scolari[2] or Milton and Cobelo,[3] who analyze the role of

DOI: 10.1201/9781032625362-4

fans in articulating the relation between media—that is, their convergence—as well as in their remediation.

Third, following Adorno's description of *pseudo-individualization*, it can be argued that music and music-mediated commodities are presented to the gaming community to create the impression of access to new materials, when they have, in fact, already been chosen for them.[4] This implies that, although the strategy followed by the developing companies is set to expand their objective audiences, there is a compromise around maintaining the engagement of existing fans, so "the 'old' game concept that is sold is somehow 'new' and catered specifically for these consumers."[5] The products and events that will be discussed in the following correspond to maintaining and expanding a *brand community*[6] into what Scolari called "transmedia branding,"[7] which is directly linked and in continuous engagement with the games' overall lore.

Although these intersections speak of a close collaboration between music and gaming, their work toward shared goals has presented challenges derived from their different approaches to (and understanding of) the market. On the one hand, professionals filling gaming and esports roles have found the reticence derived from the traditional music industry hard to accommodate. Articles in magazines like *Billboard Pro* have shown the experiences of esports agents such as consultors and licensing teams, pointing to the difficulties faced by games when incorporating outsourced music. As described by former *Rioter* Toa Dunn, "If anything creates more cost in ways that aren't really driving what a game is going after, they tend to think, 'We probably shouldn't be spending time and resources on that'."[8] This has encouraged developers such as Riot Games to create their own labels, and to close agreements with studios such as Universal Music Publishing[9] to bypass potential setbacks in their audiovisual production. Furthermore, as suggested by licensing and production expert Carmen Rodríguez, this relates to companies such as Universal being able to afford subeditors or agreements with smaller companies, so they can access their catalog in return for expanding it through new incorporations, as a *win-win* strategy.[10]

On the other hand, music industry teams working on introducing popular music in video games relate to a different experience, which requires balancing expenses with product placement. Since the first approaches from esports to the well-established music industry came from an exploratory perspective,[11] early conversations between parties created points of dissonance, especially regarding the understanding of music usage, which often requires more than one-stop licensing.

In this sense, the requirements for sync placements or live usage have benefited from the incorporation of music teams and supervisors in gaming companies. Initiatives such as Stryngr's[12] have also afforded ways of incorporating music into gaming products by creating a bypass between labels and gaming platforms that eases the licensing process. Likewise, enterprises such as the association between Republic Records and Universal Publishing to include *Boombox* into *Roblox* suggest an "opportunity for labels to dynamically launch playlists and integrate them into the gaming space."[13] Nevertheless, out-of-game experiences in esports fall outside of these initiatives, which require an approach closer to that of half-time shows in traditional sports events.

Many esports games and events, as well as industry agents, have included popular music in their universes and promotional activities through different means, balancing the potential issues of the quoted dissonances between parties, in the form of special events, promotional videos, and different forms of integration of fan and official products. These are frequently built around the main titles, yet not necessarily in continuity with the specific sonic identity of their OSTs. However, they afford a sense of coherence through their use of music, which often features well-known participants in the scene.

SPECIAL EVENTS AS COMMUNITY DYNAMIZERS

Esports require specific content to support their dynamics and the socialization of their complete ecosystem, in ways that can sometimes differ from non-competitive games. Although their musical and sound basis is reliant on elements such as those discussed in previous chapters, their competitive contexts include a wider number of agents than those involved in a game per se—professional players, casters, competition hosts, etc.[14]

One way to address the continuity among game and esports content is through special events. These include happenings in the games which are only available at specific moments and for short spans of time, that serve the promotion of their respective competitions. Special events are defined by each developer to fit their necessities, create momentum to maintain the engagement of players, and attract new publics. In consonance with the existing marketing literature,[15] they can be defined through the intersubjective meaning afforded by game and esports developers to *non-ordinary and non-replicable occurrences* that add value and attraction to the product from an experiential standpoint. That is, their added value is set around time rather than place.

The implication of such events has been previously observed in the context of esports by authors such as Mora-Cantallops and Sicilia,[16] who assessed character selection in *League of Legends* and their influence on engaging players in immersing themselves into the lore of the title, as promoted by special events in the game. They analyzed the 2015 *Bylgewater Event,* which offered a free rotation of characters for two weeks with aims to, it can be argued, encourage players to purchase them in the future. This initiative included a soundtrack that was produced as a variation of the *Howling Abyss'* map theme, reimagined as "pirate-y."[17] The scores of both themes, when superimposed, although on different tonalities and beats per minute—A minor, 75 bpm versus D minor, 124 bpm—show to be complementary of one another.

During the ten years since this event, which was replicated in 2023 in a mod,[18] similar dynamics have extended not only toward the purchasable items in the game, but also toward esports marketing.[19] A clear example is that of purchasable items such as team banners or skins for characters, although these do not mostly influence the sonic development of the game.

However, it proves difficult to find special events that are music-based *and* strictly directed to esports: the relations between music-and-game and music-and-esports are often separate, in line with the separate teams in charge of the audiovisual production

FIGURE 3.1 Howling Abyss' theme *versus* Butcher's Bridge theme.

for the games and esports divisions. But there are cases in which special event content has been related to esports promotional products.

Following the *League of Legends* case, an example is that of the *Star Guardians Event*, which introduced a parallel universe to the main storyworld through different media—including music videos, skins in the game, artwork, etc. The characters in this series of skins, which are a reference to Japanese anime series like *Sailor Moon*, were first launched in 2016 along with different animated music videos. These ultimately served as a source for later content for the 2022 LEC Championship (*League of Legends* EMEA [East, Middle East and Africa] Championship). The music video featured the players of opposing teams Misfits and G2 as animated characters in *Star Guardian* costumes, and included similar music to that of videos launched in the same year.[20] Furthermore, founder of G2 Carlos "Ocelote" Rodríguez dressed up as one of the characters to promote their collaboration with Riot Games during a live event,[21] which added to its popularization.

In a more direct relation to the music industry, one of the videos launched prior to the championship also benefited from the collaboration with DJ Porter Robinson, which as of March 2024 has accumulated more than 23 million views on YouTube and 61 million reproductions on Spotify. The echo of the song on social and traditional media can be underlined as an embedding piece for the different elements

FIGURE 3.2 Game-music-esports triangle of special content.

surrounding the central event in the game. Likewise, in other titles such as *Fortnite*, special events have taken their own entity in articulating the game's narrative and introducing participatory virtual spectacles, which are also often accompanied by specific music inputs.

Fortnite's plot articulates the mechanics of the game and gives meaning to the (somewhat repetitive) nature of each match. The game's background story includes a *beginning of time event,* an explosion of energy that created the Zero Point, which gave rise to multiple realities. This point was discovered by the scientist Geno while seeking to create the perfect civilization and founded the Imagined Order (IO) to control it and use it to travel to different realities. However, these travels affected the space-time continuum, causing various events.[22]

The scientists in the IO use a 22-minute time Loop to trap all the island's visitors–the characters controlled by the players–erasing their memory, and depriving them of speech. The Loop uses a Storm that pushes all fighters together progressively, forcing them to fight each other until only one remains standing; this person would then respawn to start the battle again. On the other hand, a group of seven members gathered to release the Zero Point and stop the "possible catastrophic damage to the Omniverse as a whole,"[23] and they developed an environment that allows them to escape the Loop.

These main points, along with secondary characters and plots, have helped outline the different chapters of the game and smoothly introduce significant patches, but they have also been key to presenting performances by popular music artists. Events that are not specifically built around a musical performance, nevertheless, they usually include their own soundtracks.

A good example of this is that built around Marshmello's in-game concert, which offered a referent for the music industry to invest in virtual performances. The artist was introduced in *Fortnite* with a battle pass that included different purchasable items and game missions for players to accomplish during a short period of time. Furthermore, the inclusion of the artist allowed a connection between the game and the esport when incorporating him both as a game character and a live performer at the World Cup finals in 2019. As will be discussed in Chapter 4, the DJ's live show in *Fortnite* was a first exploratory approach to the possibility of introducing virtual concerts and music performances in the game, an idea later taken to its maximum expression through *Fortnite Creative* and Epic Games' Unreal Engine.[24]

But despite the number of events that have taken place in *Fortnite: Battle Royale*, the in-game references included in competitive events that feature music have not yet been exploited specifically as a bidirectional marketing tool—one that attracts new users to the game and viewers to the competitions (Table 3.1).

Similarly, *Free Fire*'s collaboration with Brazilian DJ Alok contributed to aligning the game with its esports division by incorporating the artist as a playable character, launching different music videos featuring him, and staging a live performance for the

TABLE 3.1 Special Events in *Fortnite: Battle Royale* (2018–2024)

EVENT	*DATE*
Blast-Off	30th June 2018
Cube Sinking	19th September 2018
The Butterfly Event	4th November 2018
New Year's Event 2019	30th December 2018–1st January 2019
Ice Storm (Ice King Event)	19th January 2019
Showtime (Marshmello's Concert)	2nd February 2019
The Unvaulting of the Drum Gun	4th May 2019
The Final Showdown	20th July 2019
The End	13th October 2019
Live at Risky Reels Event (Star Wars Event)	14th December 2019
New Year's Event 2020	30th December 2019–1st January 2020
Astronomical Event (Travis Scott's Concert)	25th April 2020
The Device Event	15th June 2020
The Devourer of Worlds Event	1st December 2020
New Year's Event 2021	30th December 2020–1st January 2021
The Zero Crisis Finale	16th March 2021
Rift Tour (Ariana Grande's Concert)	6th August 2021
Operation Sky Fire	12th September 2021
The End of Chapter 2	4th December 2021
New Year's Event 2022	30th December 2021–1st January 2022
Intro to Chapter 3	4th January 2022
Collider Firing	22nd March 2022
The Collision	4th June 2022
Summer Event	21st July 2022–9th August 2022
Chrome Arrives	18th September 2022
Fracture Event	3rd December 2022
New Year's Event 2023	30th December 2022–1st January 2023
Wild Dreams (Kid LAROI's Concert)	27th January 2023
Heist Event	28th February 2023
Summer Scape	4th July 2023–18th July 2023
Fortnimares	10th October 2023
Time Machine	3rd November 2023
The Big Bang (Eminem's Concert)	2nd December 2023
Winterfest	14th December 2023–2nd January 2024
New Year's Event 2024	30th December 2023–1st January 2024
Pandora's Box	27th February–3nd March 2024
Zeus' Lightning & Sandstorm	13th May 2024–16th May 2024
Metallica: Fuel. Fire. Fury (Concert)	2nd August 2024–5th August 2024
Refinery Event	10th August 2024

Continued

TABLE 3.1 Continued

EVENT	*DATE*
MSB Fortnite (Karol G Concert)	23rd August 2024–26th August 2024
Absolute Doom	5th October 2024
Remix: The Prelude (Snoop Dog & Ice Spice Concert)	1st November 2024
Remix: The Finale (Juice WRLD Concert)	30th November 2024
New Year's Event 2024	30th December 2024–1st January 2025

World Series of 2019 in Rio.[25] Like with Marhsmello, this strategy allowed a connection between the game's storyworld and the overall lore built around it, and, more essentially, it created an opportunity to gather new fanbases around either product.

It is not unusual to find esports-branding elements in the games as homages to championship winners, or to encounter brands introduced as collaborations with different titles—e.g., Hawaianas x *Fortnite*, Onitsuka Tiger x *Street Fighter*, etc.—other video games and audiovisual media—e.g., *PUBG Mobile* x *Resident Evil 2*, *Fortnite* x *LEGO*, etc.—or popular culture characters. Nevertheless, the other way around, regarding the use of in-game events as promotion opportunities for live competitions, has been scarce, especially when considering special events that do not feature pop artists as a main attraction.

PROMOTIONAL (MUSIC) VIDEOS

Some events are developed exclusively for esports, promoting competitive events, team milestones, or other relevant occurrences. Such audiovisual content can be considered special events in that they refer to time-specific, non-ordinary, and non-replicable circumstances—even if they remain accessible after their launch dates. Nonetheless, live participation and belonging to the games' community are dependent on updated interaction with official content. In most cases, music emphasizes the designed visual narratives and connects with the audiences, appealing to their taste. However, despite the possibility of creating crossed references, it is not always linked to the games' OSTs, but it is expressly composed or inserted from generic libraries. If available to the developers and publishers, these occasions provide the ideal context to assemble productions featuring popular music artists.

These promotional items are frequently produced and consumed as adjacent materials to the games, becoming part of their overall lore despite their separation from the playable content. That is, although it is related to the lore around the games and refers to the intersubjective knowledge of the participants, it does not necessarily relate to the central storyline that carries the plot of a title. This differs from the story-developing videos and events included as in-game content in games such as *Fortnite* (e.g. *The Collision*, *Fracture*, etc.), which serve the engagement of users in a continuously

FIGURE 3.3 Tentative classification of promotional event videos, from more to less music-specific.

developing virtual world. These can take different forms in and out of the game, and they are usually—if not exclusively—marketed through short animated or film videos, ranging from story-based narratives to competition-driven strategies.

Developer-produced videos are usually closer to the story world of each game than organization—or league-produced videos. They can be considered more "traditional" in that they are frequently produced to commercialize esports. Developer-produced videos tend to use music as narrative support and do not always explicitly interact with the popular music industry, e.g., by introducing collaborations with popular music artists.

An example of this is the promo videos created for the *PUBG* Global Championships, which have included from short movie-like clips to edited videos featuring the players on professional stages along with animations from the game. If we take past Global Championships as a reference, we will find videos featuring official songs to represent and market the competitions, while others exhibit compilations of video highlights, launched to encourage participation, attract new viewers, and serve as an introduction to the respective live events.

For instance, in 2019, the song *Stand United*, produced by the game's developing company, was released along with a short film featuring characters from an *in-game* perspective. The lyrics appealed to the sense of community and non-ordinariety of the competitive event: "Fist clenched to my side/blood burning in my veins / hands-soaked sweat for battle / this is more than just a game."[26] The song presented an opportunity for commercialization besides the game that also functioned to appeal to the sense of belongingness of the participants in the game and the competitive encounter.

Other songs that have carried the weight of audiovisual action in music videos include *Phoenix* for the 2019 *League of Legends* World Championship, *All In* for the 2021 *Free Fire* World Series, *Ticking Away* for the *Valorant* Championship Tournament, or *Rise to the Top* for the 2022 *Brawl Stars* Championship, among others. These are frequently produced in collaboration with external music partners, and tend to feature popular music artists who align with each game's sonic identity (Table 3.2).[27]

Examples including players and live footage are also frequent, as it is part of their core responsibilities,[28] although they do not necessarily center their attention on music, they include it to agglutinate and provide continuity to their designed narratives. For instance, the announcements for the *Counter-Strike* Intel Extreme Masters (IEM) usually include upbeat music that contrasts a paused introductory cinematic. If we review the 2022 announcement for the competition in Cologne,[29] or the announcement for the 2023 IEM in Sydney,[30] we can see how the beginning of each video is designed to

TABLE 3.2 *Valorant* Championship Tournament's Official Music Videos

TITLE OF THE MUSIC VIDEO	*FEATURED MUSIC ARTISTS*	*YEAR*
Die For You	Grabbitz	2021
Fire Again	Ashnikko (written along Grabbitz and Slinger)	2022
Ticking Away	Grabbitz and bbno$	2023
Superpower	Julie & Natty (Kiss of Life), & Mark Tuan	2024

somewhat represent the location in which the competition is taking place: the first portrays the vitrines of a cathedral, a bell, old books, portraits, and candles, that can be reminiscent of *the Old Continent*, of Medieval Europe; the second is situated on a desert, with a cabin, a hat and knife, that conventionally take the viewer to inner Australia. This is, however, contrasted with the introduction of live footage of the competing teams along a hard rock and electronic soundtrack which enhances the action on screen.

When the videos shift toward the players and stage action, the soundscapes of the described locations give way to a piece of frenetic music, which progressively increases in volume while blending video game and competition footage. In these cases, the music has the function of providing what Vernallis called an *intensified audiovisual aesthetic*, which is "increasingly based on smaller units"[31] that resonate with the rapid dynamics of 21st-century capitalism. These videos provide the feeling of immediacy, velocity, and culmination, while following the discourse of a *teaser* or *trailer* for a bigger event. Furthermore, the separate tracks are also uploaded on streaming platforms, creating a new channel for extended consumption and connection with the community.

This format has been followed by games such as *DotA 2*, *Overwatch*, or *Rocket League*, for competitive promotion and recapitulation videos of their respective competitions. In the balance between cinematic and stage content, these tend to portray specific competition footage, including in- and out-of-game images. For instance, following *PUBG*'s case, the YouTube channel *PUBG Esports* periodically publishes promos, compilations of best moments, and other clips.[32] The number of clips included in this and similar channels vouch for the variety of audiovisuals that are derived from official competitions, and the relevance that music has in articulating them. However, due to the volume and regularity of such releases, most launched videos—that do not have a central promotional intent—tend to include non-specific tracks, likely extracted from free license music libraries. These seek to build a *mood* for the viewer more than a specifically tailored music base to carry the visual product, and could be further explored to determine their unity or divergence, as well as their efficacy in indirectly commercializing the games.

It can be stated that the diversity of promotional videos ranges greatly depending on the type of video and their intent, and that despite the relevance of music to carry narrative action, it is only in some cases that it is tailored as a conscious marketing component. The assiduity in the release of promotional videos by each company, and the reduced size of sound and music departments in most cases,[33] makes it reasonable that the efforts around music-lead products are strategized for big competitions and announcements, rather than compilations and daily reports for regular consumers.

In this sense, the pseudo-individualization process argued by Adorno makes it that music-centric videos are mostly set to expand their objective audiences and consolidate existing ones, while regularly released videos of best moments and recaps are mostly focused on loyal players that consume them rapidly,[34] making them less exigent with the tracks chosen to illustrate them.

EXTERNAL PROMOTIONAL VIDEOS

In addition to official videos, external agents in the esports ecosystem, such as professional clubs, teams, and organizations, have benefitted from the creation of audiovisual products aimed at promoting their own events of those in which they participate. Besides videos in similar categories to those already discussed, it is worth highlighting the music-specific clips launched by esports organizations such as the Valorant Championship Tournament (VCT) for *Valorant*, the Professional Gamers League (PGL) for *Counter-Strike*, or the Call of Duty League (CDL) for *Call of Duty* in North America, among others, as they have produced specific songs—or *anthems*—for their events featuring well-known popular artists, as well as audiovisual to accompany them—trailers, music videos, etc.

A good case study is that of the LEC, the lead esports league in Europe, the Middle East, and Africa for *League of Legends*, as it regularly produces music videos that serve the promotion of their competitions, as well as the expansion of the popularity of the organization and its most representative members (Table 3.3).

In these, the LEC casters are portrayed as the faces of official teams—e.g., Sjokz has represented MAD Lions on several occasions. The organization's *mediocre rap battle* videos, an initiative first pursued in 2019 and extended until 2022 to promote the game's Summer Playoffs, have received considerable attention regarding their aesthetics and participants. In these videos, each caster represents one of the finalist teams and their fanbases.

The verbal battles allude to the confrontational nature of the event and allow viewers to feel connected to the wider *League* community—more especially to the teams and fans of their preferred teams. The lyrics often include intersubjectively agreed-upon terms and incorporate what can be read as rap conventions that may appeal to existing and potential new audiences. Nevertheless, the language is mostly codified for players and fans with close knowledge of past competitions.

For instance, in 2020 host and caster Froskurinn, in representation of Rogue, included the following verses when facing Vadius, representing Fnatic:

> Broxah died for this? A Graves lock in barely makin' fifth,
> Soraka bot with sinner picks, does Rekkles need his Janna fix?
> Cause L9, barely 9/9, dragged across the finish line,
> End 50/50 for clear reasons, coin flipped your whole season.[35]

In this, not only players (e.g. Broxah, Rekkles) or game characters (e.g. Graves, Soraka, Janna) are mentioned, but also their relation (e.g. the assiduous use of Janna by

TABLE 3.3 LEC Promotional Music Videos (2019–2023)

TITLE	*FEATURING*	*YEAR*
Mediocre Rap Battle of LEC	Drakos, Vedius, G2, Misfits	2019
Mediocre Rap Battle of the LEC	Drakos, Vedius, Sjokz	2019
Rap Rivals	CaptainFlowers, Drakos, Ovilee May, Vedius	2019
Count on Us	Comp, Crownie, ElYoya, Finn, Hans Sama, Humanoid, Jankos, Markoon, Odoamne, Perkz	2019
The Best Promo Ever!	All teams (players)	2019
Everything We Got (Winter Promo)	Drakos, Vedius	2019
Dance with me	KIA Motors, Sjokz	2020
On My Mind by Diplo & Sidepiece	Drakos, Laure, Quickshot, Sjokz	2020
Mediocre Rap Battle of the LEC	Drakos, Froskurinn, Sjokz, Vedius, G2, MAD Lions, Rogue, Fnatic	2020
We are EU	Drakos, Ender, Froskurinn, Laure, Medic, Quickshot, Sjokz, Vedius, Yamatocannon,	2020
Our Drive	All teams (avatars)	2020
Reckless with my heart	Drakos, Ender, Vedius	2021
Crown	Drakos, Ender, Vedius	2021
Arcane x Mediocre Rap Battle: Fists to a Gunfight	Drakos, Vedius	2021
Mediocre Rap Battle of the LEC	Drakos, Vedius	2021
Wildfire (Spring Promo)	Against the Current	2022
Mediocre Rap Cypher of the LEC	Caedrel, Dan Bull, Drakos, Falconshield, Rustage, Sjokz, Vedius	2022
Edge of Infinity	Caedrel, Drakos, Vedius	2022
Awakened	Cassyette	2022
Heartbreaker	Drakos, Ender, Vedius	2023

Rekkles) elements from recent competitive events (e.g. the struggle in reaching the final stages of the competition, Broxah leaving Fnatic), or the results of the season (e.g. 9/9 referring to 9 wins, 9 losses). In addition, the use of the word *mediocre* to describe the confrontation puts space between rapped events among specific communities and the comedy tone set for the occasion.

In a similar vein, regional league organizers have followed this path and produced their own promotional songs and videos. For instance, in 2021 the Spanish Professional Video Game League (LVP) released a reggaeton/trap song featuring both players and casters. Ainoha Campos, a professional caster for LVP, described the process as a response to the music videos of the LEC—executed with fewer resources and in a shorter time:

> The idea was to do something cool, especially because it was the first time we were doing an in-person event after the pandemic. (...) In Spain, we study English from the second year of primary school, but it still feels very foreign to the audience. Maybe the type of music wasn't the closest to the audience either, because it's true that [their taste]'s very reggaeton/trap. (...) When we received the first mix, suddenly this project became more tangible, and people started to get on board, saying, "wait, that doesn't make us cringe, okay, let's do it."[36]

Despite the moderate success of this initiative, the regional league has not centered its energy on music products, but has favored other audiovisual proposals such as short competition compilations. Nevertheless, the aforementioned song, *Ready Pa' To'* (*Ready for Everything*),[37] showed attention toward the taste of fans in the targeted geographic areas and their objective public, as it has been done more extensively and in-depth by other companies such as Garena in Asia and South America.[38]

Organizations for other games, such as the CDL with *Call of Duty*, have also followed music video formats to promote their competitions through esports agents such as players, often acting as the producers of their own promotional materials. In their intro videos for the Majors—the final event that culminates the game's competitions—they have explored different forms to present the protagonists for the events. These take a similar function as the videos mentioned earlier in preparing the championships with specifically designed audiovisual content, although they do it through their own take. In this case, it is the teams participating in the championship that contribute their own videos as promotion of the competition, creating their own music face-off each season.

These short music videos usually feature licensed popular music and voice-overs, along with footage from the game and the players on set. In 2024, different teams included hip-hop tracks in their initiatives, that resonated with their team names and alluded to the competition. For instance, Los Angeles Thieves included music by Sounds of Red Bull, Frankie P, and Audubon; while Optic Texas featured rapper 808 BEEZY. Other teams such as Seattle Surge or Boston Breach opted for electronic with tracks by STRLGHT and Roonin, or IamDayLight, respectively. The trends followed in each case can be read as a mirror reaction of the preferences of gamer fans, that are afforded an identity to be collectively reflected.

Esports clubs with divisions in different games such as Team Liquid—in *Starcraft 2, Counter-Strike 2, DotA 2, Super Smash Bros,* etc.—have also closed independent productions beyond these initiatives, along with music artists and as a means to engage their fanbases and expand their popularity. For instance, in 2023 Team Liquid's *League of Legends* team released the song *Turn the Tide*[39] with industry musicians 2WEI, Edda Hayes, and Kataem. The theme did not only include elements that seem close to Riot Music Group's sonic identity, such as the combination of urban styles—electronic, hip-hop, pop—but also visual elements in the music video that are reminiscent of the brand—such as the color palettes, the use of dark and neon atmospheres, etc.

Similarly, G2 Esports—with teams in *League of Legends, Rainbow Six Siege, Fortnite*, etc.—have also engaged in music-promotional strategies through non-game-specific videos alongside artists Jeris Johnson, Yonaka, Luke Holland, Tina Guo, and others. The music videos launched for each song usually feature players and other esports agents belonging to the clubs, making them esport-exclusive products that can be consumed as additional lore around the games and the brands.

A third example, taking a step further in this direction, is that of Fnatic, which released its own music label, Fnatic Music, in 2022. The *label* features lo-fi beats designed to "chill and game."[40] Their first album, *Fnatic Island Vol. 1*, included "40 of the world's most-streamed lo-fi hip-hop artists,"[41] such as No Spirit, Cassio, or Hoogway.

These initiatives have begun intersecting with popular music artists and the wider music industry more recently than did developers or esports leagues, slowly extending toward specific exchanges at individual levels, which is only proof of the efficacy and appeal to pursue it as a marketing route—with consequently increased budgets. For instance, *Valorant* player ZmjjKK gained mediatic traction in 2023 when he briefly performed a rap by Chinese artist GAI for the camera during a competition,[42] who later responded to the gamer in a short video showing his support toward his team.[43] This exchange vouches for the perceived relevance of both industries and their growing proximity, as underlined throughout this chapter.

In short, this brief analysis exemplifies a trend toward a growing presence of existing collaborations between esports and the music industries as a means to find bidirectional feedback, which is backed by the attention of other media.[44] The success of the incorporation of popular music and specifically created music in esports marketing has extended the interest in the strategy toward smaller groups and even individual participants in the industry, in what can be argued is a growing transmedia popular culture panorama. This idea can be linked to the earlier-mentioned *transmedia branding*, in that it creates a continuity that works for the marketing of the game products at the epicenter of the esportive ecosystem. Likewise, traditional media has echoed this increasing trend and bidirectional feedback between industries, especially since the hatching of the international competitive scene in the late years of the 2010s.[45]

FAN-LED MUSIC STRATEGIES

In the landscape described so far, fans have been relegated to the receiving end of the communication channel, although they are key in defining the trends and the music products that each brand bets on through their active participation in the esports scene. Although authors such as Jenkins argued in favor of fandom as a way of resistance,[46] more recent contributions to fandom theory have advocated for a more casual definition of their relation to their reference products and franchises.[47] In this vein, Coppa recovered the *fans* versus *followers* debate and made a call for action as in "an industry convention disguised as a fan convention, we run the risk of reducing all fans to followers,"[48] urging her readers to recognize fandom as "more than its economic/revenue potential."[49]

In this epigraph, I do not pursue a thorough discussion of these terms, but intend to underline the relevance of esports consumers in establishing marketable lines and strategies for the developers to follow. Likewise, it is worth highlighting the resignification of different elements from the games once they enter the *consumer end* of esports, and how they are reappropriated and held as identification standards, separated from the mainstream industry.

The extension of music products and interpretations by fans will be discussed in more detail in Chapter 6, but as some of their behaviors around esports events and the overall ecosystem have been incorporated by game developers and brands into their competitive contexts, they require a brief space here.

A worth-noting case study is that of the *Silver Scrapes* theme in *League of Legends'* competitive events. As with any game, *League of Legends'* players hold a dialogue with an intersubjective understanding of the game, which is based on the experiences of the gaming community and not so much on the conception of the game's developers. An example of this could be the use of in-game signals—e.g., "enemy missing from line"—with a new meaning—e.g., "what are you doing?"—. This phenomenon extends into socializing environments that do not hold an implicit competitive element for attendees, like big tournaments.

In these, the game is the center of attention but not necessarily the turning point for how individuals will unfold emotionally or socially. For this purpose, the organizing company has found that promoting its most creative departments, including Riot Music Group, is especially useful in favoring a unified experience for attendees. However, not everything is under corporate control—at least not from the beginning.

Silver Scrapes has become a well-known piece, which is expected by *League* followers when two teams tie on a Best of 5.[50] The song was composed by Danny McCarthy for the second competitive season of the game, but the function for which it was conceived was quickly resignified by event viewers, who naturally adapted to unforeseen circumstances.

On *League of Legacies*, a fan-created website that works as a repository of memorable moments within the competitive scene for the game, this track is reaffirmed as a reference piece, which was accidentally brought into the game's culture:

> It was the Season 2 World Championships broadcasted live for the world to see. Riot Games was still in its infancy when it came to live productions and fortunately through technical errors, they introduced Silver Scrapes to the world audience. Whenever the production team faced difficulties, they would take large breaks to attempt to resolve the issues. When this happened, they would temporarily display a static stream to the online audience and have Silver Scrapes play in the background. However, these breaks lasted for hours and were very often.
>
> Silver Scrapes was replayed so much that the community began to really enjoy the music for its heavy dubstep drops and electronic dance vibes. Season 2 World Championships lead the frontiers of Esports expansion at the time and Silver Scrapes

FIGURE 3.4 *Silver Scrapes'* melody.

> had evolved to be its anthem. As a tribute, whenever a Best of 5 series reaches the last game, Silver Scrapes is played to commemorate how far Esports has come and celebrate the hype for the final game![51]

This event can be seen as a key moment that afforded a sense of union for veteran fans and a reference for newcomers. Furthermore, it created a point of reference that emphasizes the importance of a tiebreaker, which helps give a structural sense to competitive events.

But does this piece count with specific structural elements that serve to construct an experience for the listener, as it does the OST on *The Summoner's Rift*? Maybe, but probably not. It is a short piece, originally under 2 minutes—although it has been somewhat rewritten to better adapt to its new role—that works well as a loop due to its repetitive melodic theme on G major. As it was not originally intended to guide the listener to a deeper experience, such as World Finals opening ceremonies do, its meaning relies strongly on function.

However, the case shows how music serves to support group identity, socializing it within a ritual that has slowly been configured *not only* by Riot Games, but by the fan community. More essentially, it demonstrates how the mainstream industry incorporates consumer trends to engage them in interacting with their products. This can be seen through events such as the LPL (*League of Legends* Pro League, in China) 2023 production for Hanfu Day,[52] in which they invited the Ancient Music Orchestra of Xaiu to perform *Silver Scrapes* with traditional instruments and costumes. With this, the organization incorporated the theme into their yearly reproduction of *League of Legends*-related songs with folklorized Chinese elements for this very holiday.[53]

It can be stated that these audiovisual initiatives are specially tailored to appeal to the taste of fans, and to their contributions to the incorporation of music elements to the game's scene. In this sense, the production of new materials that have already been chosen and previously presented to the community contributes to the transmedia branding of the game, appealing to old and new consumers alike.

Although similar developments may not always be easily traceable, the fluidity of social media and the continuous exchange of ideas and opinions make it easier for alternative and mainstream to blur into one another. A turning point appears once these *memes*[54] are absorbed by the official discourse in a process of cooptation,[55] leaving the domain of group resilience to be transferred into the dominant storytelling—producing a restart of the same cycle. Even so, they are to be taken into account in the vast panorama of esports product marketing for specific gaming products, such as those described here.

STREAMING AND INFLUENCER INITIATIVES

Streaming is central to esports, as it contributes to the dissemination of the games and their competitions, providing democratic access to diverse events. In this sense, like in the previous case, it is essential to distinguish between fan-streaming, dedicated to commenting on games and related products, performing covers of themes and songs, etc., and organization-guided content.[56] Platforms such as Twitch, YouTube, and Kick, have served as audiovisual content disseminators for both, that showcase esports content in a more interactive context than music videos or other unidirectional initiatives. In other words, streaming platforms allow live participation and dialogue among fans, creating an effective way to afford visibility to different games.

As stated by Koskimaa and colleagues, "livestreams appear more accessible than official website content" and can function "as the main entrance for new players."[57] These afford additional options to enter the esports universes that do not imply hands-on play, but allow engagement with the game and, it could be argued, closer interaction with other members of the fan community.

Global and regional streamers, frequently *influencers*, are key figures in this field, as they contribute to keeping the esports gears in motion through their continuous interaction and proximity to fans. As suggested by Lenhert, Walz, and Christianson:

> Another common promotional tactic is for game publishers to pay streamers to play their game on stream. Electronic Arts (EA) published a new battle royale shooter game called Apex Legends and paid Twitch's top streamers to play it. Not surprisingly, Ninja was one of these streamers, and it was reported from a "reliable anonymous source" that he may have earned as much as $1m for doing so.[58]

Furthermore, it has become common for esports teams to associate with influencers to represent them in exchange for benefits—ranging from online *visibility* to stipulated salaries—or for big influencers to invest in esports clubs. The first is usually contracted to create virtual content around the games, engage with the community, and gain traction for the brand, while the second tends to rely on external companies or other influencers to promote their own content.

> It's very common for game companies to partner with streamers and influencers during new game/content releases. But most game companies don't have music as a "core product," so the collaborations are usually to promote a core product (i.e., game/new content/events). If there is a partnership to promote "music," it's usually the music artist fulfilling this role. Even then, the music still acts as a marketing driver for a core product. As an example, K/DA skins were the core product that the Riot sold. The music acted as a marketing driver for the skins.[59]

In this scheme, music videos or music-centric products are not necessarily at the epicenter, but are commonly present as a binding element. For this matter, music content creators are especially relevant.

Diverse music artists have been hired by esports teams to be their visible faces, perform on their behalf, or stream for their brands, in collaborations that range from influencer agreements—e.g. *YouTuber* and musician Misho Amoli with Case Esports, or Brazilian rapper GUXTA with LOUD—to contracts with big names in the music industry—e.g., Ariana Grande with *Fortnite*, or BTS with T1—whose contributions are usually more sporadic.

GUXTA's case is a good example to study how the rapper leverages the use of music to gain traction toward the brand and vice versa—how esports can serve to attract new fans toward his music—as the production of esports-theme songs serves a bidirectional benefit. In songs such as *O Brazil é a LOUD*,[60] produced for the club's *Valorant* team, the lyrics revolve around the game and its professional players (e.g. "tô piqué Cauanzin, só sendo frio e calculista" or "eu tô fazendo barra igual Tuyz na academia girando tipo aspas, munição nunca vazia"), and the music video includes both footage from the game and these same characters.

Besides individual music initiatives and associations of streamers with regional clubs,[61] some intersections have been led by music agents themselves, who have seen potential in the worldwide growing popularity of esports. This includes musician-investors as well as music artists that have founded their own clubs, such as Steve Aoki—co-owner of Rogue—, Jam Hsiao—founder of the Taiwanese esports organization The Jams—, or FaZe Clan investors like DJ Paul, Ray J, or Pitbull, among others.[62]

Artists such as American rapper T-Pain or Lil Yachty have not only invested in creating their own brands—Nappy Boy Gaming—or participating in existing clubs—FaZe Clan—respectively, but they are also regular streamers on platforms like Twitch. These spaces serve as transmedia points of encounter for these personalities, that momentarily coexist as artists, gamers, and brand representatives. The audiovisual content produced through these means adds to other official content within a more traditional video frame, such as the above-quoted music videos and recapitulations. However, the restrictions placed on streaming platforms imply that non-performer users have to carefully select the music that they include in their broadcasts, often resulting in its omission when not prearranged.

These collaborations have not been oblivious to the music industry either, which has actively engaged in forming alliances between games and artists, as well as with influencers in esports and related fields. Mediatic partnerships between esports brands and personalities have included alliances between Universal Music Group and ESL—the largest esports company in the world—and Spotify and ESL; Riot Games and Universal for the development of the *League of Legends* World Championship, in 2020, and with BMG in 2024; Epic Games and Bandcamp, which was sold to Songtradr 2023; among others. These vouch not only for the relevance of esports in the current entertainment market, but also for the growingly multimediated environment in which they take place.

Montsercat is a good case study in this scenario, as it does not only rely on *Rocket League* as a key partner through which to channel its productions, but also on its marketing system, based on the affordability of its music. Streaming and content creator communities can use their music to support their broadcast and audiovisual products, which is used as a strategy to popularize the label and its associated games. Furthermore, their vision behind the investment in music as a way to engage the audiences and create new music referents has been essential to their positioning in a competitive market. As stated by Director of Sync and Partnerships, Gavin Johnson:

> I find personally it's precious to games if they're able to break an artist. And because if you're bringing an artist in and you break that act and contribute towards their fandom and their fame, at the end of the day, that game becomes permanently attached to their identity and makes it so that that game has longevity beyond just the gameplay and the game itself.[63]

However, and despite the growing interest of the music industry to participate in one of the most rapidly growing markets of our century,[64] the agreements between esports and music parties might encounter different impediments during the following years. According to consultant and former Head of Music at Riot Games, Toa Dunn, elements such as the oversaturation of the market, the complexity of the music industry and its rightsholder ecosystem, or the potential difficulties aligning the timelines for games and ready-to-release songs,[65] may imply rethinking and restructuring how common projects are built within the next few years.

CONCLUSION

Music revolves around esports and their promotion through a wide variety of channels, that reflect a growingly virtual, multi-, and transmediated panorama. The relevance of social media and its rapidly changing content makes it so that most of the music products built to communicate esports are reliant on up-to-date trends, and their effectiveness to engage worldwide audiences. These products are frequently situated *around* the games and may not relate strictly to their soundtracks or storyworlds, but rather complement them and add to the games' overall lore—including their social scene. Such content tends to intersect with the music industry more directly than the original soundtracks of the games, especially in those that do not include popular music as a core element of the games, like *Rocket League*.

In the global esports scene, music has become key, as it has grown to be directly involved with the marketing of the games but also their competitions, participating teams, and other collaborating agents. The transmedia presence of these elements is afforded through diverse audiovisual channels, including special and promotional events, videos, fan and influencer-lead strategies, which become part of the shared knowledge and identity of the participants.

As shown, special events are non-ordinary and non-replicable occurrences destined to engage existing and new audiences, that despite being frequently communicated through music hardly transcend into the esports scene. This responds in great part to the separation of the teams working on each element—the video game, and the esports scene in which it is embedded. Therefore, the relation between music-and-game and music-and-esports frequently fails to hold continuity, despite the relative assiduity in the incorporation of esports elements into the games, such as character skins. Furthermore, this implies that, despite the presence of popular music artists and bands in the games, the crossover between special in-game and out-of-game events may not be consistent.

On the other hand, promotional videos, which I have defined as those produced and consumed adjacently to the playable content of the games, tend to refer to socializing contexts such as live competitions to construct their narratives, in addition to game content. These videos can be strictly musical in nature, like in the case of game competition anthems, which serve the brands to attract new potential audiences, while creating a well-awaited moment for existing fans.[66] However, returning to the rapid-fire release of content intrinsic to social media, the wide variety of promotional videos makes it so that the majority of content—summaries, recaps, etc.—is illustrated with preexisting library music.

Some videos expressly created around popular music are produced externally by esports agents such as leagues or professional teams. Although not all organizations are able to outsource these products, some widely popular cases have invested in promotional videos featuring players, coaches, casters, and hosts, directly appealing to the sense of community and belongingness of fans. A good case example is that of the above-mentioned LEC *mediocre rap battles*, which relocate the dynamics from a popular music context transforming them into self-tailored products. These initiatives have slowly begun intersecting with popular music artists also at individual levels, showing the mutual interest of both industries in being part of the other's respective cultural niche.

Another category is music initiatives built and communicated around esports, which have been led by fans, as they not only participate in competitive contexts but continuously assimilate and resignify the sonic elements around them. These music initiatives are different from fan-created content since, despite being socially formulated, they are rapidly coopted by brands and *mainstreamed*. From a sociological perspective, this can be read as double-edged, as developers take into account the preferences and movements of fandoms across media while absorbing their intersubjective language and reappropriating it.

Last but not least, streaming platforms and influencers appear to be core elements to the esports industry, since they have become the socializers of esports across the globe. The rise of streaming platforms such as Twitch happened virtually at the same time as esports competitions began to popularize,[67] resulting in interdependently working businesses to an extent. However, music streamers have intersected with esports agents mostly tangentially, and esports streamers have rarely engaged specifically with esports-music products. This does not mean that streamers-influencers have not engaged with music products outside of their live broadcasts or that popular musicians have not developed an interest in esports clubs. On a step removed, this has effectively created traction toward specific artists and teams, and has worked toward the promotion of specific titles.

In sum, the intersection of the music and esports industries is not only consistent at an in-game level, but has directly benefited from the surrounding products to the games and the global esports scene to create momentum. The participation of popular music artists from a performative to an investment level assesses the impact of the competitive gaming scene in the global cultural panorama, and vouches for the rapidly blurring lines that have traditionally separated entertainment media. The categorization and examples outlined here offer a possible—yet not exclusive—approximation to the variety of music-related products that orbit around the games and make them permeate through various social and cultural layers, which will likely continue to expand in the near future.

NOTES

1 Henry Jenkins, *Convergence Culture: Where Old and New Media Collide*. New York: New York University Press, 2006, 3.
2 Carlos Alberto Scolari, "Más allá del pentagrama: Transmedia y música", *Hipermediaciones*, 2014. Available at: https://hipermediaciones.com/2014/01/19/transmedia-y-musica/. Accessed 15 March 2024.
3 John Milton and Silvia Cobelo, *Translation, Adaptation and Digital Media*. New York: Routledge, 2023.

4 Theodor W. Adorno and George Simpson, "On Popular Music", *Zeitschrift für Sozialforschung*, 1941, 9, 17–48.
5 Juan Sebastián Díaz Gasca, "Music Beyond Gameplay: Motivators in the Consumption of Videogame Soundtracks" (Doctoral Thesis, Griffith University, 2015), 144.
6 Albert M. Muniz and Thomas C. O'Guinn, "Brand Community", *Journal of Consumer Research*, 2001, 27(4), 412–332; as quoted in Díaz Gasca, "Music Beyond Gameplay", 144.
7 Scolari, "Más allá del pentagrama".
8 Elias Leight, "Is the Music Business Out of Synch with Game Developers?", *Billboard*, 2024. Available at: https://www.billboard.com/pro/video-games-music-song-licensing-system-out-synch/. Accessed 15 March 2024.
9 Nádia Linhares, "Riot Partners with Universal Music Group to Create Promotional Songs for League of Legends World Finals", *Dot Esports*, 2020. Available at: https://dotesports.com/league-of-legends/news/riot-partners-with-universal-music-group-to-create-promotional-songs-for-league-of-legends-worlds-finals. Accessed 15 March 2024.
10 Carmen Rodríguez, Head of Sync and Production at OEO&Parser. Interview by Eulalia Febrer-Coll. 19 September 2023.
11 Mariana Migliore, Director and Creative Synch at BMG. Interview by Eulalia Febrer-Coll. 17 September 2023.
12 Stryngr, "Music for Gaming", n.d. Available at: https://www.styngr.com. Accessed 28 March 2024.
13 Universal Music Group, "Universal Music Group, Republic Records, & Stryngr Bring Boombox to Roblox – Pioneering Opportunities for Labels and Players", 2024. Available at: https://www.universalmusic.com/universal-music-group-republic-records-styngr-bring-boombox-to-roblox-pioneering-opportunities-for-labels-and-players/. Accessed 25 March 2024.
14 See Nico Bésombes, "Esports Ecosystem and Landscape", *Medium*, 2019. Available at: https://medium.com/@nicolas.besombes/esports-ecosystem-and-landscape-3dbbd653dc2c. Accessed 10th March 2024.
15 Joe Goldblatt and Seungwon Lee, *Special Events: The Brave New World for bolder and Better Live Events*. Hoboken, NJ: Wiley, 2020; Michaela-Oana Tară-Lungă, "Major Special Events: An Interpretative Literature Review", *Management & Marketing Challenges for the Knowledge Society*, 2012, 4, 759–776.
16 Marçal Mora-Cantallops and Miguel-Ángel Sicilia, "Motivations to Read and Learn in Videogame Lore: The Case of League of Legends", *ACM International Conference Proceeding Series*, 2016, 585–591.
17 SkinSpotlights, "Bilgewater Map Music (Butcher's Bridge), *Youtube*, 2015. Available at: https://www.youtube.com/watch?v=MrcHugDsc4Y. Accessed 20 March 2024.
18 Leischii, "Butcher's Bridge", *Runeforge*, 2023. Available at: https://www.runeforge.io/post/butchers-bridge. Accessed 20th March 2024.
19 Tobias M. Scholz, "The Business Model Network of Esports: The Convergence of Overwatch", in Dal Yong Jin (Ed.), *Global Esports: Transformation of Cultural Perceptions of Competitive Gaming*, 99–114. New York: Bloomsbury, 2021.
20 LEC, "Fight the Darkness | LEC x Star Guardian | 2022 LEC Summer", *Youtube*, 2022. Available at: https://www.youtube.com/watch?v=e1ASc0gahy8. Accessed 20 March 2024.
21 Kristine "Kurisu" Tuting, "They Told Him He Could Become Anything, So He Became Star Guardian Soraka", *One Esports*, 2022. Available at: https://www.oneesports.gg/cosplay/g2-ocelote-star-guardian-soraka-cosplay/. Accessed 20 March 2024.
22 Fortnite Wiki, "Lore (Battle Royale)", *Fortnite Wiki*, n.d. Available at: https://fortnite.fandom.com/wiki/Lore_(Battle_Royale). Accessed 18 March 2024.
23 Fortnite Wiki, "Lore (Battle Royale)".
24 The *Unreal Engine* is a free-to-access tool that allows developers to create simulations, edit videos, sounds, and render animations. See Epic Games, *Unreal Engine*, n.d. Available at: https://www.unrealengine.com/. Accessed 17th March 2024.

25 Garena Free Fire LATAM, "ALOK en VIVO | Free Fire World Series", *Youtube*, 2019. Available at: https://www.youtube.com/watch?v=23kZuvuER9w. Accessed 20 March 2024.
26 PUBG Esports, "PUBG – Stand United: PGC 2019 Trailer", *Youtube*, 2019. Available at: https://www.youtube.com/watch?v=GepTXVT4n0Y. Accessed 21st March 2024.
27 Tommi Toivonen, Audio Designer at Supercell. Interview by Eulalia Febrer-Coll. 5th April 2024.
28 See Hee Jung Hong & Dario Wünsch, "Esports Players", in Seth E. Jenny et al. (Eds.), *Routledge Handbook of Esports*, 167–176. Oxon: Routledge, 2024.
29 ESL Counter-Strike, "IEM Sydney 2023 Official Trailer", *Youtube*, 2023. Available at: https://www.youtube.com/watch?v=DtxxF0W1tI0. Accessed 21st March 2024.
30 ESL Counter-Strike, "IEM Cologne 2022 Official Trailer", *Youtube*, 2022. Available at: https://www.youtube.com/watch?v=UBPfySaDGDc&t=66s. Accessed 21st March 2024.
31 Carol Vernalis, *Unruly Media: Youtube, Music Videos, and the New Digital Cinema*. New York: Oxford University Press, 2013, 13.
32 PUBG Esports, "Home", *Youtube*, n.d. Available at: https://www.youtube.com/@PUBGEsports. Accessed 1st April 2024.
33 Tommi Toivonen, Audio Designer at Supercell. Interview by Eulalia Febrer-Coll. 5th April 2024.
34 Vernalis, *Unruly Media*.
35 LEC, "Mediocre Rap Battle of the #LEC | 2020 Summer Playoffs", *Youtube*, 2020. Available at: https://www.youtube.com/watch?v=weXb561sJl0. 8th April 2024.
36 Ainoha Campos, Professional Caster for *League of Legends* at LVP. Interview by Eulalia Febrer-Coll. 9th April 2023.
37 LVPesLoL, "READY PA'TO – FINALES 12 DE AGOSTO – SUPERLIGA SUMMER 2021", *Youtube,* 2021. Available at: https://www.youtube.com/watch?v=Hr3MT3RwO3Y. Accessed 8th April 2024.
38 Tommi Toivonen, Audio Designer at Supercell. Interview by Eulalia Febrer-Coll. 5th April 2024.
39 Team Liquid Valorant, "Turn the Tide ft. 2WEI, Edda Hayes & Kataem (Official Music Video) // Liquid VALORANT Champions 2023", *Youtube*, 2023. Available at: https://www.youtube.com/watch?v=M9UeetXVsw0. Accessed 8th April 2024.
40 Max Thielmeyer, "Fnatic Launches New Music Label With 'Lofi Beats To Chill And Game To' Album", *Forbes,* 2022. Available at: https://www.forbes.com/sites/maxthielmeyer/2022/11/09/fnatic-launches-new-music-label-with-lofi-beats-to-chill-and-game-to-album/?sh=77e344cf4d33. Accessed 8th April 2024.
41 Thielmeyer, "Fnatic Launches New Music Label With 'Lofi Beats To Chill And Game To' Album".
42 Alan Gai, professional caster for *Overwatch* and *Valorant*. Interview by Eulalia Febrer-Coll. 16th April 2024 See Hip Shop, "GAI本人回应! 无畏契约EDG选手康神现场唱GAI周延《朝天门", *Sina*, 2023. Available at: https://k.sina.cn/article_1163858357_v455f11b5019017ux0.html. Accessed 10th April 2024.
43 Huya.com, "#无畏契约#无畏契约东京大师赛 #gai #说唱歌手 #zmjjkk GAI周延为EDG无畏契约分", 2023. Available at: https://www.huya.com/video/play/881543415.html/. Accessed 10th April 2024.
44 Epidemic Sound, "The Sound of Gamers: Music Trends in Gaming Content", 2023. Available at: https://www.epidemicsound.com/blog/sound-of-gamers/. Accessed 10th April 2024.
45 See Cherie Hu, "Why the Intersection of Music and Esports Is Bigger Business Than Ever", *Forbes*, 2018. Available at: https://www.forbes.com/sites/cheriehu/2018/10/25/why-the-intersection-of-music-and-esports-is-bigger-business-than-ever/. Accessed 5th April 2024; Alexander Lee, "Why Musicians Are Partnering with Gaming Companies to Produce Original Songs and Content", *Digiday*, 2022. Available at: https://digiday.com/marketing/why-musicians-are-partnering-with-gaming-companies-to-produce-original-songs-and-content/. Accessed 5th April 2024.

46 Henry Jenkins, *"Star Trek Rerun, Reread, Rewritten: Fan Writing as Textual Poaching"*, in *Fans, Bloggers, and Gamers: Exploring Participatory Culture*. New York: New York University Press, 2006.
47 Melissa A. Click & Suzanne Scott, "Introduction", in Melissa A. Click & Suzanne Scott (Eds.), *The Routledge Companion to Media Fandom*. New York: Routledge, 2018.
48 Francesca Coppa, "Fuck Yeah, Fandom Is Beautiful", *The Journal of Fandom Studies*, 2014, 2(1), 80.
49 Coppa, "Fuck Yeah, Fandom Is Beautiful".
50 A Best of 5 (Bo5) refers to a match format where two teams compete in a series of five games, of which the first to win three games becomes the winner.
51 League of Legacies, "Silver Scrapes", n.d. Available at: http://legacies.lol/silverscrapes/. Accessed 5th October 2021.
52 See LPL, "LPL Dragon Boat Festival | Silver Scrapes | Chinese Traditional Version", *Youtube*, 2023. Available at: https://www.youtube.com/watch?v=XVEOKg3fIWI. Accessed 15th April 2024.
53 Josep Martí i Pérez, "La tradición evocada: folklore y folklorismo", *Tradición Oral*, 1999, 81–107.
54 Kevin Pauliks, "Memeing against Mainstream. An Analysis of Dank Memes and the Pictorial (Counter.) Practicers of Meme Culture", *AoIR Selected Papers of Internet Research*, 2021. Available at: https://spir.aoir.org/ojs/index.php/spir/article/view/12006/10380. Accessed 2nd March 2024.
55 Reebee Garofalo, "How Autonomous Is Relative: Popular Music, the Social Formation and Cultural Struggle", *Popular Music*, 1987, 6, 77–92.
56 Diego Martín Muñoz & Luis Miguel Pedrero, "Deporte y espectáculo en la narrativa de los 'e-sports': el caso de 'League of Legends'", *index.comunicación*, 2021, 11(2), 59–79.
57 Raine Koskimaa, Tanja Välisalo, Maria Ruotsalainen & Veli-Matti Karhulahti, "Esports Transmedia Universes: The Case of *Overwatch*", in Dal Yong Jin (Ed.), *Global Esports: Transformation of Cultural Perceptions of Competitive Gaming*, 149–165. New York: Bloomsbury, 2021.
58 Kevin Lehnert, Anna Walz & Ryan Christianson, "The Booming eSports Market: A Field Day for Fans", *Journal of Business Strategy*, 2021, 43(2), 126.
59 Toa Dunn, former Head of Music at Riot Games. Personal communication, 27th April 2024.
60 LOUD VALORANT, "O Brasil é a LOUD" – LOUD ft. GUXTA", *Youtube*, 2021. Available at: https://www.youtube.com/watch?v=DYvHCN4cEhQ. Accessed 16th April 2024.
61 See Chapter 6.
62 H. B. Duran, "A Guide To: Celebrities in Esports – Music, Film, and TV", *Esports Insider*, 2021, Available at: https://esportsinsider.com/2021/09/celebrities-esports-music-film-tv. Accessed 11th April 2024.
63 Gavin Johnson, Director of Sync and Partnerships at Monstercat, Interview by Eulalia Febrer-Coll, 13th December 2023.
64 Ashley Hancock, "Esports Market Size, Share & Trends Analysis Report by 2030", *Vantage Market Research*, 2023. Available at: https://www.linkedin.com/pulse/esports-market-size-share-trends-analysis-report-2030-ashley-hancock-pbs7c/. Accessed 18th April 2024.
65 Toa Dunn, "Music Partnerships in 2024 and Beyond", *Convergence: The Future of Video Games, Music and Transmedia*, 2024. Available at: https://www.linkedin.com/pulse/music-partnerships-2024-beyond-toa-dunn-0dnnc/. Accessed 10th February 2024.
66 Juan Tejada, *League of Legends* fan. Interview by Eulalia Febrer-Coll. 3rd September 2020; Aitor Crugeira, *League of Legends* fan. Interview by Eulalia Febrer-Coll. 4th September 2020.

67 Desoniq Studio, "The Influence of Streaming Platforms on Gaming", *Linkedin*, 2024. Available at: https://www.linkedin.com/pulse/influence-streaming-platforms-gaming-desoniqstudio-5xflc/. Accessed 18th April 2024.

REFERENCES

Adorno, Theodor W. & Simpson, George. "On Popular Music", *Zeitschrift für Sozialforschung*, 1941, 9, 17–48.

Bésombes, Nicolas. "Esports Ecosystem and Landscape", *Medium*, 2019. Available at: https://medium.com/@nicolas.besombes/esports-ecosystem-and-landscape-3dbbd653dc2c. Accessed 10th March 2024.

Click, Melissa A. & Scott, Suzanne. "Introduction", in Melissa A. Click & Suzanne Scott (Eds.), *The Routledge Companion to Media Fandom*, 1–4. New York: Routledge, 2018.

Coppa, Francesca. "Fuck Yeah, Fandom Is Beautiful", *The Journal of Fandom Studies*, 2014, 2(1), 80.

Desoniq Studio. "The Influence of Streaming Platforms on Gaming", *Linkedin*, 2024. Available at: https://www.linkedin.com/pulse/influence-streaming-platforms-gaming-desoniqstudio-5xflc/. Accessed 18th April 2024.

Díaz Gasca, Juan Sebastián. "Music Beyond Gameplay: Motivators in the Consumption of Videogame Soundtracks" (Doctoral Thesis). Griffith University, 2015.

Dunn, Toa. "Music Partnerships in 2024 and beyond", *Convergence: The Future of Video Games, Music and Transmedia*, 2024. Available at: https://www.linkedin.com/pulse/music-partnerships-2024-beyond-toa-dunn-0dnnc/. Accessed 10th February 2024.

Duran, H. B. "A Guide To: Celebrities in Esports – Music, Film, and TV", *Esports Insider*, 2021, Available at: https://esportsinsider.com/2021/09/celebrities-esports-music-film-tv. Accessed 11th April 2024.

Epic Games. *Unreal Engine*, n.d. Available at: https://www.unrealengine.com/. Accessed 17th March 2024.

Epidemic Sound. "The Sound of Gamers: Music Trends in Gaming Content", 2023. Available at: https://www.epidemicsound.com/blog/sound-of-gamers/. Accessed 10th April 2024.

ESL Counter-Strike. "IEM Cologne 2022 Official Trailer", *Youtube*, 2022. Available at: https://www.youtube.com/watch?v=UBPfySaDGDc&t=66s. Accessed 21st March 2024.

ESL Counter-Strike. "IEM Sydney 2023 Official Trailer", *Youtube*, 2023. Available at: https://www.youtube.com/watch?v=DtxxF0W1tI0. Accessed 21st March 2024.

Fortnite Wiki. "Lore (Battle Royale)", *Fortnite Wiki*, n.d. Available at: https://fortnite.fandom.com/wiki/Lore_(Battle_Royale). Accessed 18th March 2024.

Garena Free Fire LATAM. "ALOK en VIVO | Free Fire World Series", *Youtube*, 2019. Available at: https://www.youtube.com/watch?v=23kZuvuER9w. Accessed 20th March 2024.

Garofalo, Reebee. "How Autonomous Is Relative: Popular Music, the Social Formation and Cultural Struggle", *Popular Music*, 1987, 6, 77–92.

Goldblatt, Joe & Lee, Seungwon. *Special Events: The Brave New World for Bolder and Better Live Events*. Hoboken, NJ: Wiley, 2020.

Hancock, Ashley. "Esports Market Size, Share & Trends Analysis Report by 2030", Vantage Market Research, 2023. Available at: https://www.linkedin.com/pulse/esports-market-size-share-trends-analysis-report-2030-ashley-hancock-pbs7c/. Accessed 18th April 2024.

Hip Shop. "GAI本人回应 ！ 无畏契约EDG选手康神现场唱GAI周延《朝天门", Sina, 2023. Available at: https://k.sina.cn/article_1163858357_v455f11b5019017ux0.html. Accessed 10th April 2024.

Hong, Hee Jung & Wünsch, Dario. "Esports Players", in Seth E. Jenny et al. (Eds.), *Routledge Handbook of Esports,* 167–176. Oxon: Routledge, 2024.

Hu, Cherie. "Why the Intersection of Music and Esports Is Bigger Business Than Ever", *Forbes,* 2018. Available at: https://www.forbes.com/sites/cheriehu/2018/10/25/why-the-intersection-of-music-and-esports-is-bigger-business-than-ever/. Accessed 5th April 2024.

Huya.com. "#无畏契约#无畏契约东京大师赛 #gai #说唱歌手 #zmjjkk GAI周延为EDG无畏契约分", 2023. Available at: https://www.huya.com/video/play/881543415.html/. Accessed 10th April 2024.

Jenkins, Henry. *Convergence Culture: Where Old and New Media Collide*. New York: New York University Press, 2006.

Jenkins, Henry. "Star Trek Rerun, Reread, Rewritten: Fan Writing as Textual Poaching", in Henry Jenkins (Ed.), *Fans, Bloggers, and Gamers: Exploring Participatory Culture*, 37–60. New York: New York University Press, 2006.

Koskimaa, Raine, Välisalo, Tanja, Ruotsalainen, Maria & Karhulahti, Veli-Matti. "Esports Transmedia Universes: The Case of *Overwatch*", in Dal Yong Jin (Ed.), *Global Esports: Transformation of Cultural Perceptions of Competitive Gaming*, 149–165. New York: Bloomsbury, 2021.

League of Legacies. "Silver Scrapes", n.d. Available at: https://legacies.lol/silverscrapes/. Accessed 5th October 2021.

LEC. "Fight the Darkness | LEC x Star Guardian | 2022 LEC Summer", *Youtube*, 2022. Available at: https://www.youtube.com/watch?v=e1AScOgahy8. Accessed 20th March 2024.

LEC. "Mediocre Rap Battle of the #LEC | 2020 Summer Playoffs", *Youtube,* 2020. Available at: https://www.youtube.com/watch?v=weXb561sJl0. Accessed 8th April 2024.

Lee, Alexander. "Why Musicians Are Partnering with Gaming Companies to Produce Original Songs and Content", *Digiday,* 2022. Available at: https://digiday.com/marketing/why-musicians-are-partnering-with-gaming-companies-to-produce-original-songs-and-content/. Accessed 5th April 2024.

Lehnert, Kevin, Walz, Anna & Christianson, Ryan. "The Booming eSports Market: A Field Day for Fans", *Journal of Business Strategy,* 2021, 43(2), 126.

Leight, Elias. "Is the Music Business Out of Synch with Game Developers?", Billboard, 2024. Available at: https://www.billboard.com/pro/video-games-music-song-licensing-system-out-synch/. Accessed 15th March 2024.

Leischii. "Butcher's Bridge", *Runeforge,* 2023. Available at: https://www.runeforge.io/post/butchers-bridge. Accessed 20th March 2024.

Linhares, Nádia. "Riot Partners with Universal Music Group to Create Promotional Songs for League of Legends World Finals", *Dot Esports,* 2020. Available at: https://dotesports.com/league-of-legends/news/riot-partners-with-universal-music-group-to-create-promotional-songs-for-league-of-legends-worlds-finals. Accessed 15th March 2024.

LOUD VALORANT. "O Brasil é a LOUD" – LOUD ft. GUXTA", *Youtube*, 2021. Available at: https://www.youtube.com/watch?v=DYvHCN4cEhQ. Accessed 16th April 2024.

LPL. "LPL Dragon Boat Festival | Silver Scrapes | Chinese Traditional Version", *Youtube*, 2023. Available at: https://www.youtube.com/watch?v=XVEOKg3fIWI. Accessed 15th April 2024.

LVPesLo L. "READY PA'TO – FINALES 12 DE AGOSTO – SUPERLIGA SUMMER 2021", Youtube, 2021. Available at: https://www.youtube.com/watch?v=Hr3MT3RwO3Y. Accessed 8th April 2024.

Martí i Pérez, Josep. "La tradición evocada: folklore y folklorismo", in Eloy Gómez Pellón (Ed.), *Tradición Oral*, 81–107. Universidad de Cantabria, Aula de Etnografía, 1999.

Martín Muñoz, Diego & Pedrero, Luis Miguel, "Deporte y espectáculo en la narrativa de los 'e-sports': el caso de 'League of Legends'", *index.comunicación*, 2021, 11(2), 59–79.

Milton, John & Cobelo, Silvia. *Translation, Adaptation and Digital Media.* New York: Routledge, 2023.

Mora-Cantallops, Marçal & Sicilia, Miguel-Ángel. "Motivations to Read and Learn in Videogame Lore: The Case of League of Legends", *ACM International Conference Proceeding Series*, 2016, 585–591.
Muniz, Albert M. & O'Guinn, Thomas C. "Brand Community", *Journal of Consumer Research*, 2001, 27(4), 412–332.
Pauliks, Kevin. "Memeing against Mainstream. An Analysis of Dank Memes and the Pictorial (Counter.) Practicers of Meme Culture", *AoIR Selected Papers of Internet Research*, 2021. Available at: https://spir.aoir.org/ojs/index.php/spir/article/view/12006/10380. Accessed 2nd March 2024.
PUBG Esports. "Home", *Youtube*, n.d. Available at: https://www.youtube.com/@PUBGEsports. Accessed 1st April 2024.
PUBG Esports. "PUBG – Stand United: PGC 2019 Trailer", *Youtube,* 2019. Available at: https://www.youtube.com/watch?v=GepTXVT4n0Y. Accessed 21st March 2024.
Scholz, Tobias M. "The Business Model Network of Esports: The Convergence of Overwatch", in Dal Yong Jin (Ed.), *Global Esports: Transformation of Cultural Perceptions of Competitive Gaming*, 99–114. New York: Bloomsbury, 2021.
Scolari, Carlos Alberto. "Más allá del pentagrama: Transmedia y música", *Hipermediaciones*, 2014. Available at: https://hipermediaciones.com/2014/01/19/transmedia-y-musica/. Accessed 15th March 2024.
SkinSpotlights. "Bilgewater Map Music (Butcher's Bridge), *Youtube*, 2015. Available at: https://www.youtube.com/watch?v=MrcHugDsc4Y. Accessed 20th March 2024.
Stryngr. "Music for Gaming", n.d. Available at: https://www.styngr.com. Accessed 28th March 2024.
Tară-Lungă, Michaela-Oana. "Major Special Events: An Interpretative Literature Review", *Management & Marketing Challenges for the Knowledge Society,* 2012, 4, 759–776.
Team Liquid Valorant. "Turn the Tide ft. 2WEI, Edda Hayes & Kataem (Official Music Video) // Liquid VALORANT Champions 2023", *Youtube,* 2023. Available at: https://www.youtube.com/watch?v=M9UeetXVsw0. Accessed 8th April 2024.
Thielmeyer, Max. "Fnatic Launches New Music Label with 'Lofi Beats to Chill and Game to' Album", *Forbes,* 2022. Available at: https://www.forbes.com/sites/maxthielmeyer/2022/11/09/fnatic-launches-new-music-label-with-lofi-beats-to-chill-and-game-to-album/?sh=77e344cf4d33. Accessed 8th April 2024.
Tuting, Kristine "Kurisu". "They Told Him He Could Become Anything, So He Became Star Guardian Soraka", *One Esports,* 2022. Available at: https://www.oneesports.gg/cosplay/g2-ocelote-star-guardian-soraka-cosplay/. Accessed 20th March 2024.
Universal Music Group. "Universal Music Group, Republic Records, & Stryngr Bring Boombox to Roblox – Pioneering Opportunities for Labels and Players", 2024. Available at: https://www.universalmusic.com/universal-music-group-republic-records-styngr-bring-boombox-to-roblox-pioneering-opportunities-for-labels-and-players/. Accessed 25th March 2024.
Vernalis, Carol. *Unruly Media: YouTube, Music Videos, and the New Digital Cinema.* New York: Oxford University Press, 2013, 13.

Artists on Esports Stages *In-Game*

4

Popular music has converged with video games on online concerts since the last decades of the past century, from early online initiatives such as *Second Life*, which started experimenting with the insertion of life music experiences into virtual worlds, making them accessible in real-time for delocalized attendees.[1] In 2006, Suzanne Vega debuted on this platform,[2] in which she performed through her avatar for a virtual audience, also formed by avatar attendants. Since then, technological improvements and the idea of the *metaverse*[3] have afforded increasingly immersive stages for real-flesh and virtual artists to perform in, including from live shows to participatory music videos.

The presence of staged in-game music has been widely explored by authors such as Rambarran,[4] Breese and colleagues,[5] or Çelik,[6] among others. However, its embeddedness into the esports panorama as a marketing as well as socializing opportunity has yet been scarcely researched. The in-game concerts that have served as the promotion of competitive events and participating agents have been especially relevant to the gaming-music industry dialogue, as they have opened opportunities for the introduction of esports brands in the music market, and music brands in the gaming ecosystem. Furthermore, this multimedia convergence has contributed new music-mediated social contexts for attendees, in complement to social platforms such as X or Instagram. As underlined by Arditi:

> Music industry and video game industry executives think that by including concerts in other games, they may be able to attract die-hard music fans to a game and spend more money on the game. For instance, there may be little connection between *Madden NFL* players and BTS fans, but the BTS army has demonstrated an appetite to purchase anything BTS related. If EA Sports were to include a BTS concert within the game, they would be able to sell more copies of the game. By cross promoting these types of shows, music industry and video game industry companies develop a model of unending consumption by targeting fans who may not otherwise be interested in a product.[7]

The illusion of non-mediation provided by these video games, which can be attended virtually—as a virtual first-person—, was addressed by Calleja,[8] who described the

 DOI: 10.1201/9781032625362-5

interfaces through which they are presented as *transparent*. This illusion makes the users feel like they can modify and intervene directly with the contents on-screen, momentarily erasing the technological interface that mediates them. In this sense, what approaches the viewer-participant to the experience is the sense of belongingness to the event.

Frith also underlined the relevance of the perception of *liveness* in the context of traditional sports, when stating that "one of the recurring pleasures of popular culture is the difficult or spectacular act, the drama of which lies precisely in its liveness."[9] This, according to the author, means that the value of an event is placed on the perceived effort that has been put into creating an experience for the receiving audience. For this reason, and for the successful development of live music events in video games, the concept of *incorporation* is essential.

Calleja uses *incorporation* to refer to the inhabiting of virtual environments as (a) the incorporation of the environment in the mind of the player, as a part of the immediate environment that can be navigated and interacted with, and (b) the incorporation—in the corporeal sense—of the character in a specific location of the virtual environment at any moment in time. Therefore, the player assimilates the environment of the game into their consciousness while incorporating it through their avatar in that very environment.[10,11]

This does not exclude the physical world of the player, as the two realities become coexistent: for instance, someone playing next to a friend would become part of the same reality. Other authors, such as Breese and colleagues, have contrasted in-flesh live concerts to their virtual homonymous, and found that sharing the same experience simultaneously with a community of similarly engaged individuals contributed to the construction of their experience in both cases.[12] Furthermore, the possibility of living—and reliving—these events contributed to developing new socialization spaces, which do not appear in substitution to preexisting ones but in their complement.[13] Trevor S. Havey likewise underlined how the music presented in virtual environments represents social spaces "in which interpersonal relationships are actualized and individual avatars negotiate the simultaneity of their social identity as both online and offline social actors."[14]

It is fundamental that in-game performing bands are presented in a shared context, as they contribute a space for (digital) socialization—that despite being technologically mediated, is not perceived as such. These opportunities provide a shared experience with meaning for assistants, as supported by the music as a binding element. However, it is in the delocalization of these events, in the ubiquitous space that they create, where their value is most noticeable, as thousands of people can access the experiences simultaneously, at the same time, from widely diverse locations.

One of the arguments of this chapter is that these events have not only been key in providing a marketing opportunity for video game brands, their esports divisions, and the record labels and artists featured in their metaverses,[15] but also in affording a digital socializing space for game fans and other attendants, which is mainly articulated by music.

ABOUT IN-GAME PERFORMANCES

Live performances in video game worlds can rely on different elements, from the performing artists to the worlds in which they are staged. The cases discussed here differ from non-online (or non-synchronous) game events in that they try to effectively recreate a face-to-face context which participants can attend simultaneously, a virtual gathering mediated by music.[16]

Similarly to Calleja, Xu describes how participants in virtual environments tend to coexist in three body forms: their physical body in the real world, a second body constructed by culture and society, and a third one that exists "between body one and body two through technological means,"[17] which is crucial in the performing arts.

These categories can be applied to our discussion, as virtual artists and bands featured in video games can hold and combine different forms of embodiment. These include strictly virtual interventions—e.g., bands like the Bad Randoms in *Brawl Stars*—avatarized real artists—e.g., Marshmello in *Fortnite*—or non-virtual artists—e.g., Fall Out Boy in *Fortnite*'s iHeartLand. Furthermore, they can be contextualized on both virtual stages, which can be accessed in a virtual world—including "physical" stages in the game, or the game as a general stage—and on non-virtual stages, which

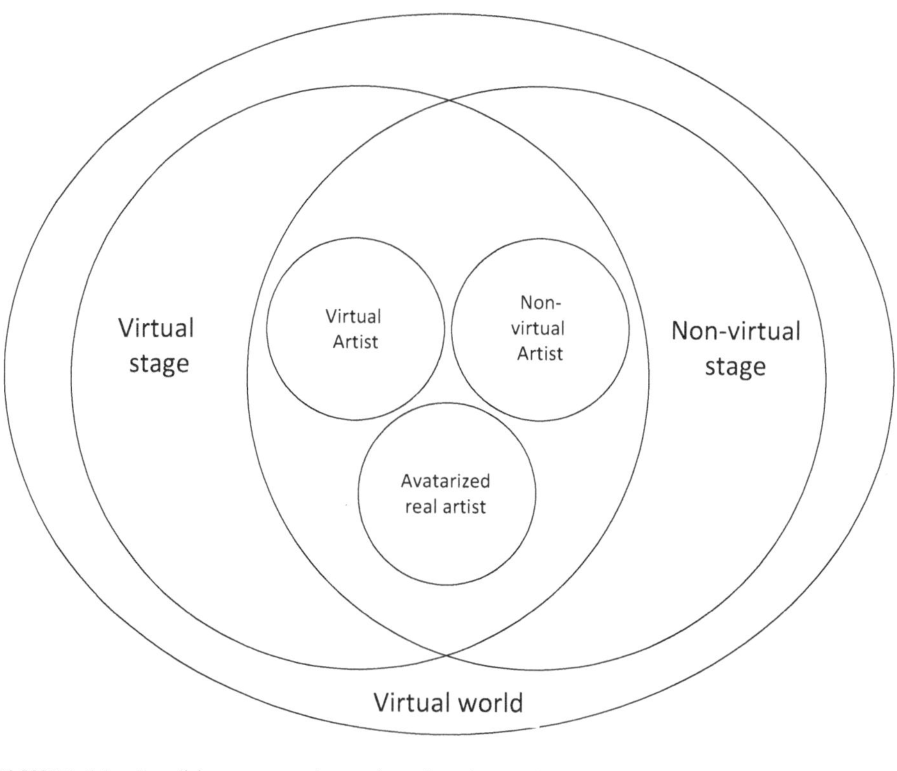

FIGURE 4.1 Possible presentations of performing artists in virtual worlds.

are projected into a virtual world—e.g., through a virtual screen. In all cases, the artists are inserted in virtual environments corresponding to the fictional worlds in which the games are developed.

An example of these is Fall Out Boy's performance in the *Fortnite Creative* island iHeartLand, sponsored by iHeart Media, who have also contributed to building the music scene in *Roblox*. In this case, the band's participation occurred as a projection in the virtual world through an in-game screen, that showed the musicians performing on a real stage in the real world. This screen was accessible for game users in the game's *Creative* mode. The investment of the media company in this and other events can be read as an example of the interest in Epic Games' *metaverse*,[18] but also as an investment in the whole ecosystem surrounding the game, including its esports scene.

A different case is Travis Scott's performance in *Fortnite*,[19] which implied the avatarization of the artist as well as the dissolution of the traditional stage in favor of using the whole imaginary world of the game as a performative space. This allowed users to become part of the experience rather than receive it passively, as will be discussed in the following epigraphs.

To these performances, virtuality is a key concept that, although behind the scope of this chapter, can be comprehended through the detailed analyses offered in *The Oxford Handbook of Music and Virtuality*, edited by Whiteley and Rambarran.[20] In this volume, the authors offer the opportunity to each collaborating scholar to suggest

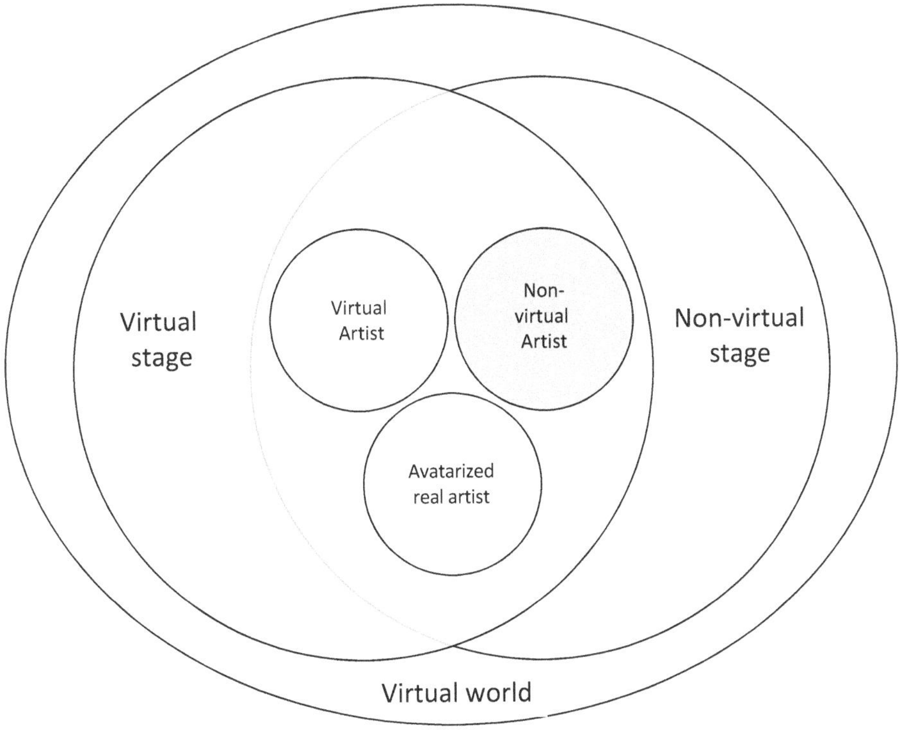

FIGURE 4.2 Disposition of the Fall Out Boy concert on iHeartLand.

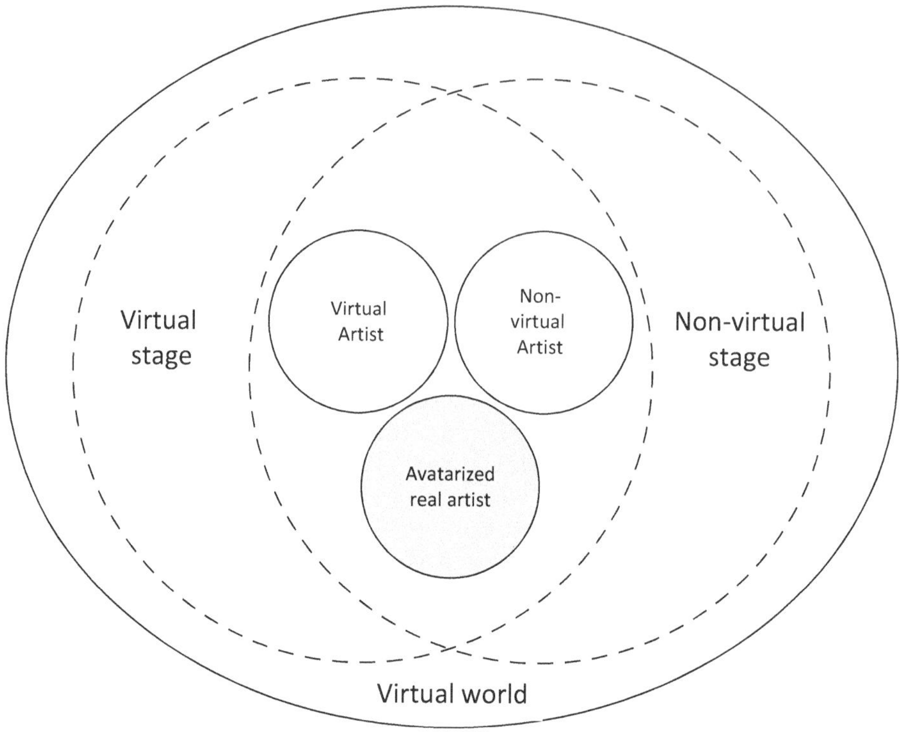

FIGURE 4.3 Disposition of Travis Scott's concert in *Fortnite*.

their take on the concept, underlining the progressive blurring boundaries between reality and fantasy, as afforded by continuously evolving technologies. An example of this continuous exploration is the partnership between platforms like Netflix and *Roblox*, set to create experiences between expectation and participation[21]—that undoubtedly hold music as a cornerstone in articulating their collaboration.

Concerning this, the idea of the *metaverse* has been linked to virtuality and discussed in the music context since the beginning of the 21st century by scholars such as Richard Elen,[22] or more recently by Gizem Çelik[23] or Pat Healy and Hannah Standiford—[24] who preferred calling it the *paraverse*. Some of the elements mentioned by these authors, like the parallelism to the real world, social interactivity, or the use of avatars, can help fit games such as *Fortnite* under a wider label. However, this would be only fitting for a few cases in the esports industry.

The possibility of creating and attending music in real-time through self-representation has been attractive in transforming passive listeners into active participants for brands around games. It is no surprise that the music industry is growingly interested in placing its products in the context of *esportified* games,[25] as their vision has become growingly transmediatic.

Water & Music founder Cherie Hu pointed to the interest in the esports-music synergies in 2020, when underlining the potential channels of connection between both through direct and indirect ways of engagement.[26]

15 WAYS TO INCORPORATE GAMING INTO YOUR MUSIC STRATEGY, C. HU (2020)

GAMING AS A BUSINESS MODEL

1. Direct content licenses with game developers.
2. Blanket licenses with user-generated content (UGC) platforms.
3. Exclusive partnership deals with UGC platforms.
4. Live, in-game events.
5. In-game digital goods and microtransactions.
6. Performances and syncs at competitive esports events.

GAMING AS A TALENT AND AUDIENCE OPPORTUNITY

7. Collaborations with gaming influencers and streamers.
8. Investments in esports leagues and brands.
9. Label imprints and management arms focused on gaming and esports.

GAMING AS A CREATIVE TOOL

10. Hardware: Creation using game consoles.
11. Software: Creation using interactive mobile apps.
12. Hardware/Software: Creation using mixed-reality tools.

GAMING AS A BRANDING AND NARRATIVE ARCHITECTURE

13. Album release campaigns with games.
14. Album release campaigns as games.
15. Parasocial artist-branded games.

Among the categories pinpointed by the author, esports-related music performances occupy a transversal position, that is present in different categories including "Live, in-game events". Previously, Lee had underlined how music companies needed to shift toward the gaming industry to scale virtual concerts, as "the digital gaming industry's expertise in pricing models and user engagement—and the cultural *cache* and social glue that games like *Fortnite* have amassed over the last several years—could help finally rewrite this narrative for good."[27] In this vein, the intersection between games and the music industry becomes more direct than that specifically with esports, which appear as a branch emerging from the same connection.

VIRTUAL CONCERTS AND ESPORTS

The relationship between virtual concerts and esports has not been as explicit as that of live performances during competitive events,[28] since they do not occur in a direct intersection with show matches, but as promotional tools in esportified video game environments. As such, they do not fall far from other games such as *Minecraft* or *Roblox*, whose open virtual metaverses have been home to multiple artists and music brands to date. Nevertheless, it can be argued that these in-game events function as loyalty and engagement tools for consumers of tournaments and related products, as they constitute a form of experiential marketing.[29]

For this purpose, including popular music artists and bands in video games has become an increasingly tackled strategy around esports and in overall gaming, as transmediality grows across audiovisual popular culture.[30] In the specific field that concerns us, including popular artists on virtual stages is key to the reception of the created experiences,[31] as they can potentially act as a link between competitive and non-competitive content. In this sense, esports marketing permeates through and benefits from the transversality and continuous exchange afforded by digital socialization.

> *Fortnite* is an interesting example as well as it used to run the one-off concerts with the biggest artists, but those have evolved with *Fornite* actually implementing the artists and their music into the "seasonal" cycle, meaning there is loads of the artist-related content (and the actual in-game concert as well) inside the game for a limited time. For example, *Fornite* just had a collaboration with Lady Gaga, and are having one with Metallica right now. And regarding the impact of these, those surely are impactul, especially with the bigger artists, increasing both player engagement (not many players want to miss these limited-time concerts, especially when there are limited-time in-game rewards to be earned as well) but also marketing and attracting new players to the game.[32]

The range of formats regarding digital performance quoted in the following makes Auslander's thesis on liveness especially relevant, as a "historically contingent concept"[33] that relies on specific cultural context. Liveness is to be experienced differently in prerecorded immersive performances than in screened-stage live broadcasts, despite a common factor around the time-specific access to the events. In other words, the perception of liveness for in-game events depends not only on the artists and the public's copresence, but also on the *eventuality* of the performance, which is accessible first-hand only during specific moments, increasing product value.

Marketing the Experience

On another note, not only does each form of mediatization provided by in-game concerts imply a different level of interaction between the artist and the public, but at an industry level their articulation holds specific legal implications. The reproduction of artistic performances through digital means—specifically *digital clones*—is also to be considered:

> Because it is understood that digital captures and clones are not primarily records of particular performances but, rather, matrices from which an infinite number of new

> performances may be produced, the digital has made it inevitable that aspects of performance beyond the voice and the face (e.g., facial expression, physical movement) will be understood as proprietary and regulated by some combination of copyright, trademark, business law, and right of publicity.[34]

With this, Auslander appeals to the economic and marketable value of digital performance beyond music as its only means, making it a sort of transistor that regulates artistic performance to amplify its effect and impact on the public of the game in which it is placed.

Despite the interest in producing live shows with the live presence of artists, the feasibility of such initiatives presents restraints derived from the introduction of effects and in-game tie-ins,[35] that have tilted the balance toward prerecorded interactive music videos, presented as one-time in-game events. To date, there have been few interventions in esports video games including performances with the live copresence of the featured artists, as most brands have shown a preference for preset audiovisual interventions that benefit the aesthetics of the shows. Live interventions have mostly included screened shows in the metaverses of the games, which afford a straightforward presentation of liveness, although cases such as Marshmello's have been able to transcend this model.

The most popular cases of artists that have performed in esports games are led by the Western influence on the global market, which is translated into the inclusion of artists such as Ed Sheeran or Post Malone in *Pokémon GO*, or Justin Bieber in *Free Fire*. Other cases with non-Western artists are mostly defined by the cooptation of the global music industry, like in the cases of Blackpink, New Jeans, or Iraqi singer Rahma Riad, which have been featured in *PUBG Mobile*. Besides the regional events scheduled by different developers, concerts have become a more transversal and globalized occurrence.

Despite the potential liveness and interactive restrictions around big performance shows, creative modes such as those offered by *Fortnite Creative* and mods in virtual worlds include a potential for a continuous extension of the convergence between music, games, and their real-world competitive settings. The presentation of the artists and the special effects built around them to create a unique audiovisual experience cannot compete directly with the interactive video clips produced by Epic Games or Krafton, but have become effective virtual socializing points for consumers.

> But if it's live from the artist's part, it's very hard. I guess it's one of those things like as a live producer you want to try to minimize the mistakes. If you're a live music producer you want to make it as best of a performance as possible, and that's why a lot of people end up going with the pre-recorded option, just to make sure that everything is perfect. It also allows bigger effects, you can do touch-ups after. And there's a third reason, like in China, you have to go through censorship anyway, so it has to be pre-recorded. Because the Chinese government doesn't want to take any risk of you saying anything inappropriate live. So that's one of the reasons why, especially in China, it's mostly pre-recorded.[36]

Virtual festivals have become an extended model for face-to-face events such as Coachella, and have created new gathering opportunities for game fans. This virtual model was especially popularized during the COVID-19 pandemic, as "reformatting live music experiences, the virtual environment, and more specifically *games*"[37] provided new possibilities for fans and melomaniacs. These events, as well as the introduction of improved engines, have allowed the construction of highly creative and interactive spaces, which provide an alternative space of shared leisure for users and brands around the globe.[38] A preceding case is that of *The Lord Of The Rings Online*, which has held a yearly music festival since 2007, in which people can meet and play side by side, and[39] which can be deemed informative for later occurrences like the *Pokémon GO Festival.*

Potential and Restraints

Although the benefits of such spaces add to the experiences in the real world, as well as to the popularization of *esports*, it is essential to also underline their (current) weaknesses. Most essentially, the nature of virtual spaces implies a limited potential for spontaneous, transgressive, or resistant behaviors that might be contrary to company policies or the social mainstream. Because of this, the potential of virtual spaces to hold virtual performances cannot be separated from the marketing goals behind the connection of music and games.

The participation of artists in in-game performances must follow preset rules regarding copyright and allowed elements, much like what is established for streaming platforms such as Twitch or YouTube—e.g., in Kid Laroi's concert in *Fortnite*, the word *fuck* was censored, following the game's PEGI code (12).[40] These limitations can be trespassed to an extent once the spectacles are moved outside the virtual arena and onto face-to-face stages, although being held by similar policies. In any case, their in-game placement is nothing but significant for the popularization of titles toward the consumption of esports, both from economic and social perspectives.

However, the restraints around including popular music artists and the difficulties derived from the contractual arrangement between involved parties are not necessarily a determining factor. Developers like Supercell or Riot Games have developed

FIGURE 4.4 Bad Randoms stage in *Brawl Stars*.[41]

brand-based bands and music products, as already stated in previous chapters, which allow them to loop over licensing external artists. A good case study is that of the Bad Randoms, who not only served as an engaging music placement, but also were introduced in the game as a feature during its seventh season.

Prior to their appearance in the game, the stage on which they performed was progressively (virtually) built to let players know that an event was taking place. They were finally featured in August 2021, with their first hit, *We Won't Cooperate*. These are not the most common mechanics in in-game concerts today, as they tend to be set apart from the main gameplay into extra-ordinary spaces that contribute a sense of rituality similar to live performances. However, it presents an available model to incorporate music products in games that not require special accesses or modes.

FROM DJ MARSHMELLO TO A HIP-HOP REMIX IN *FORTNITE*

Some of the most celebrated cases of in-game concert activations that superposes with esports have been promoted by Epic Games with *Fortnite*. Since their first exploration of the format with DJ Marshmello in 2019, following predecessors from *Second Life* or *Minecraft*, the game has resonated across media for its collaborations with world-recognized music artists. Furthermore, the metaverse of the game has expanded to include diverse music-participatory environments for fans such as *Fortnite Creative*, that offer from viewing parties to virtual-instrument playing opportunities.

As backed by Soto de la Cruz and other authors, *Fortnite's* user base can be described as "one of the reasons that facilitates organizing large-scale activities within the game," which has become "more than a leisure artifact" for players, as it "enables interaction, integration, collaborative work and the development of players' social skills."[42] This has not passed unnoticed by brands, film, or music producers around the globe, who have shown a growing interest in collaborating with Epic—and vice versa.[43] The progressive intersection with adjacent industries is shown in Figure 4.5, which despite not being comprehensive of all developments in the game, includes key elements involving popular music.

Regarding the products under *Fortnite*'s title, the music events placed on each sub-product can differ in format—e.g., to date, the concerts in *Battle Royale* have had a different outline to those on *Fortnite Creative*. First and foremost, the title has gained mediatic recognition through events held with first-line artists such as DJ Marshmello (2019), Travis Scott (2020), Ariana Grande (2021), Eminem (2023), Metallica (2024), Karol G (2024), or Snoop Dogg and Juice WRLD (2024), mainly on *Battle Royale* and *Fortnite Festival*, which have been strategically designed to be visually and interactively appealing. It can be argued that these cases—especially the first two—have been definitory for the game and the trends in metaverse concerts.

Calleja's thesis of non-mediation promoted by the transparent illusion of digital media is reaffirmed through these cases, as they can be understood through the two dimensions mentioned earlier: firstly, regarding incorporation into the immediate environment,

FIGURE 4.5 Events on *Fortnite*'s timeline.

Fortnite's universes materialize digitally with their own physical and spatial rules—which are altered during concerts to create an extra-ordinary experience. Secondly, concerning incorporation in the corporeal sense, the avatars explore the virtual environment under the illusion of non-mediation—which is achieved through the game's soundscape and the binaural perception of music and sound. Thus, the events are experienced as part of a wider reality that does not rely only on the game per se, and which tends to extend toward the competitive branch of the title, mostly from a marketing and transmedia perspective.

As I argued elsewhere,[44] these events have afforded popular music artists and brands new performative spaces to explore, largely due to the improvement in technological media, which contributes to the illusion of non-mediation for participants. However, the level at which this illusion is achieved may depend on the presentation of the performing artists,[45] which, in the cases at hand, is that of avatarized real artists on virtual stages—including the game's world as a performative space.

The following cases also exemplify the evolution of the game and the brand's technological possibilities between 2019 and 2024, ranging from a first more modest concert on the game's island to full-on interactive shows including different game modalities, embedded in week-long events revolving around the featured artists.

DJ Marshmello at Pleasant Park

Marshemello's collaboration with *Fortnite* in 2019 was essential in proving the concept of open-world virtual concerts as bidirectional promotional content and assessing the possibilities of including virtual artists in the game.[46] The event took place in Pleasant Park, a specific location on the *Battle Royale* map. Although it lasted for approximately ten minutes, it gathered more than ten million concurrent viewers,[47] of whom many were not previously familiar with the DJ.

The event began with a ten-minute countdown preceding the concert, visible from all around the virtual island. To fit the event into the game more explicitly, at the end the attendees were drawn into a two-team match—50 versus 50—in each of the parallel rooms that were generated. This afforded a sense of embeddedness in the game and provided the feeling of a shared experience for attendees, as gamers and concertgoers.

Differently from other virtual concerts, Epic Games introduced interactive items and fantastic elements that elevated the experience beyond mere hearing. As stated by Senior Producer on Decoder at *The Verge*, Nick Statt:

> And it was quite visually impressive. The stage came to life with building-sized holograms of Fortnite characters, while a custom set of graphics played behind Marshmello's avatar. At certain points, timed to the shifts in the fast-moving dance music, the stage would alter gravity, sending players bouncing into the sky and even floating in place at one point. All the while, a majority of players, at least in my match, were dancing using in-game emotes and generally goofing off in various spots around the stage and up close right in front of Marshmello's avatar. It finally felt like a Fortnite event that wasn't punctuated by guns and chaos, as most prior ones have been.[48]

These elements fit into the game's reality and, while fantastic, were perceived as plausible for the world in which they were placed. The six songs featured in the show included

TABLE 4.1 Marshmello's Concert Setlist for *Fortnite*

SETLIST	*FEATURED ARTISTS*
Alone	–
Chasing Colors	Ookay Feat. Noah Cyrus
Flashbacks	–
Everyday	Logic
Fly	–
Happier	Bastille

live commentary by the artist, and each featured special effects to accompany its respective track, such as changes in gravity during *Fly* or the appearance of giant yellow beach balls with a smiley face during *Happier* (Table 4.1).

The impact of the artist was extended toward esports with a live show for the Fortnite Champion Series (FNCS) in 2019, in which he reaffirmed his key role in establishing a music scene around the game, and showed the close link between in-game developments and the corresponding competitive scene. That is, in addition to all in-game elements—from skins to gliders or banner icons—that were translated into millions of microtransactions. The DJ saw an increase in social media visibility—more than 20,000% on his streams—and song consumption—e.g., the song in collaboration with Ookay increased its sales by 1,543% during the week of his performance.[49] Although it is the only case among the described in the following that fits into the "in-game to esports scene" case, it set a precedent in its potential to appeal to massively played titles, especially those with global competitive visibility.

Travis Scott's Astronomical

During the pandemic, online concerts and overall culture consumption increased dramatically, creating a clear path for Epic Games to follow music-wise. The exploration with DJ Marshmello was clearly successful, and the game was steadily increasing revenue from its expansion as a metaverse platform,[50] thus fostering the investment in more ambitious projects. Although it can be argued that Travis Scott's performance during the first months of the state of alarm was coincidental and not specific to the social situation, as preparation for the event had to be already in motion, it served the consolidation of new forms of virtual socialization mediated by music.

On this occasion, the event's stage was set on Sweaty Sands, another location on the *Battle Royale* map, although the show was not designed as an artist-on-stage event but as a *world-as-stage* event. It was advertised and merchandized under the name *Astronomical*, following his Astroworld tour, and was likewise linked to the digital show, as the artist arrived on the island on a meteor. Differently from Marshmello's case, the intervention became an interactive video of sorts, in which the participant was guided through different scenarios. As written by user Will Gendron, in a chronicle for *Paper:*

> As at physical venues, players are encouraged to show up before doors opened to secure their spots, and despite Fortnite's capacity to handle millions of concurrent players I find myself developing new habits. Prior to the performance, everyone is dropped into

> a standard team rumble game where a small countdown stage is situated at Sweaty Sands (...) And then the unmistakable intro to "Sicko Mode" begins playing as an Astroworld-like terraform descends toward us emitting a purple beam that gives birth to a 100-foot, shirtless Travis Scott. (...) For this concert, the stage is the entire world of Fortnite. Lighting isn't provided by digital AV equipment but rather the atmospheric layers of the game, and the artist himself is immortal.[51]

The five pieces featured added up to ten minutes approximately, including both hits—*Sicko Mode, Stargazing, Goosebumps,* and *Highest in the Room*—and a new track, *The Scotts*—in collaboration with Kid Cudi—which has become one of the most successful songs of the artist.[52] On this occasion, the music was not reproduced nor commented live in situ, but he reacted to the event on Instagram as the show developed,[53] providing a sense of proximity for fans that could not be reached by other virtual means.

Like in the previous case, the event was wrapped by a final match between the attendees, linking the performance to the actual game. In both the preparation for the concert and during this last interactive act, users were able to use specific emotes and items, such as a flaming microphone that served as the luminescent bracelets or matches in traditional concerts. However, the experience was closely tailored, and spontaneousness was limited to the possibilities of the environment, as well as any potential transgressive behaviors—e.g., "killing" assistants following in-game dynamics. In this sense, social media offers freer environments for fans and players to dialogue *out-of-limits*, proving their key role in articulating the current gaming—and audiovisual—scene.

At a music industry and organizing level, the virtuality of these events also implied a change in mindset as to how the public was approached, reached, and the extent to which it could interact with the brands and creators.[54] In other words, what changed was not only the way of mingling around the stage and peers, but the shift was rooted in the approach and disposition of the concerts. In the end, the estimated revenue for the artist was $20 million for the collaborative event, in contrast to the in-person 56-stop Astroworld tour, which made around $53.5 million total, "or roughly just under $1million per show."[55]

Ariana Grande on the Rift Tour

A year after Scott's appearance on the island, Ariana Grande was introduced as a character in the game—including items such as skins and other collectibles—and embedded into its background story "as an opportunity to build a bigger world."[56] In contrast with previous cases, the show took place on three concurrent days that covered five world regions, including the Americas (August 6th), Asia and Oceania, Europe and the Middle East, and the Americas a second time (August 8th). In addition, a global performance was held on August 7th, reaching a total of twenty-seven million live attendees over the three days.[57]

Grande was inserted in the narrative during season 7, when a spaceship arrived on the island threatening the *status quo*. After the participants were abducted, a ten-minute spectacle emerged from the ship which, following the lore, was designed to distract the inhabitants of the island while their memories were extracted. Although this case was seen as a stretch to fit into the story of the game by some users,[58] elements such as the performance of *The Way* had an obvious impact on veteran Grande fans. The popular

TABLE 4.2 Ariana Grande's Setlist for the *Rift Tour* in *Fortnite.*

PRE-CONCERT	*OTHER FEATURED ARTISTS*
Come & go	Juice WRLD & DJ Marshmello
Audio	LSD
Victorious	Wolfmother
Concert setlist	
Raindrops (an angel cried)	–
7 Rings	–
Be Alright	–
R.E.M.	–
The Way	Mac Miller
Positions	–

song was played while the avatar climbed a set of virtual stairs to "Heaven," years after the passing of coauthor Mac—who she was dating at the time.[59]

The performance was preceded by a three-song interactive sequence, in which the participants took part in different environments—sliding, jumping, and battling a monster in fantastic environments (Table 4.2). This four-minute presentation was linked to the singer's performance through a brief cinematic in which players helped each other up, while small lights rose to the sky. This was a way to "achieve a sentimental moment. An expression of support, during trying times, in a way only Fortnite [could]," as FX Art Director Tim Elek wrote on social media.[60]

Each song was designed to accompany specific interactive scenes, that had Grande at the epicenter and as a point of reference. Like in Scott's case, the performance was ideated as an interactive music video that went beyond active listening, presumably as a means to exploit the game's virtual environment and create a differentiating experience for attendees. Also like in the previous case, the artist was depicted as a giant projection, establishing a physical and social distance from the attendees' avatars.

The joint effort of game and music was reinforced by the reliance on nostalgic elements at different levels.[61] Firstly, at the beginning of the event, when the participants were abducted by the spaceship, they entered a tunnel that held images from previous seasons and game events. At a musical level, the setlist included well-known pieces by the artist, that acted both as a claim for existing fans that were not familiar with *Fortnite*, and for *Fortnite* players who were not too familiar with the singer. Related to this, the inclusion of *The Way*, or the appeal toward companionship with *Raindrops*, had a notable echo on social media.

With regards to the revenue derived from the collaboration of Epic Games' *Fortnite* with Ariana Grande's ascribed label Republic Records, owned by Universal Music Publishing Group, her participation in the game must have been similar to that of Scott's,[62] reinforcing the effectiveness of the collaborations at each end of the agreement. That is, mainly from the collectible items that were inserted in the game after the singers' inclusion, the purchase of *battle passes* for the specific season, etc.

Eminem and The Big Bang Event

In December 2023, Epic Games broke a quiet streak by releasing *Fortnite Experiences,* following their presentation of the Unreal Editor for *Fortnite* earlier in the year. The three new modes—*LEGO Fortnite, Rocket Racing,* and *Fortnite Festival*—provided new spaces in the metaverse. They were built in collaboration with the LEGO Group, Psyonix, and Harmonix, respectively.

The project was presented through a combination of a participatory video announcement and a small music intervention, which included a peak into the new game subuniverses. The event began with a rocket being shot into the island's dome, which triggered a "fracture" in the game's virtual reality—all accompanied by orchestral music, which gave the illusion of a participative cinematic. From the crack created by the rocket, emerged a ship that collided on the island creating a vortex, which swallowed everything around it and propelled players into space. After finding themselves in a pitch-black environment, they were propelled toward the different worlds—first LEGO's, then Psyonix's, and finally Harmonix's.

The orchestral music was put on hold when the characters landed on *Fortnite Festival*'s galaxy, where the first notes of *Lose Yourself* were immediately recognizable. The stage for the game—in which other artists such as Billie Eilish have starred since—was presented and Eminem appeared, rapping the well-known lyrics of the song. This offered the opportunity to show the mechanics of the game for the first time, which are very similar to *Guitar Hero* and other rhythm-based games. This dynamic was quickly interrupted by a giant avatar of the artist, who transitioned to *Godzilla,* in a fashion similar to Scott's or Grande's previous appearances. It can be argued that the choice of featured tracks was not random, as they are two of the most listened songs by the artist:[63] *Lose Yourself* (2002), which occupies the first position of most reproduced tracks, and *Godzilla* was introduced featuring Juice WRLD, who had been present in previous soundtracks, in representation of more recent work by the artist (2020).

Although it can be argued that Eminem's show was secondary to the event as it primarily served as the presentation of their newest collaborations, it afforded momentum on social media for their dissemination.[64] The participants were finally extracted from the game's environment and propelled once again to space, from where they could observe multiple constellations representing the growing metaverse of the game and the parallel realities afforded through the game's narrative in previous seasons. This served as a narrated explanation for the following pause in the game's servers before all new modes were available.

Like in prior occasions, the artist was introduced in *Fortnite*'s universe through character skins, emotes, and other items, that added to the overall experience—and the revenue for involved parties.[65] Furthermore, following Scott's lead, the rapper teased his virtual debut in the game on social media,[66] thus showing the need for engaging multimediatlly with online communities and new fanbases. This can be extended to his most recent album, *The Death of Slim Shady (Coup De Grâce),* which has been favored by his approach to younger generations through *Fortnite,* creating engagement for veteran and new fans alike.[67]

Metallica's Fuel. Fire. Fury.

Following Eminem's brief intervention, Metallica's interactive show *Fuel. Fire. Fury.* was available for users in 2024, embedded into a week-long thematic event in the game. The inclusion of the band contributed to an expansion out of mainstream pop and hip-hop trends, as well as an approach to an audience with a preference for alternative genres, as well as among wider age ranges. The concert was framed by smaller modes and challenges in *LEGO Fortnite*, *Rocket Racing*, or *Battle Royale*. Participation included items such as electric guitars that could be used to "create a lightning arc in the sky,"[68] and move around the *Battle Royale* island faster, or participation in the *Battle Royale Metallica Cup* to earn in-game-specific items. This contributed to a sense of embeddedness in the game, and allowed players who were less familiar with the band to get acquainted with their music and overall trajectory.

In *Fortnite Festival*, the pass for the season allowed competing in a "face-off" music event, built around other challenges to obtain rewards. Among these, the players could access the songs that would be played in the concert until the end of the season, along with other existing tracks, on a circular stage that allowed a match between sixteen players. Although this format could hold the potential for competition, its embeddedness in the *Fortnite* esports scene is only relevant as a marketing commodity.

The concert that culminated the event was available at six different times over two days, allowing players from different geographies to attend.

> The concert was the showcase moment, and it was like going through an interactive version of heavy metal album art. Players were whisked away in a hot rod to a pyro-heavy concert stage before moving on to a gothic bell tower and a fight with a menacing puppet master. Like past virtual concerts featuring Eminem and Ariana Grande, it was an attempt to mix the feel of going to a live show with something fantastical.[69]

Like in previous occasions, the setlist chosen for the event included band hits, in this case from the 1980s and 1990s: *Enter Sandman*, *Fuel*, *Master of Puppets*, *Ride the Lightning*, *The Unforgiven*, and *Wherever I May Roam*. With this, the argument of the band's cooptation by the mainstream can be contrasted with the will to nostalgically appeal to older audiences through reissues—while being exposed to younger generations. As underlined by Bottomley, "the repetition of previously released musical texts in our culture helps, on the one hand, naturalize the consumption of recycled recordings and, on the other hand, serves many purposes other than just maximizing industry profits,"[70] as they gain cultural significance in specific moments in time.

Although this line of thought could lead to a deeper discussion around authenticity, reissuing, and consumption, that is only pertinent here as it affords higher visibility for the game's brands in their exploitation of their competitive products. Metallica's James Hetfield outlined how the two brands working together "made sense" from what can be called both a cultural and economic exchange:

> What I kind of equate it to is we have a huge family out there. The Metallica family is international and obviously every corner of the earth, there's a Metallica family member. And Fortnite is kind of the same. They've reached many people all over the planet, so getting the two together makes sense. And they've got a lot to gain from our

> family and vice versa. So it is a really cool idea. And like it was explained to me, it's like it's a whole another continent. And we've played all seven, [so we] might as well play the eighth one.[71]

Despite the distance from gaming that was expressed by the artist in the same interview, the trans- and multimediality of the market implies a need for engaging with new communication channels to both engage new publics and retain the existing through reformulated means. Following Jone's thesis in *The Rock Canon*, Eminem's or Metallica's strategies worked in favor of relying on the popular music canon as an "arbiter of cultural value and cultural capital"[72] that needs (social) institutions to give it authority—and thus to be perpetuated. In other words, in participating in *Fortnite*, traditionally non-commercial bands find a path to extend their work and maintain it as an essential piece of the masses' cultural capital, that is not necessarily shared by recent mainstream artists such as Travis Scott or Ariana Grande.

On the other hand, even if the quoted cases did not all directly translate into esports activations, it can be inferred that the growing popularity of *Fortnite*'s competitive division has received positive feedback and popularity from the initiatives. The small amount of data available online points toward the stabilization of the electronic sports market but a growing interest in competitions such as the FNCS.

Karol G MSB Fortnite

Following the success of the metal interactive experience, Karol G was the first Latin artist to perform in the game, which served as a statement to the increasing internationality of the music and gaming industries. The Colombian singer is well known as an influential reggaeton and urban pop artist, and despite her primary appeal to Latin and Hispanic publics, she has gained international recognition through collaborations with Daddy Yankee, J Balvin, Nicki Minaj, or Shakira, and received numerous awards such as the Latin Grammy Award for Best New Artist (2018) or Album of the Year (2023).

Her performance in the game followed the format of previous concerts, as it was placed in a specifically created environment in *Fortnite Festival*, and displayed as an immersive music video in which attendees could not only get close to the artist's giant avatar, but participate in challenges including different game modalities like *Rocket Racing*. The show included five popular songs—including *Provenza*, *S91*, *Oki Doki*, *Bichotag*—, with *Tusa* as a closing piece, which had reached number 1 on many charts around the globe as the first all-female Latin song to break into Spotify's global ten Top Chart.[73]

The show was not synchronous, but it was available longer than other cases—from the 23rd until the 26th of August—, and adapted to the diverse geographies of attendees schedule-wise.[74] This format implied a reformulation of the idea of liveness, since the immediacy of Marshmello or Travis Scott's cases—yet if more restricted accessibility- and spectacle-wise—was altered. The approach by Epic Games to music consumption, in this sense, was useful for implementing the impression of access to new materials, opening the door for alternative ways of exploiting preexisting products, despite the progressive distancing from real-life reproduction.

This goes in line with the extension of the event, which was embedded in Season 5 of the game, and presented as a unique opportunity to engage with items specific to the featured artist—including music-themed elements such as the "Bichota 4-String" Bass or a Premium Reward Track of *Qlona*.[75] The participation of the artist on the platform served her as a route for attracting new audiences, as she reported on *Variety:*

> I've been amazed by the incredible response we have seen from fans across the globe. It has been a rewarding experience to receive messages and read on social media how people are discovering my music for the first time and connecting with it. This is a testament of the incredible work that Fortnite has done creating a global community and the rising popularity of Latin music.[76]

Her statement does not only attest to the consolidation of the game as a virtual socializing *metaverse*, but underlines the growing attention to cross- and multimediality by the gaming and music industries, which create a bidirectional route for continuous development, drawing remarkable mediatic attention.[77]

A Final(e) Remix by Snoop Dogg, Juice WRLD, Eminem, and Ice Spice

Lastly in the five-year period analyzed, the double event held as two consecutive concerts to close the games season represents the growth of Epic Games in the industry, also as a music mediator. For the transition from *Fortnite*'s chapter five to six, the company designed a two-part *Finale* event, whose first act was held live on the TSX's stage at Times Square in New York, on the 1st of November 2024. The square was transformed into an active part of the experience, including its characteristic screens as part of the audiovisual spectacle, which featured artists Ice Spice and Snoop Dogg.[78]

The event, attended live by hundreds of fans,[79] covered celebrated songs by both artists: *Princess Diana* by Ice Spice; *Who Am I?*, *Drop It Like Its Hot*, and Dr Dre's *The Next Episode* by Snoop Dogg. The last piece, whose lyrics were slightly modified—e.g. words like *nigga* or *fuck* were eliminated—, served as a link to a cinematic trailer aimed at illustrating the change of season on the virtual island. In this clip, both artists were featured as characters alongside Eminem and Juice WRLD, who would later be part of the in-game concert on the 30th of November. It can be argued that the concert *in the flesh* served not only as a marketing claim for their later virtual performance, or the attraction of new players toward the title, but also as a statement. As described by *Forbes* contributor Paul Tassi, "If you think Fortnite peaked years ago, you're just wrong."[80] The position of the developers as an active part of the music industry is only increasing with the progressive affordances of technology, which in turn makes it possible for the company to invest in out-of-game experiences, complementary to their videoludic content.

The second part of the event took place in the game,[81] at the very center of the *Battle Royale* map, and was included as part of the *battle pass* for the season. The mechanics included the usual skins, soundtracks for the lobby, and special challenges for players, including a battle against the rapper around (or in) his own castle. Further elements

TABLE 4.3 Tracklist for *Remix: The Finale* (2024)

SONG	*FEATURED ARTISTS*
Drop it Like it's Hot	Snoop Dogg
Cadillac Deviles	Snoop Dogg
Another Part of Me	Snoop Dogg, Dr Dre, Sting
The Monster	Eminem, Rihanna
Houdini	Eminem
In Ha Mood	Ice Spice
Oh Shhh...	Ice Spice, Travis Scott
Empty Out Your Pockets	Juice WRLD
Lucid Dreams	Juice WRLD

for the specific pass were, for instance, a gun that shot Eminem's *Rap God* lyrics, or a teams' *Red vs Blue* face-to-face with Snoop Dog and Juice WRLD as representatives.[82]

This prelude was followed by the virtual concert itself, which drew a record 14.3 million synchronous players. In this case, the experience was similar to Travis Scott's, as it did not include interactive challenges from subuniverses but depicted giant figures of the singers as points of reference for attendees. The concert was a remix that included songs by Snoop Dogg, Eminem, Ice Spice, and Juice WRLD, among other featured artists, and interactive elements to dynamize each song like on previous occasions (Table 4.3).

The show, in part designed as a tribute to the late Jarad "Juice WRLD" Higgins,[83] lasted for fifteen minutes and closed with the disappearance of the rapper into the night sky, who had collaborated with Epic before his decease. His involvement with the game was furthermore underlined by the artist's mother in stating that:

> Jarad always loved to play Fortnite – it was more than just entertainment for him, it was a way to connect with others. From a young age, video games were a part of how he bonded with friends and family, and being in Fortnite is an incredible tribute to that connection. I know he would be overjoyed to see how his love for games continues to bring people together across different spaces, just like his music does.[84]

The participation of international rappers brought an added impact to the virtual gathering, as it supported the occasion while acting as a reminiscence of past events. Likewise, the interactive music video that accompanied the concert and the previous cinematic presentation introduced on Times Square referred to the popular culture and gaming capital of viewers, in underlining popular music iconic lyrics—e.g. Eminem's *Lose Yourself*, which was translated into the trailer video as a restaurant named *Mom's Spaghetti*.

The progressive transformation of the *Fortnite* platform and the increased possibilities for creating interactive music events that participate from different modalities exemplify the steady growth of Epic Games since the pandemic. The growing interest of the music industry in being involved with the game is clear, as is the investment of the developers in creating music experiences complementary to their virtual world. Parallelly, the popularity of the game's esports division has increased in the last four years,[85] in line with the progressive stabilization of the general esports market. This, along with the diverse strategies and elements described above, reinforces the centrality of such events as transmedia promotional tools that go beyond home playing, and serve to attract potential players toward further socializing opportunities in esports.

CONCLUSION

Exploring the reception of music performances in games such as *Fortnite* allows a deeper comprehension of the implications of the new concert formats at gaming and esports consumption levels. These provide new opportunities for brands and artists to exploit their products and for fans to participate actively in the ongoing exchanges. Moreover, these contexts, developing in coexistence with real-life representations and social environments, suggest a greater presence of new communication channels that complement traditional structures and are closely linked to online media.

Although mediated by technologies such as those used in the cases described, the strategies followed by companies such as Epic Games in titles like *Fortnite* afford a feeling of involvement for players. As argued by Jem Kelly, the "co-presence of performer and spectator is an enduring generic convention in pop performance, proposing a shared experience, a sense of 'being there' at the moment," that needs to be taken into account.[86] In this sense, *liveness* is essential, despite the need to understand what the term implies when performances are preprogrammed immersive experiences—or even participatory announcements.

The extent to which attendees can self-express freely in such environments as in face-to-face occasions is likewise relevant, as are the possibilities for performer-spectator or spectator-spectator interaction, which are limited according to company policy and market code. Of course, these divergences may exist in real-life environments depending on the format or occasion surrounding a concert—the expected behavior at a Beyoncé concert would not be the same as that of a small band playing in a town bar. Yet, the non-perceived mediation of virtual environments creates more closely monitored environments.

Throughout these pages, I have underlined how virtual concerts are relevant in providing marketing opportunities for video game brands and their respective esports branches, as well as for the record labels and artists that perform in their virtual worlds. As shown through *Fortnite*'s initiatives between 2019 and 2024, these have proved effective for both parties in disseminating their products and gathering large revenues in short periods of time. Although the connection to esports is not as direct as that discussed in the following chapter, it can be argued that the embeddedness of in-game events into a larger gaming ecosystem contributes to attracting new publics susceptible to gaining an interest about competitive events. This is especially true for those cases that have effectively migrated to esports shows, such as Supercell's Bad Randoms.

These elements are intrinsically linked to the digital socializing spaces that the games contribute. These spaces can be attended through self-representation while interacting with other users in different locations, mainly through the mediation of music.

For the games under discussion to be successful, the online nature provides a channel for creating new bonds and engaging in joined virtual activities, which can be transferred to face-to-face greetings and other shared experiences.

Last but not least importantly, the trend of transmediality in the music industry has translated into an increased interest in these socially-based opportunitites, which has been shown through the inclusion of more "traditional" bands such as Metallica in *Fortnite*. In this vein, the economic and marketable value of digital performance makes in-game participation a means to generate an impact on game and music fans alike. Cases such as DJ Marshmello's or Travis Scott's have provided a cornerstone in defining the future of game trends and (esports) marketing which will, undoubtedly, continue to metamorphize.

NOTES

1 Trevor S. Harvey, "Avatar Rockstars: Constructing Musical Personae in Virtual Worlds", in Sheila Whiteley & Shara Rambarran (Eds.), *The Oxford Handbook of Music and Virtuality,* 171–190. New York: Oxford University Press, 2016; Felipe Gértrudix-Barrio & Manuel Gértrudix-Barrio, "Music in Virtual Worlds. Study on the Representation Spaces", *Comunicar*, 2012, 19(38), 175–181.

2 Lies Bouckaert, "Virtual Reality as New Concert Space: The Experience of VR Concerts Illuminated from the Perspective of Audience and Developers" (Master's Dissertation. Universiteit Gent, 2021).

3 Gizem Çelik, "A New Field in Music Production: Metaverse Concerts", *Ege Üniversitesi İletişim Fakültesi Medya ve İletişim Araştırmaları Hakemli E-Dergisi*, 2023, 12, 4–24. The author defines the metaverse in the context of online concerts, as "a huge virtual environment parallel to the physical world, where users interact with other users or environments through avatars. Users can exist in these virtual environments simultaneously with the physical world through a representation", 8.

4 Shara Rambarran, ""Feel Good" with Gorillaz and "Reject False Icons": The Fantasy Worlds of the Virtual Group and Their Creators", in Sheila Whiteley & Shara Rambarran (Eds.), *The Oxford Handbook of Music and Virtuality,* 148–166. New York: Oxford University Press, 2016.

5 Jennifer L. Breese, Mark A. Fox & Ganesh Vaidyanathan. "Live Music Performances and the Internet of Things", *Issues in Information Systems*, 2020, 21(3), 179–188.

6 Çelik, "A New Field in Music Production: Metaverse Concerts".

7 David Arditi, "Video Game Concerts: Unending Consumption on Video Game Platforms", *Critical Sociology*, 2024, 51, 319–334. Available at: https://journals.sagepub.com/doi/full/10.1177/08969205241229064. Accessed 20th May 2024.

8 Gordon Calleja, "Immersion in Virtual Worlds", in Mark Grimshaw-Agaard (Ed.), *Oxford Handbook of Virtuality*, 222–236. New York: Oxford University Press, 2014.

9 Simon Frith, "Liveness", in *Performing Rites: On the Value of Popular Music*. Cambridge, MA: Harvard University Press, 1996, 207.

10 Calleja, "Immersion in Virtual Worlds", 169.

11 Concepts such as *presence* or *embodiment* have also worked to define the involvement of participants in (music-led) virtual contexts. See Kelsey Onderdijk, Lies Bouckaert, Edith Van Dyck & Pieter-Jan Maes, "Concert Experiences in Virtual Reality Environments",

Virtual Reality, 2023, 27(3), 1–14. Available at: https://pubmed.ncbi.nlm.nih.gov/37360813/. Accessed 3rd December 2023; Bo Xu, "From Virtual-Reality Fusion to Comprehensive Virtual: The Future of the Performing Arts", *Proceedings of the 2021 International Conference on Education, Humanity and Language, Art*, 2021. Available at: https://www.atlantis-press.com/proceedings/icela-21. Accessed 3rd December 2023.

12 Breese et al., "Live Music Performances and the Internet of Things".

13 Marcel Martončik, "e-Sports: Playing Just for Fun or Playing to Satisfy Life Goals?", *Computers in Human Behavior*, 2015, 48, 208–211.

14 Trevor S. Harvey, "Virtual Worlds: An Ethnomusicological Perspective", in Sheila Whiteley & Shara Rambarran (Eds.), *The Oxford Handbook of Music and Virtuality*, 390. New York: Oxford University Press, 2016.

15 Sergio Jesús Villén Higueras & María Nieves Corral Rey, "Análisis de las relaciones intermediales entre la música y los videojuegos: una perspectiva desde los videojuegos musicales", in Nadia Alonso López, Raúl Terol Bolinches, José María Herranz de la Casa & Pavel Sidorenko Bautista (coords.), *Narrativas emergentes para la comunicación digital*, 143–164. Madrid: Dykinson, 2022.

16 See Eulalia Febrer-Coll, "Immersive Environments in Video Games as a New Stage for Popular Music Performance", in Lidia López (Ed.), *Music, Sound and Identity in Video Games*. London: Palgrave McMillan, 2025.

17 Xu, "From Virtual-Reality Fusion to Comprehensive Virtual: The Future of the Performing Arts", n.p.

18 Çelik, "A New Field in Music Production: Metaverse Concerts".

19 Travis Scott, "Travis Scott and Fortnite Present: Astronomical (Full Event Video)", *Youtube*, 2020. Available at: https://www.youtube.com/watch?v=wYeFAlVC8qU. Accessed 19th May 2024.

20 Sheila Whiteley & Shara Rambarran (Eds.), *The Oxford Handbook of Music and Virtuality*. New York: Oxford University Press, 2016.

21 Erin Corbett, "Explore Your Netflix Favorites in the New Nextworld Universe on Roblox", *Netflix*, 2024. Available at: https://www.netflix.com/tudum/roblox-nextworld. Accessed 9th May 2024.

22 Richard Elen, "Music in the Metaverse", Brideswell Associates, Paper 16, 2008. Available at: https://aes2.org/publications/elibrary-page/?id=17304. Accessed 20th July 2024.

23 Çelik, "A New Field in Music Production: Metaverse Concerts".

24 Pat Healy & Hannah Standiford, "Enter the Paraverse: Challenging Assumptions of Live Music in the Metaverse", *Proceedings of the 17th European Conference on Games Based Learning, ECGBL 2023*, 251–259. Available at: https://papers.academic-conferences.org/index.php/ecgbl/article/view/1634/1644. Accessed 20th July 2024.

25 Mariana Migliore, Director and Creative Synch at BMG. Interview by Eulalia Febrer-Coll. 17th September 2023.

26 Cherie Hu, "15 Ways to Incorporate Gaming into Your Music Strategy", *Water and Music*, 2020. Available at: https://www.waterandmusic.com/15-ways-to-incorporate-gaming-into-your-music-strategy. Accessed 1st May 2024.

27 Cherie Hu, "Why the Music Industry Needs the Video Gaming Industry's Help to Scale Virtual Concerts", *Music Business Worldwide*, 2019. Available at: https://www.musicbusinessworldwide.com/why-the-music-industry-needs-the-video-gaming-industrys-help-to-scale-virtual-concerts/. Accessed 21st May 2024.

28 See Chapter 5.

29 Mónica Valderrama Santomé & Verónica Crespo-Pereira, "Festivales de música y marketing experiencial: efectos para marca, organizador y espectador", *aDResearch ESIC International Journal of Communication Research*, 2021, 26(26), 60–74.

30 Villén Higueras & Corral Rey, "Análisis de las relaciones intermediales entre la música y los videojuegos: una perspectiva desde los videojuegos musicales".

31 Onderdijk et al., "Concert Experiences in Virtual Reality Environments".
32 Wilhelm Voutilainen, Sr. Chief Game Analyst at GameRefinery. Personal communication, 28th June 2024.
33 Philip Auslander, *Liveness: Performance in a Mediated Culture*. New York: Routledge, 2008, 63.
34 Auslander, *Liveness: Performance in a Mediated Culture*, 174.
35 Mike Ault, former Audio Director at Psyonix. Personal communication. 18th June 2024.
36 Eric Tan, Music and Publishing Director for Video Games Companies, former Riot Games and Sony Music employee. Interview by Eulalia Febrer-Coll. 9th July 2024.
37 Karina Moritzen, "Abrindo Moshpits Virtuais: Cenas Musicais e Shows ao vivo em Fortnite e Minecraft", *XXX Encontro Anual Da Compós*, 2021, 1–24.
38 See Sergio Jesús Villén Higueras y María Nieves Corral Rey, "Análisis de las relaciones intermediales entre la música y los videojuegos: una perspectiva desde los videojuegos musicales", 142–163.
39 Mat Ombler, Video Games & Music Journalist. Interview by Eulalia Febrer-Coll. 4th October 2023.
40 PEGI, "Fortnite Battle Royale", *Pan European Game Information*, n.d. Available at: https://pegi.info/search-pegi?id=110706. Accessed 10th July 2024.
41 Screenshot by I_think_good_player on *Reddit*, 2021. Available at: https://www.reddit.com/r/Brawlstars/comments/p2bwch/bad_randoms_stage_on_newest_environment/. Accessed 15th July 2024.
42 Jennifer Soto de la Cruz, Sara Cortés Gómez & Pilar Lacasa, "La reinvención del videojuego y nuevas formas de consumo en tiempos de confinamiento. Caso *Fortnite*", *Comunicación y Sociedad*, 2023, 4.
43 Matthew Wilkins, "All Fortnite Crossovers and Collaborations (Ausgust 2024)", *Sportskeeda*, 2024. Available at: https://www.sportskeeda.com/fortnite/all-fortnite-crossovers-collaborations. Accessed 15th July 2024.
44 Febrer-Coll, "Immersive Environments in Video Games as a New Stage for Popular Music Performance".
45 See Figure 4.1.
46 Stuart Dredge, "Gamefan talks Fortnite and UEFN: 'It's Opened Up a Massive Door for What We Can Do'", *Musically*, 2023. Available at: https://musically.com/2023/07/18/gamefam-talks-fortnite-and-uefn-its-opened-up-a-massive-door-for-what-we-can-do/. Accessed 18th July 2024.
47 Andrew Webster, "Fortnite's Marshmello Concert Was the Game's Biggest Event Ever", *The Verge*, 2019. Available at: https://www.theverge.com/2019/2/21/18234980/fortnite-marshmello-concert-viewer-numbers#. Accessed 18th July 2024.
48 Nick Statt, "Fortnite's Marshmello Concert Was a Bizarre and Exciting Glimpse of the Future", *The Verge*, 2019. Available at: https://www.theverge.com/2019/2/2/18208223/fortnite-epic-games-marshmello-concert-exciting-bizarre-future-music. Accessed 18th July 2024.
49 Bryan Rolli, "Marshmello's Epic 'Fortnite' Concert Boosted His Streas More Than 2,000%", *Forbes*, 2019. Available at: https://www.forbes.com/sites/bryanrolli/2019/02/08/marshmello-fortnite-concert-boost-streams/. Accessed 18th July 2024.
50 Josh Howarth, "Fortnite User and Growth Stats", *Exploding Topics*, 2024. Available at: https://explodingtopics.com/blog/fortnite-stats. Accessed 6th August 2024.
51 Will Gendron, "Travis Scott's Fortnite Experience Felt Fake in a Good Way", *Paper*, 2020. Available at: https://www.papermag.com/fortnite-astronomical-travis-scott-review#rebelltitem9. Accessed 18th July 2024.
52 Kworb, "Travis Scott – Spotify Top Songs | Current charts | YouTube stats", *Kworb.net*, 2024. Available at: https://kworb.net/spotify/artist/0Y5tJX1MQlPlqiwlOH1tJY_songs.html. Accessed 1st August 2024.

53 FTPFlame, "Travis Scott reacts to his Fortnite Event (FULL IG LIVE w/ Stormi)", *Youtube*, 2020. Available at: https://www.youtube.com/watch?v=PBQXrg8U3xc&t=1142s. Accessed 28th July 2024.

54 Tatiana Cirisano, "Game On: What Travis Scott Is Teaching Music Stars About the World's Biggest New (Virtual) Stage", *Billboard Pro*, 2020. Available at: https://www.billboard.com/pro/travis-scott-fortnite-billboard-cover-story-interview-2020/. Accessed 10th July 2024.

55 Puah Ziwei, "Travis Scott Reportedly Earned $20 Million from 'Fortnite' Event", *NME*, 2020. Available at: https://www.nme.com/news/music/travis-scott-earned-20million-fortnite-concert-event-2829792. Accessed 23rd July 2024.

56 Çelik, "A New Field in Music Production: Metaverse Concerts", 14.

57 Justin Patel, "Top 10 Most Popular Metaverse Concerts", *MetaverseMarcom*, 2022. Available at: https://www.metaversemarcom.io/post/top-10-most-popular-metaverse-concerts. Accessed 23rd July 2024.

58 Jakesauriuslol, "How Do Fortnite Concerts Fit the Lore?", *Reddit*, 2022. Available at: https://www.reddit.com/r/FortNiteBR/comments/103tb6w/how_do_fortnite_concerts_fit_the_lore/. Accessed 23rd July 2024.

59 Sam Prance, "Ariana Grande Fans Are "Sobbing" over the Mac Miller Tribute in Her Fortnite Concert", *Capital FM*, 2021. Available at: https://www.capitalfm.com/artists/ariana-grande/mac-miller-tribute-fortnite-concert-the-way/. Accessed 24th July 2024.

60 Tim Elek, "Dynamic Range: A Major Goal for Rift Tour Was to Achieve a Sentimental Moment. An Expression of Support, during Trying Times, in a Way Only Fortnite Can. Take a Moment to Help Each Other, and Elevate One Another. #RiftTour", *X*, 2021. Available at: https://twitter.com/MrElek/status/1423815410294697985. Accessed 24th July 2024.

61 For further exploration of these elements, refer to the suggestions provided in Vincent E. Rone, Can Askoy and Sarah Pozderac-Chenevey, *Nostalgia and Videogame Music*. Chicago, IL: Intellect, 2022.

62 Paul Tassi, "Ariana Grande Should Earn a Fortune from Her 'Fortnite' Rift Tour Concert", *Forbes*, 2021. Available at: https://www.forbes.com/sites/paultassi/2021/08/02/ariana-grande-should-earn-a-fortune-from-her-fortnite-rift-tour-concert/. Accessed 30th July 2024.

63 Kworb, "Eminem - Spotify Top Songs | Current charts | YouTube Stats", *Kworb*, 2024. Available at: https://kworb.net/spotify/artist/7dGJo4pcD2V6oG8kP0tJRR_songs.html. Accessed 1st August 2024.

64 Will Schube, "Eminem Stars in Fortnite's 'Big Bang' Event", *UDiscoverMusic*, 2023. Available at: https://www.udiscovermusic.com/news/eminem-fortnite-big-bang-event/. Accessed 1st August 2024.

65 Pranav Maytray, "How much Did Eminem Make from the Fortnite Live Event? Expected Earnings Explored", *Sportskeeda*, 2023. Available at: https://www.sportskeeda.com/fortnite/how-much-eminem-make-fortnite-live-event-expected-earnings-explored. Accessed 1st August 2024.

66 Marshall Mathers, "Calling All Grandmas 12.2", *X*, 2023. Available at: https://twitter.com/Eminem/status/1727061013776982431?ref_src=twsrc%5Etfw%7Ctwcamp%5Etweetembed%7Ctwterm%5E1727061013776982431%7Ctwgr%5E25034e2a6068cb457de78895495b2525f8abf300%7Ctwcon%5Es1_&ref_url=https%3A%2F%2Fwww.complex.com%2Fmusic%2Fa%2Fbrad-callas%2Feminem-teases-fortnite-appearance-ahead-of-games-next-live. Accessed 1st August 2023.

67 Juan Sebastián Díaz Gasca, "Music beyond Gameplay: Motivators in the Consumption of Videogame Soundtracks" (Doctoral Thesis, Griffith University, 2015), 144.

68 The Fortnite Team, "Metallica Lights Up Fortnite with a New Music Experience, Festival Season, and More!", *Fortnite*, 2024. Available at: https://www.fortnite.com/news/metallica-lights-up-fortnite-with-a-new-music-experience-festival-season-and-more?lang=en-US. Accessed 1st August 2024.

69 Andrew Webster, "Fortnite's Metallica Concert Showed How Sprawling the Game Has Become", *The Verge*, 2024. Available at: https://www.theverge.com/2024/6/29/24187226/fortnite-metallica-concert-interview. Accessed 1st August 2024.

70 Andrew J. Bottomley, "Play It Again: Rock Music Reissues and the Production of the Past for the Present", *Popular Music and Society*, 2016, 39(2), 171.

71 Blabbermouth, "JAMES HETFIELD Says METALLICA's Collaboration with FORTNITE 'Makes Sense': 'It Is a Really Cool Idea'", *Blabbermouth.net*, 2024. Available at: https://blabbermouth.net/news/james-hetfield-says-metallicas-collaboration-with-fortnite-makes-sense-it-is-a-really-cool-idea. Accessed 1st August 2024.

72 Carys Wyn Jones, *The Rock Canon: Canonical Values in the Reception of Rock Albums*. Hampshire: Ashgate, 2008, 136.

73 Universal Music Latino, "Karol G & Nicki Minja's "Tusa" Becomes the First All-Female Lating Song to Ever Break into Spotify's Global Top 10 Chart", *Universal*, 2019. Available at: https://www.universalmusica.com/karol-g-nicki-minajs-tusa-becomes-first-all-female-latin-song-ever-break-spotifys-global-top-10/. Accessed 27th September 2024.

74 Borja Ruete, "Karol G llega a Fortnite Festival Temporada 5 y estas son sus skins: fecha y hora del concierto", *Meristation*, 2024. Available at: https://as.com/meristation/noticias/karol-g-llega-a-fortnite-festival-temporada-5-y-estas-son-sus-skins-fecha-y-hora-del-concierto-n/. Accessed 27th September 2024.

75 The Fortnite Team, "Superstar Karol G Brings the Rhythm to Fortnite Festival Season 5!", *Fortnite*, 2024. Available at: https://www.fortnite.com/news/superstar-karol-g-brings-the-rhythm-to-fortnite-festival-season-5?lang=en-US. Accessed 27th September 2024.

76 Katcy Stephan, "How Karol G and 'Fortnite' Pulled Off Her 'Fantastical' In-Game Concert (EXCLUSIVE)", *Variety*, 2024. Available at: https://variety.com/2024/gaming/news/karol-g-fortnite-concert-festival-manana-sera-bonito-1236115883/. Accessed 27th September 2024.

77 See Google Trends, "Fortnite", *Google*, 2024. Available at: https://trends.google.com/trends/explore?date=today%205-y&q=%2Fm%2F0k9bc90&hl=en-GB Accessed 29th September 2024.

78 Fortnite, "Remix: The Prelude | Fortnite Takes Over NYC with a LIVE Snoop Dogg & Ice Spice Show", *Youtube*, 2024. Available at: https://www.youtube.com/watch?v=oVNGSMDo58Y. Accessed 17th December 2024.

79 Andrew Webster, "Snoop Dogg's Times Square Concert Showed the Ambitious Future of Music in Fortnite", *The Verge*, 2024. Available at: https://www.theverge.com/2024/11/4/24288014/fortnite-chapter-2-remix-snoop-dogg-times-square-music. Accessed 17th December 2024.

80 Paul Tassi, "'Fortnite' Hits 14.3 Million Players with Juice WRLD, Ice Spice, Snoop Dogg, Eminem Concert", *Forbes*, 2024. Available at: https://www.forbes.com/sites/paultassi/2024/11/30/fortnite-shatters-playercount-record-with-juice-wrld-ice-spice-snoop-dogg-eminem-concert/. Accessed 17th December 2024.

81 Perfect Score, "Fortnite Remix the Finale: Juice WRLD, Eminem & Snoop Dogg Concert (Full Live Event Gameplay!)", *Youtube*, 2024. Available at: https://www.youtube.com/watch?v=ojgZU99hlPU. Accessed 17th December 2024.

82 Fortnite, "Juice Wrld vs Snoop Dogg (Red vs Blue)", *Fortnite*, 2024. Available at: https://www.fortnite.com/@drac10/5048-7778-5228?lang=es-ES. Accessed 17th December 2024.

83 Rubén Martínez, "Here's Fortnite's Touching Tribute to the Late Singer Juice WRLD", *MeriStation*, 2024. Available at: https://en.as.com/meristation/news/heres-fortnites-touching-tribute-to-the-late-singer-juice-wrld-n/. Accessed 17th December 2024.

84 Paul Tassi, "'Fortnite' Hits 14.3 Million Players with Juice WRLD, Ice Spice, Snoop Dogg, Eminem Concert".

85 Andrea Memoli, "Fortnite's Highest Viewership in Four Years: FNCS Global Championship 2023!", *Fortnite Tracker*, 2023. Available at: https://fortnitetracker.com/article/2236/2023-fncs-global-championship-fortnites-highest-viewership-in-four-years. Accessed 4th August 2024.

86 Jem Kelly, "Pop Music, Multimedia and Live Performance", in Jamie Sexton (Ed.), *Music, Sound and Multimedia: From the Live to the Virtual*. Edinburgh: Edinburgh University Press, 2007, 106.

REFERENCES

Arditi, David. "Video Game Concerts: Unending Consumption on Video Game Platforms", *Critical Sociology*, 2024, 51, 319–334. Available at: https://journals.sagepub.com/doi/full/10.1177/08969205241229064. Accessed 20th May 2024.

Auslander, Philip. *Liveness: Performance in a Mediated Culture*. New York: Routledge, 2008, 63.

Blabbermouth. "JAMES HETFIELD Says METALLICA's Collaboration with FORTNITE 'Makes Sense': 'It Is A Really Cool Idea'", *Blabbermouth.net*, 2024. Available at: https://blabbermouth.net/news/james-hetfield-says-metallicas-collaboration-with-fortnite-makes-sense-it-is-a-really-cool-idea. Accessed 1st August 2024.

Bottomley, Andrew J. "Play It Again: Rock Music Reissues and the Production of the Past for the Present", *Popular Music and Society*, 2016, 39(2), 171.

Bouckaert, Lies. "Virtual Reality as New Concert Space: The Experience of VR Concerts Illuminated from the Perspective of Audience and Developers" (Master's Dissertation). Universiteit Gent, 2021.

Breese, Jennifer L., Fox, Mark A. & Vaidyanathan, Ganesh. "Live Music Performances and the Internet of Things", *Issues in Information Systems*, 2020, 21(3), 179–188.

Calleja, Gordon. "Immersion in Virtual Worlds", in Mark Grimshaw-Agaard (Ed.), *Oxford Handbook of Virtuality*, 222–236. New York: Oxford University Press, 2014.

Çelik, Gizem. "A New Field in Music Production: Metaverse Concerts", *Ege Üniversitesi İletişim Fakültesi Medya ve İletişim Araştırmaları Hakemli E-Dergisi*, 2023, 12, 4–24.

Corbett, Erin. "Explore Your Netflix Favorites in the New Nextworld Universe on Roblox", *Netflix*, 2024. Available at: https://www.netflix.com/tudum/roblox-nextworld. Accessed 9th May 2024.

Cirisano, Tatiana. "Game On: What Travis Scott Is Teaching Music Stars about the World's Biggest New (Virtual) Stage", *Billboard Pro*, 2020. Available at: https://www.billboard.com/pro/travis-scott-fortnite-billboard-cover-story-interview-2020/. Accessed 10th July 2024.

Díaz Gasca, Juan Sebastián. "Music Beyond Gameplay: Motivators in the Consumption of Videogame Soundtracks" (Doctoral Thesis). Griffith University, 2015, 144.

Dredge, Stuart. "Gamefan Talks Fortnite and UEFN: 'It's Opened Up a Massive Door for What We Can Do'", *Musically*, 2023. Available at: https://musically.com/2023/07/18/gamefam-talks-fortnite-and-uefn-its-opened-up-a-massive-door-for-what-we-can-do/. Accessed 18th July 2024.

Elek, Tim. "Dynamic Range: A Major Goal for Rift Tour Was to Achieve a Sentimental Moment. An Expression of Support, during Trying Times, in a Way Only Fortnite Can. Take a Moment to Help Each Other, and Elevate One Another. #RiftTour", *X,* 2021. Available at: https://twitter.com/MrElek/status/1423815410294697985. Accessed 24th July 2024.

Elen, Richard. "Music in the Metaverse", Brideswell Associates, Paper 16, 2008. Available at: https://aes2.org/publications/elibrary-page/?id=17304. Accessed 20th July 2024.

Febrer-Coll, Eulalia. "Immersive Environments in Video Games as a New Stage for Popular Music Performance", in Lidia López (Ed.), *Music, Sound and Identity in Video Games.* London: Palgrave McMillan, 2025.

Fortnite. "Juice Wrld vs Snoop Dogg (Red vs Blue)", *Fortnite,* 2024. Available at: https://www.fortnite.com/@drac10/5048-7778-5228?lang=es-ES. Accessed 17th December 2024.

Fortnite. "Remix: The Prelude | Fortnite Takes Over NYC with a LIVE Snoop Dogg & Ice Spice Show", *Youtube,* 2024. Available at: https://www.youtube.com/watch?v=oVNGSMDo58Y. Accessed 17th December 2024.

Frith, Simon. "Liveness", in Simon Frith (Ed.), *Performing Rites: On the Value of Popular Music.* Cambridge, MA: Harvard University Press, 1996.

FTPFlame. "Travis Scott Reacts to His Fortnite Event (FULL IG LIVE w/ Stormi), *Youtube,* 2020. Available at: https://www.youtube.com/watch?v=PBQXrg8U3xc&t=1142s. Accessed 28th July 2024.

Gendron, Will. "Travis Scott's Fortnite Experience Felt Fake in a Good Way", *Paper,* 2020. Available at: https://www.papermag.com/fortnite-astronomical-travis-scott-review#rebelltitem9. Accessed 18th July 2024.

Gértrudix-Barrio, Felipe & Gértrudix-Barrio, Manuel. "Music in Virtual Worlds. Study on the Representation Spaces", *Comunicar,* 2012, 19(38), 175–181.

Google Trends. "Fortnite", *Google,* 2024. Available at: https://trends.google.com/trends/explore?date=today%205-y&q=%2Fm%2F0k9bc90&hl=en-GB. Accessed 29th September 2024.

Harvey, Trevor S. "Avatar Rockstars: Constructing Musical Personae in Virtual Worlds". In Sheila Whiteley & Shara Rambarran (Ed.), *The Oxford Handbook of Music and Virtuality,* 171–190. New York: Oxford University Press, 2016.

Harvey, Trevor S. "Virtual Worlds: An Ethnomusicological Perspective", in Sheila Whiteley & Shara Rambarran (Eds.), *The Oxford Handbook of Music and Virtuality*, 378–391. New York: Oxford University Press, 2016.

Healy, Pat & Standiford, Hannah. "Enter the Paraverse: Challenging Assumptions of Live Music in the Metaverse", *Proceedings of the 17th European Conference on Games Based Learning, ECGBL*, 2023, 251–259. Available at: https://papers.academic-conferences.org/index.php/ecgbl/article/view/1634/1644. Accessed 20th July 2024.

Howarth, Josh. "Fortnite User and Growth Stats", *Exploding Topics*, 2024. Available at: https://explodingtopics.com/blog/fortnite-stats. Accessed 6th August 2024.

Hu, Cherie."15 Ways to Incorporate Gaming into Your Music Strategy", *Water and Music,* 2020. Available at: https://www.waterandmusic.com/15-ways-to-incorporate-gaming-into-your-music-strategy. Accessed 1st May 2024.

Hu, Cherie. "Why the Music Industry Needs the Video Gaming Industry's Help to Scale Virtual Concerts", *Music Business Worldwide,* 2019. Available at: https://www.musicbusinessworldwide.com/why-the-music-industry-needs-the-video-gaming-industrys-help-to-scale-vir tual-concerts/. Accessed 21st May 2024.

I_think_good_player on *Reddit*, 2021. Available at: https://www.reddit.com/r/Brawlstars/comments/p2bwch/bad_randoms_stage_on_newest_environment/. Accessed 15th July 2024.

Jakesauriuslol. "How Do Fortnite Concerts Fit the Lore?", *Reddit,* 2022. Available at: https://www.reddit.com/r/FortNiteBR/comments/103tb6w/how_do_fortnite_concerts_fit_the_lore/. Accessed 23rd July 2024.

Jones, Carys Wyn. *The Rock Canon: Canonical Values in the Reception of Rock Albums.* Hampshire: Ashgate, 2008, 136.

Kelly, Jem. "Pop Music, Multimedia and Live Performance", in Jamie Sexton (Ed.), *Music, Sound and Multimedia: From the Live to the Virtual,* 106. Edinburgh: Edinburgh University Press, 2007.

Kworb. "Eminem - Spotify Top Songs | Current charts | YouTube stats", *Kworb,* 2024. Available at: https://kworb.net/spotify/artist/7dGJo4pcD2V6oG8kP0tJRR_songs.html. Accessed 1st August 2024.

Kworb. "Travis Scott – Spotify Top Songs | Current charts | YouTube stats", *Kworb.net,* 2024. Available at: https://kworb.net/spotify/artist/0Y5tJX1MQlPlqiwlOH1tJY_songs.html. Accessed 1st August 2024.

Martínez, Rubén. "Here's Fortnite's Touching Tribute to the Late Singer Juice WRLD", *MeriStation,* 2024. Available at: https://en.as.com/meristation/news/heres-fortnites-touching-tribute-to-the-late-singer-juice-wrld-n/. Accessed 17th December 2024.

Martončik, Marcel. "e-Sports: Playing Just for Fun or Playing to Satisfy Life Goals?", *Computers in Human Behavior,* 2015, 48, 208–211.

Mathers, Marshall. "Calling All Grandmas 12.2", *X,* 2023. Available at: https://twitter.com/Eminem/status/1727061013776982431?ref_src=twsrc%5Etfw%7Ctwcamp%5Etweetembed%7Ctwterm%5E1727061013776982431%7Ctwgr%5E25034e2a6068cb457de78895495b2525f8abf300%7Ctwcon%5Es1_&ref_url=https%3A%2F%2Fwww.complex.com%2Fmusic%2Fa%2Fbrad-callas%2Feminem-teases-fortnite-appearance-ahead-of-games-next-live. Accessed 1st August 2023.

Maytray, Pranav. "How Much Did Eminem Make from the Fortnite Live Event? Expected Earnings Explored", *Sportskeeda,* 2023. Available at: https://www.sportskeeda.com/fortnite/how-much-eminem-make-fortnite-live-event-expected-earnings-explored. Accessed 1st August 2024.

Memoli, Andrea. "Fortnite's Highest Viewership in Four Years: FNCS Global Championship 2023!", *FortniteTracker,* 2023. Available at: https://fortnitetracker.com/article/2236/2023-fncs-global-championship-fortnites-highest-viewership-in-four-years. Accessed 4th August 2024.

Moritzen, Karina. "Abrindo Moshpits Virtuais: Cenas Musicais e Shows ao vivo em Fortnite e Minecraft", *XXX Encontro Anual Da Compós,* 2021, 1–24.

Onderdijk, Kelsey, Bouckaert, Lies, Van Dyck, Edith & Maes, Pieter-Jan. "Concert Experiences in Virtual Reality Environments", *Virtual Reality,* 2023, 27(3), 1–14. Available at: https://pubmed.ncbi.nlm.nih.gov/37360813/. Accessed 3rd December 2023.

Patel, Justin. "Top 10 Most Popular Metaverse Concerts", *MetaverseMarcom,* 2022. Available at: https://www.metaversemarcom.io/post/top-10-most-popular-metaverse-concerts. Accessed 23rd July 2024.

PEGI. "Fortnite Battle Royale", *Pan European Game Information,* n.d. Available at: https://pegi.info/search-pegi?id=110706. Accessed 10th July 2024.

Perfect Score. "Fortnite Remix the Finale: Juice WRLD, Eminem & Snoop Dogg Concert (Full Live Event Gameplay!)", *Youtube,* 2024. Available at: https://www.youtube.com/watch?v=ojgZU99hlPU. Accessed 17th December 2024.

Prance, Sam. "Ariana Grande Fans Are "Sobbing" over the Mac Miller Tribute in Her Fortnite Concert", *Capital FM,* 2021. Available at: https://www.capitalfm.com/artists/ariana-grande/mac-miller-tribute-fortnite-concert-the-way/. Accessed 24th July 2024.

Rambarran, Shara. ""Feel Good" with Gorillaz and "Reject False Icons": The Fantasy Worlds of the Virtual Group and Their Creators", in Sheila Whiteley & Shara Rambarran (Eds.), *The Oxford Handbook of Music and Virtuality,* 148–166. New York: Oxford University Press, 2016.

Rolli, Bryan. "Marshmello's Epic 'Fortnite' Concert Boosted His Streas More Than 2,000%", *Forbes,* 2019. Available at: https://www.forbes.com/sites/bryanrolli/2019/02/08/marshmello-fortnite-concert-boost-streams/. Accessed 18th July 2024.

Rone, Vincent E., Askoy, Can, & Pozderac-Chenevey, Sarah. *Nostalgia and Videogame Music*. Chicago, IL: Intellect, 2022.

Ruete, Borja. "Karol G llega a Fortnite Festival Temporada 5 y estas son sus skins: fecha y hora del concierto", *Meristation,* 2024. Available at: https://as.com/meristation/noticias/karol-g-llega-a-fortnite-festival-temporada-5-y-estas-son-sus-skins-fecha-y-hora-del-concierto-n/. Accessed:27th September 2024.

Schube, Will. "Eminem Stars in Fortnite's 'Big Bang' Event", *UDiscoverMusic*, 2023. Available at: https://www.udiscovermusic.com/news/eminem-fortnite-big-bang-event/. Accessed 1st August 2024.

Soto de la Cruz, Jennifer, Cortés Gómez, Sara & Lacasa, Pilar. "La reinvención del videojuego y nuevas formas de consumo en tiempos de confinamiento. Caso *Fortnite", Comunicación y Sociedad,* 2023, 4, 1–23.

Statt, Nick. "Fortnite's Marshmello Concert Was a Bizarre and Exciting Glimpse of the Future", *The Verge,* 2019. Available at: https://www.theverge.com/2019/2/2/18208223/fortnite-epic-games-marshmello-concert-exciting-bizarre-future-music. Accessed 18th July 2024.

Stephan, Katcy. "How Karol G and 'Fortnite' Pulled Off Her 'Fantastical' In-Game Concert (EXCLUSIVE)", *Variety*, 2024. Available at: https://variety.com/2024/gaming/news/karol-g-fortnite-concert-festival-manana-sera-bonito-1236115883/. Accessed 27th September 2024.

Tassi, Paul. "Ariana Grande Should Earn a Fortune from Her 'Fortnite' Rift Tour Concert", *Forbes,* 2021. Available at: https://www.forbes.com/sites/paultassi/2021/08/02/ariana-grande-should-earn-a-fortune-from-her-fortnite-rift-tour-concert/. Accessed 30th July 2024.

Tassi, Paul. "'Fortnite' Hits 14.3 Million Players with Juice WRLD, Ice Spice, Snoop Dogg, Eminem Concert", *Forbes,* 2024. Available at: https://www.forbes.com/sites/paultassi/2024/11/30/fortnite-shatters-playercount-record-with-juice-wrld-ice-spice-snoop-dogg-eminem-concert/. Accessed 17th December 2024.

The Fortnite Team. "Metallica Lights Up Fortnite with a New Music Experience, Festival Season, and More!", *Fortnite,* 2024. Available at: https://www.fortnite.com/news/metallica-lights-up-fortnite-with-a-new-music-experience-festival-season-and-more?lang=en-US. Accessed 1st August 2024.

The Fortnite Team. "Superstar Karol G Brings the Rhythm to Fortnite Festival Season 5!", *Fortnite*, 2024. Available at: https://www.fortnite.com/news/superstar-karol-g-brings-the-rhythm-to-fortnite-festival-season-5?lang=en-US. Accessed 27th September 2024.

Travis Scott. "Travis Scott and Fortnite Present: Astronomical (Full Event Video)", *Youtube,* 2020. Available at: https://www.youtube.com/watch?v=wYeFAlVC8qU. Accessed 19th May 2024.

Universal Music Latino. "Karol G & Nicki Minja's "Tusa" Becomes the First All-Female Lating Song to Ever Break into Spotify's Global Top 10 Chart", *Universal,* 2019. Available at: https://www.universalmusica.com/karol-g-nicki-minajs-tusa-becomes-first-all-female-latin-song-ever-break-spotifys-global-top-10/. Accessed 27th September 2024.

Valderrama Santomé, Mónica & Crespo Pereira, Verónica. "Festivales de música y marketing experiencial: efectos para marca, organizador y espectador", *aDResearch ESIC International Journal of Communication Research,* 2021, 26(26), 60–74.

Villén Higueras, Sergio Jesús & Corral Rey, María Nieves. "Análisis de las relaciones intermediales entre la música y los videojuegos: una perspectiva desde los videojuegos musicales", in Nadia Alonso López, Raúl Terol Bolinches, José María Herranz de la Casa & Pavel Sidorenko Bautista (coords.), *Narrativas emergentes para la comunicación digital,* 143–164. Madrid: Dykinson, 2022.

Webster, Andrew. "Fortnite's Marshmello Concert Was the Game's Biggest Event Ever", *The Verge*, 2019 Available at: https://www.theverge.com/2019/2/21/18234980/fortnite-marshmello-concert-viewer-numbers. Accessed 18th July 2024.

Webster, Andrew. "Fortnite's Metallica Concert Showed How Sprawling the Game Has Become", *The Verge,* 2024. Available at: https://www.theverge.com/2024/6/29/24187226/fortnite-metallica-concert-interview. Accessed 1st August 2024.

Webster, Andrew. "Snoop Dogg's Times Square Concert Showed the Ambitious Future of Music in Fortnite", The Verge, 2024. Available at: https://www.theverge.com/2024/11/4/24288014/fortnite-chapter-2-remix-snoop-dogg-times-square-music. Accessed 17th December 2024.

Whiteley, Sheila & Rambarran, Shara (Eds.). *The Oxford Handbook of Music and Virtuality.* New York: Oxford University Press, 2016.

Wilkins, Matthew. "All Fortnite Crossovers and Collaborations (August 2024)", *Sportskeeda,* 2024. Available at: https://www.sportskeeda.com/fortnite/all-fortnite-crossovers-collaborations. Accessed 15th July 2024.

Xu, Bo. "From Virtual-Reality Fusion to Comprehensive Virtual: The Future of the Performing Arts", *Proceedings of the 2021 International Conference on Education, Humanity and Language, Art*, 2021. Available at: https://www.atlantis-press.com/proceedings/icela-21. Accessed 3rd December 2023.

Ziwei, Puah. "Travis Scott Reportedly Earned $20 Million from 'Fortnite' Event", *NME,* 2020. Available at: https://www.nme.com/news/music/travis-scott-earned-20million-fortnite-con cert-event-2829792. Accessed 23rd July 2024.

Artists on Esports Stages

Out-of-Game

5

The rapid growth of the esports industry has implied an increasing investment in competitive events, which has come hand-in-hand with marketing opportunities from brands in and outside the gaming ecosystem. This rising interest has translated into larger stadiums for competitions, bigger screens, the incorporation of music performances on live shows, and the introduction of visual stimuli for face-to-face and online attendees—especially since the second half of the 2010s. Although it does not apply to all leagues or all games, including popular music artists has become a claim for live attendance—much like in traditional sports events like the Superbowl—[1] as well as an opportunity for fans to engage in a socializing activity that contributes a sense of belongingness to each game's social scene.

Despite music shows being included in earlier competitions, 2014 marked a turning point when the pop-rock band Imagine Dragons performed in Seoul during the *League of Legends* World Championship. The song, included in the band's second album *Smoke + Mirrors*, was used to promote the event and transcended as an identity-building anthem for the games' community. This show was not surpassed in viewership again until 2018 when the virtual K-pop band K/DA debuted on stage,[2] establishing a case for technologies such as CGI (Computer-Generated Imagery) and social media to be embedded in the promotion of brand products and by-products.

Since then, other games have bet on popular music to socialize their esports events and promote their games beyond the flatscreen, including preexisting and self-tailored bands. This does not mean that all esports games have headed down the same road, as two trends continue to coexist: one that advocates for a growingly transmediatic context that features popular artists and bands as part of their brand character, and one that anchors its sonic identity on the sobriety in establishing a distance from the mainstream. In the first case, the impact of the music generated for the events can be higher,[3] as the collaboration with labels and agents outside of video games contributes to other niches and new potential publics. A good example is the song *Enemy*, by Imagine Dragons, which has been featured in widely different settings besides the first season of the Netflix show *Arcane* for which it was composed, including the World Championship of *League of Legends* in 2021 and many popular radio stations around the world.[4]

DOI: 10.1201/9781032625362-6

Like this one, many of the strategies designed to build relatable and commodifiable experiences for attendants respond to forms of experiential marketing that seek to "engage and emotionally connect audiences with brands, create positive recall and impact through the development of an original and unique event, encourage word-of-mouth among event attendees and potential customers (friends, family, etc.) through media such as social networks."[5] This is reaffirmed by the increasing number of collaborations that different organizations have closed during the last few years, both with giants such as Warner Music, and smaller independent labels.[6]

Despite the potential difficulties in closing such agreements, as described by Sidney Fohrman,[7] autochthonous and partnered music in esports environments will presumably continue to coexist:

> I don't think what [Riot Games] is doing is going to replace doing a collaboration with Drake or Doja Cat or something, you're not going to replace that with your own label. And creating music and owning it, it certainly makes things easier for Riot. I think you're going to see people will be following Riot's footsteps because of the importance of music and because of the complicated and fraught rights profile, but again, I think consumers want to hear their favorite artists and I don't think that's going to go away.[8]

How virtual and real artists coincide in games is representative of this idea, as is the presence of other—maybe less mainstream—musicians and directors within the music scene of games. For instance, the collaboration between *Rocket League* and Monstercat's roster, or *DotA 2*'s with violinist Lindsey Stirling, do not include triple-A artists. It is likewise pertinent to remember that the stages that feature such artists are not always restricted to competitive live events, but may extend to other out-of-game environments such as social and traditional media.

LIVE SHOWS AND CEREMONIAL OPENINGS

One of the most notorious environments for artists to be featured in the context of competitive gaming is live shows preceding or enlivening different spaces during in-person and hybrid events, such as world cups and championships. The music genres and styles chosen in each case are linked to the need to appeal to the personal identity of consumers, who express themselves "through [their] deployment of other people's music."[9] Frith argued that with rock, jazz, or other music scenes "gigs and venues are essential to the mythology"[10] of fans, and so can be applied to the different esports' scene lores.

Game developers have acknowledged the marketing strength that live music affords, and have consequently pursued the building of a coherent music scene for their products, and paid special attention to the points of connection between music and their audiences' sociocultural environments. It is not uncommon to find regional artists linked to competitions in specific geographies, or that the designers for the events try to incorporate the diversity of their fanbase into their spectacles. *Free Fire* can be pointed as an example, as they have paid attention to the diversity of the geographies in which the game is most popular—Brazil, India, and other Southeast Asian countries.[11]

Although they got the most credit for their Justin Bieber in-game concert in 2021, or the music videos launched along Brazilian singer Anitta or Indian actress Shradda Kapoor, other artists have collaborated on face-to-face stages, including Brazilian DJ Alok or Vietnamese singer Sơn Tùng M-TP.

Others have incorporated artists that appeal to their global audiences in shared spectacles, like *Valorant*'s opening shows for the game's World Finals, which since 2021 have starred performers including American rappers PnB Rock, Ashnikko, Lil Nas X, or K-pop group Kiss of Life in 2024. Similarly, *Counter-Strike* has featured DJs with diverse nationalities that fit the electronic-forward sonic identity of the game, such as DJ Snake or DJ Fede, while *Call of Duty* has worked with artists ranging from Skrillex and DJ Khaled to rapper Gunna. These cases illustrate the trends in the music industry according to IFPI reports since 2020,[12] which underline pop, electronica, and hip-hop as some of the main genres in vogue, along with Latin and indie music, making pluricultural stages even more pertinent.

The virtual bands specifically assembled to be included in these shows are tailored to fit the same music tendencies, although cases such as The Bad Randoms for *Brawl Stars* have stepped outside of the mainstream, vouching for a punk-rock aesthetic. K-pop has become increasingly popular and, since the creation of Riot Games' K/DA, it has encouraged other companies to jump on the trend of creating their trademark bands, sometimes following the same genre.

In addition, following the virtual performance for the 2020 *League of Legends* World Cup finals in Shanghai, bands like T.R.A.P by *Free Fire* also started incorporating CGI technologies into their shows, mostly as prerecorded presentations for their competitions. These, however, have tended to be substituted by live performances that are more traditionally inclined stage-wise in later years.

Despite their growing popularity during the early 2020s, these bands have not always been featured on live stages and have mostly appeared in promotional music videos. Virtual groups such as those shown in Table 5.1 became especially buoyant during—or immediately after—the pandemic, when the restrictions on live performances were most severe, but their popularity decreased shortly after.

TABLE 5.1 Virtual Bands in Esports (2014–2024)

VIDEO GAME	*BAND*	*YEAR OF DEBUT*
Arena of Valor/Honor of Kings	AoV Band	2021
	Infinite King	2019
Brawl Stars	Bad Randoms	2021
	Good Randoms	2023
Free Fire	T.R.A.P.	2020
League of Legends	Pentakill	2014
	K/DA	2018
	True Damage	2019
	HEARTSTEEL	2023
Mobile Legends: Bang Bang	S.T.U.N.	2021
	S.P.A.R.K.L.E.	2024
PUBG	Power 4	2021

The advantages of developing music for these occasions had to be—and continue to be—balanced with the need for managing licenses to external music. This has been tackled by some brands transversally as a means to create a coherent link between game and esports, as well as to surpass any potential rights issues:

> A lot of traditional rights holders will think very specifically about the specific license that they're doing to where it's like, "hey, we're specifically licensing 15 seconds of this song for this trailer". Monstercats' approach is more holistic, to where we want to partner long-term with games for their entire ecosystem. So that's inclusive of everything in-game, in the trailers, esports, content creators, and that entire pipe is endemic with our music. That's what we're aiming for.[13]

It is important to remember that teams in charge of game development and esports organization are frequently different, despite them working together to achieve cohesive results. Furthermore, the *ceremonial* aspect imbued to these events, as explicitly used by developers, holds similarities to what has been done in traditional sports in the past,[14] which creates an appearance of rituality or extra-ordinariety that appeals to fans and other consumers. In other words, the structure provided by such presentations makes a statement about the necessity for normative compliance and establishes a clear hierarchy around the ritual arena,[15] regardless of the nature of the artists on stage.

In this context, as stated by Frith, live musical performance matters for two reasons: (1) "it is a public celebration of musical commitment, a deeply pleasurable event at which our understanding of ourselves through music is socially recognized," and (2) "it is a site in which to explore—for ourselves—how performance works. And, of course, where there are social desires, there will be entrepreneurs—promoters, ready, at a price, to meet them."[16] How this is approached will depend, in each case, on aspects ranging from the necessities and possibilities of the teams behind the organizations, to the will to build a sense of community and identity that submerges the spectators into the spectacles through the mediation of music.

DotA 2 versus League of Legends

DotA 2 and *League of Legends* have been known in the gaming scene for their long-lived rivalry, triggered by their common origin around the custom map Aeon of Strife (AoS)—"the first MOBA"—[17]created on *Starcraft* in 2001. This map was taken as a stencil and later duplicated on *Warcraft III* under the title *Defence of the Ancient* (*DotA*), along with similar playboards. These projects grew in popularity rapidly, and received the engagement of future Valve and Riot Games employees, who took on their own projects following the trails of that first design.[18]

Their initial steps into the competitive scene also drew from preexisting show matches by the original *DotA* in 2004, and materialized in 2011 for *DotA 2*'s The International and the *League of Legends* World Championship.[19] Since launching these events, their competitiveness did not stay at a technical or popularity level, but moved toward establishing two differentiated sonic identities. Broadly, these can be linked to the two earlier-mentioned coexisting trends—one that vouches for engaging with mainstream and transmedia content, another built more counterculturally aside from it.

TABLE 5.2 Artists Featured in *League of Legends'* World Championships (2012–2024)

YEAR	*FEATURED ARTISTS AND BANDS*
2012	Martin O'Donnell (conductor)
2013	Christopher Tin (conductor)
2014	Imagine Dragons
2015	Christian Schumann (conductor), Lisa Rowe
2016	Gerard Marino (conductor), Zedd
2017	Against The Current, Jay Chou, Chrissy Costanza
2018	The Glitch Mob, Mako, The Word Alive, K/DA (represented by Madison Beer, Jaira Burns, Miyeon, Soyeon)
2019	Cailin Russo, Chrissy Costanza, True Damage (represented by Becky G, Keke Palmer, Soyeon, Miyeon, Duckwrth, Thutmose)
2020	K/DA (represented by Madison Beer, Jaira Burns, Miyeon, Soyeon, Lexie Liu), Henry刘宪华, Max Schneider, Jeremy McKinnon
2021	PVRIS, Imagine Dragons, JID, Denzel Curry, Bea Miller
2022	Lil Nas X, Edda Hayes, Louis Leibfried, Jackson Wang
2023	HEARTSTEEL (represented by Baekhyun, Cal Scruby, ØZI, Tobi Lou), NewJeans
2024	Ashnikko, Forts and Tiffany Aris, Linkin Park

Riot Games is well-known for its audiovisual promotion efforts, especially during its opening ceremonies for *League of Legends* and *Valorant*. Since its first music-led opening ceremony in 2012, Riot Games has collaborated with renowned artists and bands from different nationalities and often incorporated them as alter egos to represent the voices of singers in their own bands. This, together with a keen use of cutting-edge technology, has helped position the company as a key voice in the esports industry musically and in overall marketing.

The first editions of the championship proved more conservative, and starred composer-conductors known for their work on triple-A series such *Halo* (Martin O'Donnell), *Battlefield* (Christian Schumann), *God of War* (Gerard Marino), as well as games like *Civilization IV* (Christopher Tin, who composed the Grammy-winning theme *Baba Yetu*). However, Imagine Dragon's success in 2014 as an event-opener made Riot Games consider the inclusion of popular music as part of their roster, along with the progressive growth of the music department at the company.[20] With this intervention, the band became one of the most recognized and representative in the last decade's esports international scene.

Another essential turn of events in the building of such spectacles came hand in hand with the incorporation of CGI technology in 2017, when Chrissy Costanza's performance of *Legends Never Die* was complemented by the appearance on-stage of the game's Elden Dragon.[21] Although this event was dependent on screens for viewers at the stadium, virtual attendees were able to follow an uninterrupted show that displayed the potential of technology as an experienced mediator. This trend was fully embraced in 2018 with the performance of K/DA characters side by side with the singers who voiced them, and again in future shows.

Other technologies introduced include holograms, which were first tested with Zedd's performance of *Ignite* in 2016, and fully incorporated in 2019 with the virtual band True Damage;[22] or screens situated as extensions for the stage show—e.g., in 2023, during the World Finals in Seoul, which featured two K-pop bands: Riot's HEARTSTEEL, and girl group New Jeans.

On the other hand, Valve's *DotA 2* has not fallen short in spectacle-building, yet their reliance on less-known artists or mainstream agents in the industry has put them in a less mediatic position. Differently from other titles, they have frequently included theme music from the game by in-house composer Tim Larkin, who has also acted as the conductor in several opening ceremonies.[23] The game publishers have collaborated with professional orchestras such as the Shanghai Philharmonic Orchestra or the Seattle Symphony Orchestra, but have rarely announced it as a differential point. They have, however, occasionally counted with individual artists such as violinist Lindsey Stirling (in 2016 and 2021) or pianist JJ Lin (in 2021), as well as music groups like The Live Voices (in 2017) or Kuné (in 2018).

Their spectacles have emphasized a structured opening with the intervention of the games' president and cofounder Gabe L. Newell—"Gaben"—who since the first show matches in 2011 has acted as the facilitator for the events. His presentation has been preceded or followed by different connections to the main show, including progressively larger opening ceremonies.[24] Differently from the previous case, his speech and the formality afforded by the choices of spectacle are frequently supported by a symphonic orchestra, which performs arranged pieces from the game, conducted by the main composer for the title. This choice can be seen as resonating with the game's community, as stated by caster Anders Blume:

> I think for *DotA*, if you ever watch some of the music they play in The International where it's like drums and violins and a big cello and stuff like this, that to me makes so much more sense. I'm like, this fits what we're about to watch, a huge battle with swords and axes. Of course I'm gonna have this kind of feel, like it makes sense to me. So I just think they are doing a better job in my opinion.[25]

This does not imply a lack of visual spectacle, as the game has explored widely diverse experiences like aerial dance or the characterization of artists. Furthermore, in 2016, they already incorporated CGI into their opening, briefly featuring five game characters on stage[26]—anticipating Riot Games' use of the tool—and have included a wide array of tools to accompany their music visually.

Although these are only two of the MOBAs on the market, their position as the most viewed esports[27] and their contrasting approaches to music inclusion in face-to-face events make them relevant for analysis and discussion. However, many other popular esports titles have invested in spectacles to frame their championships, frequently moving closer to Riot's initiative than that of Valve's. Some examples are *Mobile Legends: Bang Bang,* which has included prerecorded virtual performances featuring self-tailored bands such as S.P.A.R.K.L.E., a J-pop band first presented for the AllStars competition in 2024; and *Arena of Valor,* whose character alter ego DJ Butterfly was the introducer for their International Championship in 2022.

Likewise, on-stage performers "in the flesh" have also been key in marketizing these events in other cases, like *Honor of Kings*' International Championship, which has featured popular singers Jike Junyi[28] and GEM.[29] Other esports categories—shooters, sports games—have also followed similar approaches when including opening shows into their physical gatherings—e.g., TheFatRat's 2017 performance at ESL One in Cologne for *Counter-Strike*—[30]vouching for the value of thinking about esports marketing from a transmedia perspective, that considers the continuous exchange between different forms of entertainment.

As an example, *Counter-Strike*'s collaboration with TheFatRat in 2017 was built around his well-known song *Fly Away*, mixed with sonic elements from the game, such as off voices or gun sounds, which were accompanied by videos and play of lights. However, the success of the agreement with Universal Music Group and the record of viewers reached on that occasion[31] was not replicated with on-stage performers in later years. Rather, the organizers have taken on a specific approach to opening their competitions that vouches for multimedia spectacles that are not necessarily live.

Despite including tracks from other artists, such as Josh Powell's *Leviathan* in 2021 or Ros Stephen's *Dissidence* in 2023, ESL One has placed an emphasis on building an immersive spectacle that takes into account the experience of the player-attendees. This implies the inclusion of carefully selected music—from electronic to orchestral—along with visual elements such as light shows, which are frequently accompanied by voice-overs and excerpts from previous competitive events. Although not strictly *live*, these events include the need for crossing paths with diverse music industry agents and contribute to the dissemination of pieces that could not be known to fans otherwise. Furthermore, the case works as yet another key example to argue in favor of the spectrum of possibilities for introducing popular music artists in esports (live) contexts.

"Heavy Is the Crown": Linkin Park at Worlds 2024

During the writing of this book, Linkin Park's collaboration with Riot Games was the last case available for analysis, as they participated in the opening show for the *League of Legends* World Championship and as part of the Riot Games show *Arcane* (season 2) on Netflix. The case illustrates the contents discussed so far, and exemplifies the growing implications of competitive gaming and game publishers as mediators for factual and potential popular music fanbases.

The collaboration was teased indirectly in the first announcements for the championship, as the design of the creative content for social media was seen as similar to Linkin Park's recent rebranding.[32] The first song launched to make the partnership official was *The Emptiness Machine*, although it was the second piece presented, *Heavy is the Crown*, which was fit as a theme for the game's 2024 events.

Linkin Park's appearance on stage for Worlds, which attracted a record 4.2. million viewers,[33] began on earlier conversations between both parties and implied the trust of each side in projects that were still in the building. As described by Mike Shinoda:

> We had to let you in the door on our secret first and, you know, I've had a relationship with different folks from Riot for a while, with Brandon years ago. I don't even remember how we met, but Brandon Beck and I kind of talked once in a while and I eventually met Christian from *Arcane*, and I met various people from the Worlds side,

> and one of my favorite games is *Valorant* as well. So, as we were putting together our new music and the band started kind of jelling it was almost natural that the conversations began about Worlds. I think there's a lot of synergy between the way they look at things creatively and the things that we're doing creatively, and there's a lot of synergy in the fan bases.[34]

To build the songs and the creative content around it—including the music video for *Heavy is the Crown*, which gained nearly ten million views on the first day of its release—[35]Linkin Park musicians and Riot Music Group agents worked side by side since early in the process. As stated by the band members, the composition was meant to appeal to game and music fans—together and separately. In this sense, the song can be analyzed transmediatically from the multiple meanings that it contributes to its diverse receptors: from the new role assumed by singer Emily Armstrong to the pressure of T1 and Lee "Faker" Sang-hyeok in representing the *League of Legends* community, or regarding the representation of *Arcane*'s plotline.

The convergence of elements surpasses a single use and moves toward a cross-media popularization beyond the game's target—similar to what happened in 2023 with *Enemy* by Imagine Dragons. Furthermore, the incorporation of the well-known band, representative of the early 2000s rock scene, underlines how video games have elevated their status to that of popular music.

The music video created by Brunch Studio to accompany the song's presentation can be seen as following *Arcane*'s visual aesthetic. The clip's narrative is set in and around a castle, that serves the introduction of the animated characters of Linkin Park members and *challenger*—competitive-level—players, drawn as embodying their usually picked characters' powers. The animation follows the persecution of the crown, which is finally placed on a thrown by Faker, who walks in "contemplating the weight" of the object.[36] The centrality of this player as an engager for fans is key, as he only enters the castle last before the final battle between players begins, creating a momentary silence that is only resumed by the final chorus of the song.

Linkin Park is not shown simultaneously to the players in this animation, but they are separated visually and narratively through lighting palettes to create parallel lines, despite all being placed in the same space. The lyrics and music describe the struggle of being in a position of influence in popular culture, as is well depicted by using a fry scream technique, already used by the singer's predecessor, Chester Bennington. Likewise, the lyrics may be read as emphasizing the competitiveness of the esports event: *Turn to run, now look what it's become / Outnumbered, ten to one / Back then, should've bit your tongue / 'Cause there's no turnin' back this path once it's begun.*

During the *League of Legends* finals, the opening ceremony featured the band as a closing act, following Ashnikko's *Paint the Town Blue*, and Forts and Tiffany Aris' *Still Here*. For their on-stage presentation, the castle's rose window depicted in the first seconds of the animated video was projected as the band members emerged, performing for live and online audiences, creating a continuity between products. The finalist teams, BLG and T1, were lastly introduced as the song continued playing to sustain the momentum of the event, affording a momentary co-staging of the rock band and the esports players, that culminated in the presentation of the competition trophy.

The song, along with the products created around it, represents a peak in the collaboration of popular music and esports, as well as the wider entertainment industry, as it merges diverse niches, providing an opportunity for global fans to combine diverse interests under a single event.

Identity Representation in Competitive Environments

Among the elements that raise analytic interest in the cases mentioned above, beyond the use of technological advances and the inclusion of live music, is the attention to the cultural identities of the fans of the games. Despite the creation of globalized performances that appeal to a wide range of publics, games like *DotA 2* and *League of Legends* have followed strategies that aim to commercialize or commodify their spectacles within the music market and create connections with their fans. This is also true for other games most popular in Eastern countries, like *Honor of Kings*, whose need to appeal to Western audiences has been less urgent—since the title was launched as the Chinese homonymous to *Arena of Valor*. In this sense, turning to popular options in the territories with larger consumer groups is a common tangent, aside from the selection of worldwide-known artists that can resonate transversally with each game's fanbase.

The locations at which the competitions take place are definitory of the performances to an extent. For instance, the opening show for The International in Shanghai in 2019 included a performance by the National Philharmonic Orchestra, Chinese traditional dances, and a tanggu ensemble. It can be argued that including some of the country's cultural practices and autochthonous groups was intended to bring forward the value of the host's traditions and move aside the mainstream, in line with the approach to ceremoniality followed by Valve. However, especially around Riot Games' model, it is the artists that are placed on stage and the music genres selected for the performances that mostly afford a connection with globalized fan identities.[37]

An example of this is found in the artists selected to open the different global championships depending on their target audience. For instance, in 2023 *Mobile Legends: Bang Bang*—whose main audiences are in Asia and Southeast Asia—[38]featured songs by Indonesian singer and rapper KZ Tandingan, which was more comprehensive than including DJ Alok, who performed for the *Free Fire* World Final in 2017—and whose audience is mostly located in Brazil.[39] This also applies to regional and cultural practices such as Ramadan in several Asian countries, which in cases such as the earlier mentioned are taken into account not only for the performance of specific events, but also regarding their marketing.[40]

In aims to differentiate the influence of localization on video game music, Gibbons established three broad categories that come in especially handy for this matter: basic localization, which includes information "localized for target markets (e.g. subtitles), with few or no musical changes;" complex localization, whose "culture-specific musical markers are removed or altered, typically with the goal of making a game seem internationalized, or perhaps universal;" and blending, where "the music is significantly or completely altered for international release, typically to strip the game of markers of cultural identification and replace those markers with those of the target demographic's culture."[41] This applies to the establishment of live or prerecorded performances in esports contexts, as the aim of the spectacles follows similar rules to those in the videogames themselves.

Eric Tan, who has worked with Riot Games in artist casting and show management for opening performances for *League of Legends* World Finals, described this very attention to fan engagement:

> When we look at the way we do our casting, on who gets to perform, we want to make sure that either Chinese players get represented or make Korean players get represented. And that is why we had Jackson Wang to come perform at the World Championship in 2022, as a way to say that, okay, we also want to have Chinese representation. And then again, with HEARTSTEEL last year, where we had Ozi from Taiwan and also Baekhyun from EXO, so that we make sure that we have Chinese and Korean representation for those markets. And it was an unbelievable experience to see them performing live in front of 18,000 people at the Sky Dome in Seoul.[42]

Speaking strictly about world championship dynamization shows, the opportunities to appeal to worldwide audiences have become more globalized. It is not unusual to include artists from different countries on the same stage to create references for attendees in diverse geographies, yet this usually responds to the attention placed on music market trends. For instance, the singers mentioned in Table 5.2. include K-pop stars that can be attractive to Eastern and Western publics alike—e.g., Baekhyun—especially in gaming environments.[43]

Virtual bands such as True Damage addressed this inclusion idiomatically—including singer alter egos for their game characters—as well as linguistically. The lyrics of the song *Living Like Giants,* launched for the *League of Legends* World Finals in 2019, contemplated verses performed in English, Korean, and Spanish.[44] Furthermore, the slang used in English appealed to the cultural knowledge of the fans as well as to the music genre of the song in a more localized way.

Excerpts from *Living Like Giants* by Riot Music Group

[English] Homie, better put your pride aside
I'm a Benz and you're more like a Volvo.
[Korean] 날카로운 날로 뭐든 베어
빨리 달려 넌 못따라 와.
[Spanish] Ay, nada nos puede parar, oh, no.

This is not to say that games with fanbases from around the globe and which consciously consider their diverse backgrounds, including religious practice, do not incorporate in-game events and music elements that afford a sense of connection and consideration to their cultural practice more specifically—e.g., *Wild Rift*[45] or *Fortnite.*[46] These include skins and theme songs to smaller championships, like GG Ramadan Rivals by *Counter-Strike*[47] or the *Free Fire* Ramadan Championship, and are not as transversally spread among the games' general community.

Especially when referring to globalized approaches to music, the *crisis of identity* described by Muriel and Crawford in *Video Game as Culture*, which leads to what they label as an era of *post-identity*, becomes patent. According to the authors, these would imply a flexibility that "cannot find accommodation in the spectrum of solidity/liquidity,"[48] as it is transitory and everchanging. That is, the music framing esports competitions does include specific elements that appear in continuation to the idiosyncrasies of modernity, while accommodating globalized dynamics that appeal to each individual experience. The music identities created around esports can thus be argued to work in balance with this fluctuation, as it appeals to both regional influences and global references.

CGI AND CHARACTER ALTER EGOS

Artist interventions during opening and dynamization shows have taken two main formats: regular on-stage performances or technologically mediated spectacles. The range of possibilities between these two poles has entailed singers and bands participating as themselves or adopting alter ego personalities to merge with the characters of the games that they represent.

The adoption of alternative identities has been discussed in popular music studies by authors such as Ken McLeod—regarding the "uses of space, alien and techno futuristic themes in popular music and the construction of various marginalised identities"–[49]and Larissa Irrizarry—in reference to the alter egos of Black women in popular music.[50] However, the adoption of game character identities by popular singers in esports contexts has not held notorious countercultural implications to date, and has been focused on breaking the fourth wall of the games as marketing and community-binding strategies.

Especially with the support of CGI and hologram technologies, the embodiment of characters by real-flesh artists has worked as a means to transcend the barrier between fantasy and reality. This field has also been previously tackled in the work of scholars like Shara Rambarran[51] or John Richardson[52] regarding the virtual band Gorillaz. However, for on-stage performances, the range of possibilities goes beyond contributing a singing voice to a projection—e.g., in hologram-based shows like Hatsune Miku's.[53] The range of possibilities for the relation between artists/game characters can go from dressing up professional "anonymous" musicians—e.g., during the Bad Randoms' performance for the *Brawl Star* World Finals in 2022—to setting up the stage for real artists and character projections simultaneously—e.g., with K/DA's performance during the *League of Legends* finals in 2018.

Among these possibilities, alter egos specifically refer to artists representing game characters while being recognizable as themselves, which contributes a temporary new identity to the artists while exploring an alternative side for the characters. As stated by the former Head of Music at Riot Games, regarding K/DA:

> It's a really cool blend because we worked with Madison Beer, we worked with Jaira Burns, and G-Idle. We still had to negotiate with their team, their legal team and everything. But instead of having the artists up front and center and all about them, it just became about their craft and what they could really lend to it. And we found actually

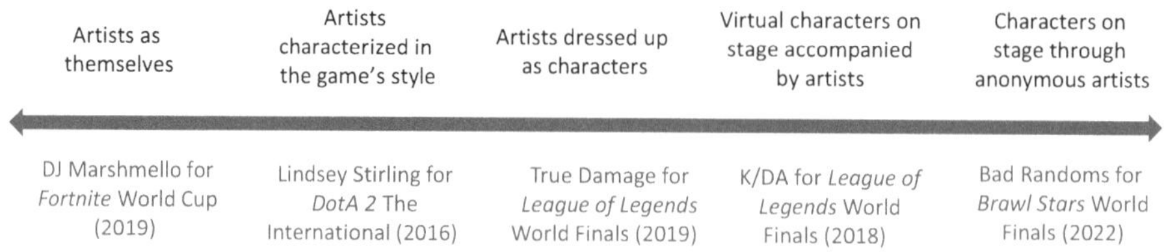

FIGURE 5.1 Artist/Character representation on stage during esports competitions.

> a lot of artists really liked it because, for example, you could have an artist who maybe isn't so diva, but the character is. And so she gets to really lean into being a diva maybe more than she normally would for her brand or something like that. And I think they got a kick out of that to an extent.[54]

K/DA's case may be one of the most discussed in academic literature to date,[55] as the band encapsulates the trends and initiatives of the current connections between the music and esports industries. Their staging through computer-generated imagery was not only mediatically transcendent, but it allowed a revitalization around the discussion on virtual bands and video games. In this sense, Ivănescu describes how "the development of K/DA follows many (...) generic conventions, including the crafting of their portrayed personas, the musical style, and the band structure,"[56] which are characteristic of K-pop, and links the success of the group to the rapid growth of the genre.

Despite the inclusion of K-pop idiosyncrasies, the experience of embodying the game characters, as Soyeon and Miyeon pointed out, presented a way of exploring their performativity beyond what can be considered the tighter limits of *idol* representation:

> I performed as "Akali" today. Compared to other champions on the stage, she felt more "hip" ... cooler. That was my impression, so I tried to express that in my performance.
>
> I performed as "Ahri" today. I understand she is a character that represents the nine-tail fox. I played a few games on Ahri myself in order to understand the champion better, and I felt that she is a very attractive champion.[57]

The co-shared stages with their respective CGI characters established an amusing dynamic for the singers and the audiences at home, despite their limitations for attendees *in situ*. These impediments derived from the reliance on secondary screens to *see* the performing characters, and were later addressed by incorporating other technological tools. For instance, the presentation of True Damage through holograms in 2019, contributed to blurring the barrier between reality and virtuality on in-person events. In this case, the public was able to actually see the created effects that contributed to the illusion of the singers as alter egos of the characters. For instance, Lysandra's ability which throws a giant claw toward her enemies, or Ekko's space-time jumps were more easily reproduced through these means—yet if they required specific positioning in the public to see properly.

However, one of the key features that allows such illusions to work and for them to be sustained in time is precisely the prolongation of the presence of the artists—especially the game characters on different platforms. In this sense, the transmedia promotion of the virtual personas and the companies' following virtual-influencer trends is essential in providing a continuous stream of content and potential for brand adherence among the public.

VIRTUAL ARTISTS BEYOND THE STAGE

The elements that contribute to breaking the barrier between fantasy and reality are strongly linked to the concept of *hyperrealism*, which places game characters on the threshold of corporeality. This term, which Rambarran develops concerning Baudrillad's "order of simulacra,"[58] allows us to label these bands as a *simulation* of real pop groups. Among the different stages of representation that the author describes, simulation refers to those cases in which an "'original' cannot be detected,"[59] as the boundaries separating reality and illusion become blurred, frequently through digital means. In other words, an "original" cannot be found as it does not exist in the real world, despite being part of it.

In the case that concerns us, this is achieved by including band members in interviews on well-known face-to-face and online platforms, or by creating personal accounts on social media that allow them to communicate directly with fans. In cases like K/DA or HEARTSTEEL, Instagram, TikTok, and X have allowed them to share stories and thoughts in "real-time." Similarly, Infinite King assiduously engages with a two-million-fan online community on Weibo, and bands like S.P.A.R.K.L.E by *Mobile Legends: Bang Bang* have posted "behind the scenes" videos of the characters on YouTube, contributing a sense of proximity to followers.

These elements afford the construction of the artists' personae as if they were in control of their words and behaviors, taking to an extreme the manufacturing of pop stars that initiated in the 1990s,[60] or in K-pop more recently. The virtual bands allow control of their assets to the companies that produce them, despite the need for collaboration and agreement with music industry agents. What is in continuous tension in these cases is, thus, the effort in producing complex products and their marketing and revenue. However, the model's success can be measured through the increasing number of avatar-based bands in the global music panorama, such as the virtual K-pop band Eternity.[61] Their images are inserted in what Stark defines as the dichotomic nature of virtual bands, that exist in universes that are specifically built for them, in realities created for them, with their own background stories and characteristics.[62]

An example fitting the bands mentioned above is K/DA's presentation of their second single, *More*, which was launched for their performance in the *League of Legends* World Finals of 2020 in Shanghai. This social presence helped consolidate the band's popularity and propelled Riot Games' initiative by placing their music-related products on the market as part of a cohesive experience for their fans. Some of the interventions by the band members included audiovisual interviews with Chinese producer Zhang Yadong,[63] and Genius,[64] as well as written interviews with media such as *Hypebae*.[65]

These platforms served for K/DA developers to speak through their characters and explain their work through the voices of *League of Legends* champion alter egos. Likewise, they allowed an expansion of the storyworld of the game and its overall lore:

> Without True Damage, we wouldn't have connected with Yasuo, who Akali also brought as a producer of our new EP (...) MORE celebrates the next evolution of K/DA. We wanted this triumphant pop sound: an anthem of queens.[66]

Additionally to the impact of the first-hand content on these platforms, including the virtual artists talking to the camera and "studio photographs," their relevance in the international (gaming) music scene grew enough to be considered a phenomenon itself. Škripcová already pointed out how "in the era of V-tubers and other virtual celebrities or influencers, it could easily happen that the accounts gained popularity with the audience without knowing about the characters' affiliation to the game,"[67] an idea that could be illustrated by this very case.

These elements have not been transversally integrated into all cases with esports bands or specifically created characters that work for their promotion, but Riot Games' initiative has been somewhat replicated on a smaller scale by other brands such as Power 4 by *PUBG*[68] on X, while titles such as *Free Fire* have developed videos in which characters appear to talk to camera, breaking the fourth wall, as a means to communicate with fans—even if they are not strictly linked to music content.[69]

An example of this is *The Kelly Show*, which *Free Fire* was first introduced in 2020[70] as a means to update players about new patches in the game, changes, and overall news around the game. The virtual show starring the game character Kelly was launched in different languages, aimed at the wide public of the title in diverse geographies, as a medium through which the game developers get to talk to their fanbase and express their creative processes. Furthermore, they have used this channel to highlight

FIGURE 5.2 Character Kelly from *Free Fire* performing for a YouTube short. Copyright © 2024 Garena Online. All rights reserved.

the involvement of players in the day-to-day decisions of the company and create a sense of belongingness for the community. As the character explained in the very first episode of the series: "The developers and I have been reading your feedback, and we've made changes. We appreciate your voices, so please keep them coming!"[71]

Although music takes a secondary role in these clips, it works as a cohesive element for the audiovisual content and is often used to emphasize the message transmitted in the video. Despite this, some of the vertical content—YouTube shorts, Instagram reels, etc.—has used music specifically to break the fourth wall and engage the audience in related products such as soundtracks or event songs. For instance, in July 2024 they uploaded a short vertical video depicting Kelly as a streamer, in front of a microphone and with headphones on, singing over the original version of the game's theme, as a means to engage old fans as well as creating a hyperrealistic situation in which she performed for her "online audience"—who were shown in the video comments as other characters from the game.[72]

These elements show how characters' transmediality becomes an essential part of the current gaming and social media panorama. They are imbued with the music and gaming industries' tendencies to cross platforms to reach wider audiences. Likewise, they reinforce the relevance of new technologies in creating a well-articulated ecosystem that blends with reality through different formats, from live face-to-face shows to social media interventions.

TV Scenarios

Continuing with Riot Games' universe, in November 2021 the *League of Legend*-based series *Arcane* was released on Netflix, reaching first position on the platform's charts in over 50 countries, following 34 million reproductions during the first six days.[73] This, it can be argued, allowed approaching an audience outside of the game's main target, who was also put in touch with the popular music soundtrack of the show.

The adaptation of video games to TV formats had precedents in cases like the *Resident Evil* saga, and has been reproduced in other mediatic successes such as *The Witcher, The Last of Us*, or *Fallout*. Inversely, Jenkins had already tackled the transmediation of *The Matrix* series into video game format, as have other authors with other movies, music videos, and video games.[74] In 2006, he described the postapocalyptic content of the franchise as a form of entertainment "for the age of media convergence, integrating multiple texts to create a narrative so large that it cannot be contained within a single medium."[75] This idea has continued to extend and be explored in later decades, including narratives that revolve around esports games. In line with this, the story developed for *Arcane* was designed as a complement to the content of the brand, which, as a TV show, was new to both existing fans of *League of Legends* and non-gamer viewers, and therefore appealing to different niches.

However, concerning the music of these parallel products, the soundtracks created for each case are not necessarily common. In adaptations like *The Last of Us*, composer Gustavo Santaolalla was also involved in creating the OST for the TV series, which implied a continuity in style for the music and sound. In this sense, the arrangements can be seen as tailored to attend to the specific scope of the television format. This is different from the case under analysis here, which served as a marketing standpoint for the promotion of the *League of Legends*.

Arcane's soundtrack was linked to the overall lore built around the title, but not necessarily around the game per se. This implied the inclusion of artists who had collaborated with Riot Games in past events, such as Bea Miller, Curtis Harding, or Imagine Dragons, among others. Thus, although the story was new for existing players as well as to new viewers, *League of Legends* users were "given a certain advantage when watching Arcane,"[76] including familiarity with the music and knowledge of audiovisual content—which appeared as multiple easter eggs during the show.[77] Most clearly, the exploitation of Imagine Dragons' *Enemy* as the opening theme and their insertion in episode 5 as animated characters implied a direct relation to past events that symbolize key moments in the game's history—e.g., the band's first bet on popular music with *Warriors* in 2014. The success of these past joint projects culminated, as described by the Riot Games team, as a "love letter to you, the players and fans who, over the years, have been with us to help make League of Legends what it is today."[78]

The audiovisual result was accomplished in collaboration with Fortiche Productions, an illustration company with whom Riot Games had previously worked—e.g., in creating the music video for *Get Jinxed*. Furthermore, the show's visual aesthetics followed the preexisting lines of the companies' joint projects. Musically speaking, the intersection of artists who had already collaborated with the brand and new associations afforded a close design of the pieces that accompanied the narrative of the different chapters.

Some examples of the adaptation to the narrative can be found in the songs' lyrics, as well as in the tonalities or instrumentation used in each case. For instance, Bea Miller's *Playground*, which is introduced when the underground city of Zaun is shown for the first time, reinforces the visual aspects of the scene:

> Welcome to the playground, follow me
> Yell me your nightmares and fantasies
> Sink into the wasteland underneath
> Stay for the night, I'll sell you a dream.

Likewise, the track by Sting and violinist Ray Chen titled *What Could Have Been*, helps the viewer understand the feelings of disillusionment and anger of one of the protagonists:

> I want you to hurt like you hurt me today and
> I want you to lose like I lose when I play
> what could have been.[79] [80]

However, what makes the show and the participation of the artists in Table 5.3. most relevant—besides story enhancement—is the inclusion of the songs and the artists in products between the series and competitive events. On the one hand, the opening ceremony video launched for the World Finals of 2021, as well as its teasers, acted as

TABLE 5.3 Artists Featured in *Arcane*, Season 1 (2021) and 2 (2024)

TRACK TITLE	*ARTISTS*	*SEASONS AND EPISODES*
Enemy	Imagine Dragons ft. JID	Opening theme S1&2
Playground	Bea Miller	S1, E1
Our Love	Curtis Harding and Jazmine Sullivan	S1, E2
Goodbye	Ramsey	S1, E3
Get Jinxed!	Agnete Kjølsrud (Djerv)	S1, E4
Dirty Little Animals	Bones UK	S1, E4
Guns For Hire	Woodkid	S1, E6
Misfit Toys	Pusha T, Mako	S1, E7
Dynasties & Dystopia	Denzel Curry, Gizzle, Bren Joy	S1, E7
I Can't Hear It Now	Freya Ridings	S2, E
Sucker	Marcus King	S2, E
Renegade (We Never Run)	Stefflon Don, Raja Kumari ft. Jaina de Marco	S2, E
Hellfire	Fever 333	S2, E
To Ashes and Blood	Woodkid	S2, E
Paint The Town Blue	Ashnikko	S2, E
Remember Me	d4vd	S2, E
Cocktail Molotov	Zand	S2, E
What Have They Done To Us	Mako, Grey	S2, E
Rebel Heart	Djerv	S2, E
The Beast	Misha Mansoor	S2, E
Spin The Wheel	Mick Wingert	S2, E
Ma Meilleure Ennemie	Stormae, Pomme	S2, E
Fantastic	King Princess	S2, E
The Line	Twenty One Pilots	S2, E
Blood Sweat & Tears	Sheryl Lee Ralph	S2, E
Come Play	Stray Kids, Young Miko, Tom Morello	S2, E
Wasteland	Royal & The Serpent	S2, E

a connecting piece to link *Arcane* and the championship, contributing to a feeling of continuity in Riot's universe. This was a unique occasion in which the opening show for Worlds did not include a live performance, but rather a prerecorded sequence that blended diverse agents under one medium.

The footage was staged in the world of Runeterra, with the featured artists of the soundtrack walking the fantastic city of Zaun. The first minutes of the video belong to scenes from the series, which transition toward a music video featuring the artists and their respective tracks. The successive performances in this short film were articulated through the appearance of the animated characters, who helped link different scenes and give way to the face-to-face stage on which the players were standing before the competition started. In this way, Imagine Dragons, JID, Denzel Curry, Bea Miller, and PVRIS, were presented as part of the official soundtrack for the series as well as for the esports event.

On the other hand, the inclusion of the artists in the TV series as animations has also raised attention as a form of transmediality. The opening song *Enemy* appeared in one of the chapters in which the band members were featured as additional characters of the imaginary world, creating an opportunity for what we may call a case of *inverted hyperreality*, which vouches for the significance of the band around the game's lore.

Arcane's first season success can be measured by the award of different prizes at the Annie Awards and the Golden Reel Awards, as well as in the increase of video game users in the weeks following the show's release. Imagine Dragons, at the same time, with their enthusiasts and detractors, hit first positions on billboards around the world, which makes the success of the strategy designed by the show creators tangible regarding their bet on bands that have helped them become part of a wider international scene. The band's success can also be analyzed from complementary perspectives, as may the rest of the participants in the series' soundtrack, including experience, sociocultural, and economic standpoints.

The series' second season shows the investment in including popular music artists as key promoters in the vast array of names included in the soundtrack, as the featured musicians have doubled in volume for this occasion. The earlier-mentioned crossover with Linkin Park, with *Heavy is the Crown,* brings another key element to the series as well as the competition. It appeals to veteran fans in a similar way to Imagine Dragons, evoking a sense of nostalgia from past decades and the listeners' cultural capital.

A different—yet successful—case in adapting an esports game narrative to a TV series format is the anime *Dragon's Blood*, based on *DotA 2*. Although conceptually different, this show afforded a point of connection for fans to extend their knowledge of the game and its overall lore. The soundtrack of the show was created separately from the game by the composer Dino Meneghin, who did not know about the game before being offered the opportunity to create the show's soundtrack. Despite this, and to create a better sense of continuation with the game, the author approached *DotA 2*'s composer Tim Larkin:

> We talked about some of the most important themes that he had written, the ones that were sort of fan favorites, and we actually incorporated some of those into the music, as a bit of a "fan service" (...) That was something that we were really conscious of, I was conscious of with the music, and I think that was also part of the reason for not wanting to do the music in a similar style as the game.[81]

The intersection with the popular music industry is, therefore, not as present as in *Arcane*'s case, despite the presence of the soundtrack in the OST consumer circuit.[82]

This implies another approach to creating a sense of continuity between the game and its related products, which favors the introduction of new music material that is reminiscent yet separated from the gaming title. Similarly, the *Halo* TV series based on the homonymous game was designed with a specific soundtrack to illustrate the story, which was intentionally separated from the sonic content of the original game series.

The *Halo* series was first announced in 2013 to be put into production,[83] but was not released until almost a decade later. There have been two seasons released so far, of which the first was scored by Sean Callery, and the second by Bear McCreary. Both composers were encouraged to approach the sound of the game and include it in their proposals to orchestrate the series. As pointed out by the authors themselves:

> The main title was a kind of a bridge between the original *Halo* theme, and the Gregorian chant melody that everyone knows. They were thinking it'd be nice if we could, quote the theme. Not exactly the same as in the game. So I thought of doing it with a cello and a female voice singing at the same time. It's a very interesting sound.[84]

> The first thing that I wanted to do is go back to the music of the games and try to bring it to the forefront, and feature it in a way that would make me, as a long-time gamer, smile when I heard that main title (…). In the music of the *Halo* games, underneath all the propulsion and the action, there is this sense of drama. Simple melodies and lush harmonies that I always admired. I wanted to take that regal nobility that I always loved about the music of *Halo* in the games and bring it to the series.[85]

Although these cases have not directly intersected with the esports events corresponding to each title, they have worked to reach a wider public than that targeted through their playable content. Furthermore, they are good examples of how the gaming and music industries intersect at different levels and how their relation to competitive game events may be more or less distant depending on the intention of developers or other agents involved.

Specifically to esports, it is not an irrational endeavor to speculate on possible future series,[86] especially given the increasing interest in creating transmediatic products that complement each other and extend each game's universe and lore beyond their playable contents. The intersection with popular music artists in cases that are more inclined to delve into the mainstream, like *Fortnite*, can be hypothesized to become relevant in the future to work on a bidirectional promotion between industries.

CONCLUSIONS

As shown throughout this chapter, the increasing interest in competitive events as investment and collaborative opportunities for music agents has translated into the recurrent presence of popular music artists as dynamizers on and around esports stages. As in other activities in which music is present as a socializer, the inclusion of figures of reference for attendees to collectively approach, discuss, and engage with, has contributed to a sense of belongingness to the games' social scenes.

Despite the impact of these cases, some developers have opted for less mediatic options when building the sonic backgrounds of their championships. While some developers and publishers have followed transmedia strategies that include artists and bands as part of their brand's identity and lore—e.g., *Valorant* or *Free Fire*—others have opted for investing in self-tailored music soundtracks, distancing themselves from the mainstream—e.g., *Counter-Strike* or *DotA 2*. These are, of course, not black-or-white possibilities, but two in a scale of grays, that includes an array of ways to engage with the music industry and gaming audiences.

Live shows and opening ceremonies have been present as dynamizers and extra-ordinariety enhancers in all the events that have opted to include them. On most of these occasions, the music genres have been related to already predefined sonic identities, which tend to focus on the sociocultural preferences of game fans.

Although some competitions—and their audiovisual promotion—may be designed for specific niches within the public of the titles—e.g., *Fotnite*'s Lantern Fest—big competitions that aim to appeal to global audiences are frequently aligned with the tendencies of the global music industry.[87] As such, K-pop has been increasingly in demand, as many titles have bet on the production of virtual *idols* and bands to represent their products. K/DA has been pinpointed as the most referenced—and pioneering—case in this line of action, which was later followed by other games such as *Free Fire*, or further initiatives from Riot Games such as HEARTSTEEL. Nevertheless, other genres such as trap, hip-hop, or EDM have also gained a significant presence among music-related products surrounding the competitions.

The use of scaffolding technologies has also been a common ground in most occasions, especially when including virtual artists or alter egos based on game characters, which are strictly reliant on them. In this vein, the inclusion of CGI in performances such as K/DA's in 2017 and 2020 demonstrates the integration of traditional on-stage performances and technologically mediated interventions. This has worked as a way to bring the fans closer to both the music and the game characters, and has promoted an increasing attraction toward competitive events,[88] which appear to be not only matches, but social events for attendees.

In some cases, the presence of these virtual character-pop stars has extended beyond the events in which they have been featured, and have been imbued in transmedia strategies that have presented them in hyperrealistic contexts—as already explored in earlier decades with bands such as Gorillaz. Following this example, some of the initiatives blending the intervention of popular music artists and game characters have crossed over social media through their virtual stars, mimicking the behaviors of real-flesh influencers. For this purpose, some brands have created social media accounts for their bands or band members, who have served as a medium for producers to get directly in touch with fans, breaking the fourth wall and speaking through their voices.

This has contributed to the illusion of non-mediation explored in other concert formats—such as in-game performances—and placed the artist-characters in a non-factual position of control over their own words and behaviors. Furthermore, the investment in such characters has favored the construction of trans- and cross-media universes that expand each game's lore, as it allows the creation of shared references between products that are more difficult to achieve with non-game-intrinsic artists.

In some specific cases, like the introduction of Imagine Dragons as characters in *Arcane*, artists have also jumped from real to virtual—and not the other way around. The series establishes a successful case on how a band (Imagine Dragons), a video game (*League of Legends*), and its related esports competitions (2021 World Championship) can be linked almost seamlessly to benefit each other. In this sense, the investment of Riot Games in creating a unified narrative that is exploited through all possible channels—including different titles, events, and audiovisual productions—has become a referent.

Like in *Rocket League* and Monstercat's cases, these dynamics have created a bidirectional reward system for what are now two complementary industries in many ways. They have also contributed to establishing the foundations for a growing transmediatic market in which products are designed to blend and live in continuous exchange.

It has become clear how, in the era of communication and transmediation, sharing resources and aligning them with multiple agents in the entertainment industry is a *must*. Even if the relation between esports and the elements discussed in this chapter is not always as explicit as opening ceremonies for world championships, the audiovisual strategies designed to surround and dynamize the games have become crucial to their success—also in competitive environments. In other words, entertainment can no longer be understood as separate markets, but must be seen as a continuum that draws from different resources that complement each other—in this case, including esports as a central pillar.

The early initiative that put Imagine Dragons on the *League of Legends* stage triggered a reaction that has culminated in the involvement of first-line bands and artists under the work of multiple titles. The involvement of Linkin Park in the promotion of the 2024 Worlds Championship of the game is proof of that, as are the music videos encompassing characters, esports players, and band members, or the embeddedness of the *Heavy is the Crown* on stage and in *Arcane*.

NOTES

1 Sofie Van Bauwel & Tonny Krijnen, "Let's Get Loud: Intersectionally Studying the Super Bowl's Halftime Show", *Media and Communication*, 2021, 9(3), 209–217.

2 Jeff Benjamin, "'League of Legends' Girl Group Earns Madison Beer, (G)I-DLE & Jaire Burns No.1 on World Digital Song Sales Chart", *Billboard*, 2018. Available at: https://www.billboard.com/pro/kda-pop-stars-madison-beer-gidle-jaira-burns-no-1-world-digital-songs-league-of-legends/. Accessed 12th August 2024.

3 Emma Griffiths, "The Convergence of Music & Esports: Industry Pros Weigh in on Opportunities, Trends & What's in Store for the Future (Part 1)", *Synchtank*, 2019. Available at: https://www.synchtank.com/blog/the-convergence-of-music-esports-industry-pros-weigh-in-on-opportunities-trends-whats-in-store-for-the-future-part-1/. Accessed 21st August 2024.

4 See Eulalia Febrer-Coll, "'Everybody Wants to Be My Enemy': Popular Music and Transmediality in Arcane", *SeriArte: Revista científica de series televisivas y arte audiovisual*, 2023, 4(1), 68–86. Available at: https://helvia.uco.es/bitstream/handle/10396/26505/seriarte_4_5.pdf?sequence=1&isAllowed=y. Accessed 10th August 2024.

5 Mónica Valderrama Santomé & Verónica Crespo-Pereira, "Festivales de música y marketing experiencial: efectos para marca, organizador y espectador", *ADResearch ESIC International Journal of Communication Research*, 2021, *26*(26), 64.

6 Tom Daniels, "Singapore Showcase: Finding the Rhythm with Esports and Music", *Esports Insider*, 2023. Available at: https://esportsinsider.com/2023/06/esports-and-music. Accessed 10th August 2024.

7 Chair of Music Practice and Chair of Esports and Games Practice at law firm Sheppard Mullin.
8 Esports Insider, "Sidney Fohrman & Toa Dunn on Law, Music & Esports Converging | ESI Focus: Law in Esports #2", *Youtube*, 2021. Available at: https://www.youtube.com/watch?v=rosZiGzS7t8. Accessed 14th August 2024.
9 Simon Frith, "Live Music", in John Shepherd & Kyle Devine (Eds.), *The Routledge Reader on the Sociology of Music*. New York: Routledge, 2015, 237.
10 Frith, "Live Music", 237.
11 Akash & Joseph Kim, "Free Fire's Billion Free Downloads", *Game Makers*, 2024. Available at: https://www.gamemakers.com/p/free-fires-billion-free-downloads. Accessed 26th August 2024.
12 IFPI, "Reports & Resources", n.d. Available at: https://www.ifpi.org/resources/. Accessed 26th August 2024.
13 Gavin Johnson, Director of Sync and Partnerships at Monstercat, Interview by Eulalia Febrer-Coll, 13th December 2023.
14 Rupert Till, *Pop Cult: Religion and Popular Music*. London and New York: Bloomsbury, 2010.
15 Francesca R. Sborgi Lawson "Music in Ritual and Ritual in Music: A Virtual Viewer's Perceptions about Liminality, Functionality, and Mediatization in the Opening Ceremony of the 2008 Beijing Olympic Games", *Asian Music,* 2011, 42(2), 3–18.
16 Frith, "Live Music", 275.
17 David Dannelly, "The Origin of the MOBA: Aeon of Strife and Defense of the Ancients", *David Dannelly: Faculty, Technical Game Designer & 3D*, 2019. Available at: https://daviddannelly.com/blog/zjYm/the-origin-of-the-moba-aeon-of-strife-and-defen%20se-of-the-ancients. Accessed 30th August 2024.
18 Brian Crecente, "League of Legends Is Now 10 Years Old. This Is the Story of Its Birth", *The Washington Post*. Available at: https://www.washingtonpost.com/video-games/2019/10/27/league-legends-is-now-years-old-this-is-story-its-birth/. Accessed 30th August 2024.
19 The International Gaming Syndicate (IGS) began hosting *DotA* competitions in 2004. *DotA 2* was incorporated into the esports scene in 2011, before the game's official launch in 2013. See Felix Bammel, *The History of Competitive DotA*. Amazon, 2022.
20 Toa Dunn, former Head of Music at Riot Games. Interview by Eulalia Febrer-Coll. 4th September 2020.
21 The Elden Dragon is an NPC in *League of Legends*, a late-game neutral monster that spawns after a series of events, providing a *buff* with amplified damage and an execution effect to the team who slays it.
22 Eulalia Febrer-Coll, "Living Like Giants: 'League of Legends' from the Screen to the Stage", *Journal of Sound, Silence, Image and Technology*, 2020, 3, 71–88, https://raco.cat/index.php/JoSSIT/article/view/387496. Accessed 16th February 2024.
23 Tim Larkin, composer at Valve. Interview by Eulalia Febrer-Coll. 28th January 2025.
24 These were shortly interrupted during the pandemic, which caused the correlative numbers assigned to the events to not be coincidental with the year they were held. For example, TI12 was held in 2023.
25 Anders Blume, professional commentator for Valve, best known for his work with *Counter-Strike 2*. Interview by Eulalia Febrer-Coll. 9th July 2024.
26 dota2, "T16 Opening Ceremonies", *Youtube*, 2016. Available at: https://www.youtube.com/watch?v=aDpPyb97Xc0&t=704s. Accessed 15th April 2024.
27 J. Clement, "Leading MOBA Games on Streaming Platforms as of June 2024, by Average Concurrent Viewers", *Statista*, 2024. Available at: https://www.statista.com/statistics/1357157/moba-livestream-top-games-concurrent-viewers/. Accessed 2nd September 2024.

28 HoK Global Esports, “Let’s Take a Look at the Opening Ceremony of the KIC2023 Grand Finals!”, *Youtube*, 2022. Available at: https://www.youtube.com/watch?v=dOiLoEHyPqI&t=524s. Accessed 5th September 2024.

29 GEM鄧紫棋, “G.E.M.鄧紫棋【無雙的王者】LIVE版（王者榮耀2021共創之夜)”, *Youtube*, 2021. Available at: https://www.youtube.com/watch?v=0ZiksZsU6PM&list=PLKVmhoBXRGSWgK6PFJiZ7OBcTZILFwhTS. Accessed 5th September 2024.

30 ESLCounter-Strike, “ESL One Cologne 2017 | TheFatRat Opening Ceremony”, *Youtube*, 2017. Available at: https://www.youtube.com/watch?v=wCFlSZpYyBc. Accessed 5th September 2024.

31 ESL Faceit Group, “Record Attendance and Digital Engagement for ESL One Cologne 2017 Powered by Intel”, *ESL Faceit Group*, 2017. Available at: https://eslfaceitgroup.com/blog/2017/07/record-attendance-and-digital-engagement-for-esl-one-cologne-2017-powered-by-intel/. Accessed 10th October 2024.

32 Web Desk, “Linkin Park Rebrands with New Band Members, Announcer Tour and Album”, *Geo News*, 2024. Available at: https://www.geo.tv/latest/562840-linkin-park-rebrands-with-new-co-vocalist-announces-tour-and-new-album. Accessed 20th November 2024.

33 Esports Charts, “2024 League of Legends Worlds Opening Ceremony Attracts Record 4.2. Million Viewers”, *Esports Charts*, 2024. Available at: https://escharts.com/news/2024-worlds-opening-ceremony#:~:text=2024%20League%20of%20Legends%20Worlds%20opening%20ceremony%20attracts%20record%204.2%20million%20viewers,-Nov%2002%2C%202024. Accessed 20th November 2024.

34 Pedro Romero, “Linkin Park Q&A Panel | Worlds 2024 Media Day”, *Youtube*, 2024. Available at: https://youtu.be/orCSVy2RaFg?si=biCq2GQgy2jmxNN8. Accessed 20th November 2024.

35 League of Legends, “Heavy Is the Crown ft. Linkin Park (Official Music Video) | League of Legends Worlds 2024 Anthem”, *Youtube*, 2024. Available at: https://www.youtube.com/watch?v=5FrhtahQiRc. Accessed 9th December 2024. Anna Bernardo, “Linkin Park Talks about the Making of ‘Heavy Is the Crown’ for Worlds and Arcane, Plus Future Plans”, *Gosu Gamers*, 2024. Available at: https://www.gosugamers.net/features/73637-linkin-park-talks-about-the-making-of-heavy-is-the-crown-for-worlds-and-arcane-plus-future-plans. Accessed 9th December 2024.

36 Foo Zen-Wen, “Every Hidden Reference in League of Legends Worlds 2024 Anthem ‘Heavy Is the Crown’”, *Strafe*, 2024. Available at: https://www.strafe.com/news/read/every-hidden-reference-in-lol-worlds-2024-anthem/. Accessed 9th December 2024.

37 Mark Duffett, “Introduction”, in Mark Duffett (Ed.), *Popular Music Fandom: Identities, Roles and Practices*. New York: Routledge, 2015, 7.

38 Craig Chapple, “Mobile Legends Revenue Passes $500 Million as Southeast Asia Powers Explosive Growth”. Available at: https://sensortower.com/blog/mobile-legends-revenue-500-million#. Accessed 15th September 2024.

39 Esports Earnings, “Top Countries for Free Fire”, *Esports Earnings*, 2024. Available at: https://www.esportsearnings.com/games/598-free-fire/countries. Accessed 15th September 2024.

40 For example, Free Fire Esports Pakistan, “Free Fire Ramadan Championship – Final Stage | 7PM Sunday 8.05.22”, *Youtube*, 2022. Available at: https://www.youtube.com/watch?v=xIm9a_Mq8qA. Accessed 15th September 2024.

41 William Gibbons, “Open Worlds: Globalization, Localization, and Video Game Music”, in Melanie Fritsch & Tim Summers (Eds.), *The Cambridge Companion to Video Game Music*, 359–375. Cambridge: Cambridge University Press, 361.

42 Eric Tan, Music and Publishing Director for Video Games Companies, former Riot Games and Sony Music employee. Interview by Eulalia Febrer-Coll. 9th July 2024.

43 Sway, "Eric and Mat Talk All Things Roblox, SM Entertainment, Genshin Impact, HYBE, New Jeans, Fortnite etc", *Youtube*, 2024. Available at: https://www.youtube.com/watch?v=LawQhrM8F2I. Accessed 15th September 2024.
44 Febrer-Coll, "Living Like Giants".
45 Inside Riot, "Celebrating Ramadan in Wild Rift Together under the Crescent", *Riot Games*, 2024. Available at: https://www.riotgames.com/en/news/ramadan-wild-rift-event. Accessed 15th September 2024.
46 Paul McNally, "Fortnite's Lantern Fest Returns Bigger Than Ever to Celebrate Ramadan", *Readwrite*, 2024. Available at: https://readwrite.com/fortnites-lantern-fest-returns-bigger-than-ever-to-celebrate-ramadan/. Accessed 15th September 2024.
47 EGamersWorld, "GGLeague Ramadan Rivals 2024". Available at: https://egamersworld.com/counterstrike/event/gg-league-ramadan-rivals-2024-uJlyOOq1vj. Accessed 15th September 2024.
48 Daniel Muriel & Garry Crowford, "Video Gamers and (Post-)Identity", in *Video Games as Culture: Considering the Role and Importance of Video Games in Contemporary Society*. New York: Routledge, 2018, 174.
49 Ken McLeod, "Space Oddities: Aliens, Futurism and Meaning in Popular Music", *Popular Music*, 2003, 22(3), 337–355.
50 Larissa Irrizarry, "Alter Egoing: The Shifting Affects of Janelle Monáe", *Journal of the Cultural Studies Association*, 2022, 11(1). Available at: https://www.jstor.org/stable/48748050. Accessed 14th September 2024.
51 Shara Rambarran, "'Showroom Dummies': Live and Simulated Performers, Performances, and Audicenes", in *Virtual Music: Sound, Music, and Image in the Digital Era*. New York: Bloomsbury, 2021, 109–130.
52 John Richardson. *An Eye for Music: Popular Music and the Audiovisual Surreal*. New York: Oxford University Press, 2012.
53 Rambarran, "'Showroom Dummies'".
54 Toa Dunn, former Head of Music at Riot Games. Interview by Eulalia Febrer-Coll. 20th September 2023.
55 See Andra Ivănescu, "'Pop Stars': The Personas of K/DA, Transmedia Marketing, and Riot Games Music", *Persona Studies*, 2025, 10(1), 42–55; Lucia Škripcová, "Convergence in Digital Games: A Case Study of League of Legends", *Acta Ludologica*, 2022, 5(2), 86–103; Eulalia Febrer-Coll, "A Critical Review of Esports and Music from a Gender Perspective", in Annette R. Hofmann & Pascal Mamudou Camara (Eds.), *Critical Perspectives on Esports*. London: Routledge, 2024, 117–131.
56 Ivănescu, "'Pop Stars'", 46.
57 ESPN, "G-IDLE's Soyeon, Miyeon Honored to Perform K/DA – POP/STARS at Worlds 2018 | ESPN Esports", *Youtube*, 2018. Available at: https://www.youtube.com/watch?v=-WJt9xd7zbw. Accessed 29th September 2024.
58 Jean Baudrillard. *Simulacra and Simulation*. Translated by Sheila Glaser. Ann Arbor, MI: University of Michigan Press, 1994.
59 Rambarran, "'Showroom Dummies'", 152.
60 Andreas M. Kaplan & Michael Haenlein, "The Britney Spears Universe: Social Media and Viral Marketing at Its Best", *Business Horizons*, 2012, 55(1), 0–31.
61 Julie Yoonnyung Lee & Amelia Hemphill, "K-pop: The Rise of the Virtual Girl Bands", *BBC*, 2022. Available at: https://www.bbc.com/news/world-asia-63827838. Accessed 28th September 2024.
62 Alicia Stark, *Virtual Pop: Gender, Ethnicity, and Identity in Virtual Bands and Vocaloid* (Doctoral Thesis, Cardiff University, 2018).
63 K/DA Fans, "K/DA – ALL OUT behind the Scenes Full Interview", *Youtube*, 2020. Available at: https://www.youtube.com/watch?v=Hm9uxiQPFBs. Accessed 28th September 2024.

64 Genius, "K/DA "MORE" Official Lyrics & Meaning | Verified", *Youtube*, 2020. Available at: https://www.youtube.com/watch?v=j1RjqonnU7M. Accessed 28th September 2024.

65 Hypebae, "Riot Game's Virtual Pop Group K/DA is Ready to Go 'All Out'", *Hypebae*, 2020. Available at: https://hypebae.com/2020/11/kda-riot-games-debut-ep-all-out-virtual-pop-group-league-of-legends-interview-ahri-evelynn-kaisa-akali. Accessed 28th September 2024.

66 K/DA Fans, "K/DA – ALL OUT".

67 Škripcová, "Convergence in Digital Games", 98.

68 Power 4 Band, *X*, n.d. Available at: https://x.com/power4band?lang=en. Accessed 3rd October 2024.

69 Garena Free Fire, "The Kelly Show Is Here!", *Facebook*, 2024. Available at: https://fb.watch/u-N6CiP3Ao/. Accessed 3rd October 2024.

70 Garena Free Fire Global, "What's Up Free Fire S1 EP.1: Rampage | Free Fire Update", *Youtube*, 2020. Available at: https://www.youtube.com/watch?v=DWBYHj6jEvE&list=PLScKGtvu1OB9yo9MombqroTMuDLgg8sfQ&index=26. Accessed 10th October 2024.

71 Garena Free Fire Global, "What's Up Free Fire S1 EP.1: Rampage | Free Fire Update", minute 0:32.

72 FreeFireIndiaOfficial, "Kelly's Musical Performance: A Captivating Melody | Free Fire MAX", *Youtube*, 2024. Available at: https://youtube.com/shorts/s2zal5ZkMq8?si=hYGv-UWHfTXf-Joz. Accessed 10th October 2024.

73 We Are Collider, "Arcane Netflix Global Experiential Launch", *Campaign Experience Award*, n.d. Available at: https://www.campaignexperienceawards.com/finalists/arcane-netflix-global-experiential-launch-d0004. Accessed 3rd October 2024.

74 Cande Sánchez-Olmos & Eduardo Viñuela, "Transmedia Storytelling, Music and Videogames: The Case of Los Ríos de Alice by Vetusta Morla and Delirium Studios", *Icono14*, 2023, 17(1), 60–82.

75 Henry Jenkins, "Searching for the Origami Unicorn: *The Matrix* and Transmedia Storytelling", in *Convergence Culture: Where Old and New Media Collide*, 92. New York: New York University Press, 2006.

76 Škripcová, "Convergence in Digital Games", 98.

77 Brittany Vicent, "10 'League of Legends' Easter Eggs from 'Arcane' Season 1", *Tudum by Netflix*, 2022. Available at: https://www.netflix.com/tudum/articles/arcane-season-1-league-of-legends-easter-eggs. Accessed 7th October 2024.

78 Stream Wars, "Making of ARCANE – Best of behind the Scenes, League of Legends, Netflix Original Series (2021)", *Youtube*, 2021. Available at: https://www.youtube.com/watch?v=7rAbZUZCnL8. Accessed 14th April 2023.

79 League of Legends, "Worlds 2021 Show Open Presented by Mastercard: Imagine Dragons, JID, Denzel Curry, Bea Miller, PVRIS", *Youtube*, 2021. Available at: https://www.youtube.com/watch?v=1OzoFq4Q3_c. Accessed 15th October 2024.

80 See Febrer-Coll, "'Everybody Wants to Be My Enemy': Popular Music and Transmediality in Arcane", 68–86.

81 Rama's Screen, "Interview: Composer Dino Meneghin Talks Netflix DOTA: DRAGON'S BLOOD Synthesizer Score", *Youtube*, 2021. Available at: https://www.youtube.com/watch?v=wh-b9sQd2rU. Accessed 14th October 2024.

82 See Juan Sebastián Díaz Gasca, "Music Beyond Gameplay: Motivators in the Consumption of Videogame Soundtracks" (Doctoral Thesis, Griffith University, 2015). Available at: https://research-repository.griffith.edu.au/bitstream/handle/10072/367483/Diaz%20Gasca_2015_02Thesis.pdf?sequence=1. Accessed 15th October 2024.

83 The Deadline Team, "Next-Gen Xbox One Unveiled with Content Including Spielberg-Produced 'Halo' Series", *Deadline*, 2013. Available at: https://deadline.com/2013/05/xbox-one-unveiled-halo-series-steven-spielberg-505318/. Accessed 15th October 2024.

84 Becky O'Brien, "Bringing the Video Game to Life: Talking with Composer Sean Callery about 'Halo'", *Cinelinx*. Available at: https://www.cinelinx.com/uncategorized/bringing-the-video-game-to-life-talking-with-composer-sean-callery-about-halo/. Accessed 15th October 2024.

85 BearMcCreary_Official, "Replying to @Hi @Sparks and Shadows", *TikTok*, 2024. Available at: https://www.tiktok.com/@bearmccreary_official/video/7335138889608203563. Accessed 15th October 2024.

86 See Jennifer Maas, "Which Video Games Should Streamers Adapt? New Data Proposes Netflix 'Fortnite' Series, 'God of War' at Apple Over Amazon and More (EXCLUSIVE)", *Variety*, 2023. Available at: https://variety.com/lists/video-game-tv-series-ideas-study/top-cross-visitation-for-peacock/. Accessed 15th October 2024.

87 IFPI, "Reports & Resources".

88 Juan Tejada, Pablo Municio, & Daniel Fraile, *League of Legends* fans. Interviews by Eulalia Febrer-Coll, 3rd and 4th September 2020; Maye MacSwiney, *Riot Games* Marketing Communications Manager, Interview by Eulalia Febrer-Coll 9th September 2020.

REFERENCES

Akash & Kim, Joseph. "Free Fire's Billion Free Downloads", *Game Makers,* 2024. Available at: https://www.gamemakers.com/p/free-fires-billion-free-downloads. Accessed 26th August 2024.

Baudrillard, Jean. *Simulacra and Simulation*. Translated by Sheila Glaser. Ann Arbor: University of Michigan Press, 1994.

BearMcCreary_Official. "Replying to @Hi @Sparks and Shadows", *TikTok,* 2024. Available at: https://www.tiktok.com/@bearmccreary_official/video/7335138889608203563. Accessed 15th October 2024.

Benjamin, Jeff. "'League of Legends' Girl Group Earns Madison Beer, (G)I-DLE & Jaire Burns No.1 on World Digital Song Sales Chart", *Billboard,* 2018. Available at: https://www.billboard.com/pro/kda-pop-stars-madison-beer-gidle-jaira-burns-no-1-world-digital-songs-league-of-legends/. Accessed 12th August 2024.

Bernardo, Anna. "Linkin Park Talks about the Making of 'Heavy Is the Crown' for Worlds and Arcane, Plus Future Plans", *Gosu Gamers,* 2024. Available at: https://www.gosugamers.net/features/73637-linkin-park-talks-about-the-making-of-heavy-is-the-crown-for-worlds-and-arcane-plus-future-plans. Accessed 9th December 2024.

Chapple, Craig. "Mobile Legends Revenue Passes $500 Million as Southeast Asia Powers Explosive Growth". Available at: https://sensortower.com/blog/mobile-legends-revenue-500-million. Accessed 15th September 2024.

Clement, Jessica. "Leading MOBA Games on Streaming Platforms as of June 2024, by Average Concurrent Viewers", *Statista,* 2024. Available at: https://www.statista.com/statistics/1357157/moba-livestream-top-games-concurrent-viewers/. Accessed 2nd September 2024.

Crecente, Brian. "League of Legends Is Now 10 Years Old. This Is the story of Its Birth", *The Washington Post*, 27th October 2019. Available at: https://www.washingtonpost.com/video-games/2019/10/27/league-legends-is-now-years-old-this-is-story-its-birth/. Accessed 30th August 2024.

Daniels, Tom. "Singapore Showcase: Finding the Rhythm with Esports and Music", *Esports Insider,* 2023. Available at: https://esportsinsider.com/2023/06/esports-and-music. Accessed 10th August 2024.

Dannelly, David. "The Origin of the MOBA: Aeon of Strife and Defense of the Ancients", *David Dannelly: Faculty, Technical Game Designer & 3D*, 2019. Available at: https://daviddannelly.com/blog/zjYm/the-origin-of-the-moba-aeon-of-strife-and-defen%20se-of-the-ancients. Accessed 30th August 2024.

Díaz Gasca, Juan Sebastián. "Music Beyond Gameplay: Motivators in the Consumption of Videogame Soundtracks" (Doctoral Thesis). Griffith University, 2015. Available at: https://research-repository.griffith.edu.au/bitstream/handle/10072/367483/Diaz%20Gasca_2015_02Thesis.pdf?sequence=1. Accessed 15th October 2024.

dota2. "T16 Opening Ceremonies", *Youtube,* 2016. Available at: https://www.youtube.com/watch?v=aDpPyb97Xc0&t=704s. Accessed 15th April 2024.

Duffett, Mark. "Introduction", in Mark Duffett (Ed.), *Popular Music Fandom: Identities, Roles and Practices,* 7. New York: Routledge, 2015.

EGamersWorld. "GG League Ramadan Rivals 2024". Available at: https://egamersworld.com/counterstrike/event/gg-league-ramadan-rivals-2024-uJlyOOq1vj. Accessed 15th September 2024.

ESLCounter-Strike. "ESL One Cologne 2017 | TheFatRat Opening Ceremony", *Youtube,* 2017. Available at: https://www.youtube.com/watch?v=wCFlSZpYyBc. Accessed 5th September 2024.

ESL Faceit Group. "Record Attendance and Digital Engagement for ESL One Cologne 2017 Powered by Intel", *ESL Faceit Group,* 2017. Available at: https://eslfaceitgroup.com/blog/2017/07/record-attendance-and-digital-engagement-for-esl-one-cologne-2017-powered-by-intel/. Accessed 10th October 2024.

ESPN. "G-IDLE's Soyeon, Miyeon Honored to Perform K/DA – POP/STARS at Worlds 2018 | ESPN Esports", *Youtube,* 2018. Available at: https://www.youtube.com/watch?v=-WJt9x-d7zbw. Accessed 29th September 2024.

Esports Charts. "2024 League of Legends Worlds Opening Ceremony Attracts Record 4.2. Million Viewers", *Esports Charts,* 2024. Available at: https://escharts.com/news/2024-worlds-opening-ceremony#:~:text=2024%20League%20of%20Legends%20Worlds%20opening%20ceremony%20attracts%20record%204.2%20million%20viewers,-Nov%2002%2C%202024. Accessed 20th November 2024.

Esports Earnings. "Top Countries for Free Fire", *Esports Earnings,* 2024. Available at: https://www.esportsearnings.com/games/598-free-fire/countries. Accessed 15th September 2024.

Esports Insider. "Sidney Fohrman & Toa Dunn on Law, Music & Esports Converging | ESI Focus: Law in Esports #2", *Youtube,* 2021. Available at: https://www.youtube.com/watch?v=rosZiGzS7t8. Accessed 14th August 2024.

Febrer-Coll, Eulalia. "'Everybody Wants to Be My Enemy': Popular Music and Transmediality in Arcane", *SeriArte: Revista científica de series televisivas y arte audiovisual,* 2023, 4(1), 68–86. Available at: https://helvia.uco.es/bitstream/handle/10396/26505/seriarte_4_5.pdf?sequence=1&isAllowed=y. Accessed 10th August 2024.

Febrer-Coll, Eulalia. "A Critical Review of Esports and Music from a Gender Perspective", in Annette R. Hofmann & Pascal Mamudou Camara (Eds.), *Critical Perspectives on Esports,* 117–131. London: Routledge, 2024.

Febrer-Coll, Eulalia. "Living Like Giants: 'League of Legends'from the Screen to the Stage", *Journal of Sound, Silence, Image and Technology,* 2020, 3, 71–88, https://raco.cat/index.php/JoSSIT/article/view/387496. Accessed 16th February 2024.

Free Fire Esports Pakistan. "Free Fire Ramadan Championship – Final Stage | 7PM Sunday 8.05.22", *Youtube*, 2022. Available at: https://www.youtube.com/watch?v=xIm9a_Mq8qA. Accessed 15th September 2024.

FreeFireIndiaOfficial. "Kelly's Musical Performance: A Captivating Melody | Free Fire MAX", *Youtube,* 2024. Available at: https://youtube.com/shorts/s2zal5ZkMq8?si=hYGv-UWHfTXf-Joz. Accessed 10th October 2024.

Frith, Simon. "Live Music", in John Shepherd & Kyle Devine (Eds.), *The Routledge Reader on the Sociology of Music,* 237. New York: Routledge, 2015.

Garena Free Fire. "The Kelly Show Is Here!", *Facebook,* 2024. Available at: https://fb.watch/u-N6CiP3Ao/. Accessed 3rd October 2024.

Garena Free Fire Global. "What's Up Free Fire S1 EP.1: Rampage | Free Fire Update, *Youtube,* 2020. Available at: https://www.youtube.com/watch?v=DWBYHj6jEvE&list=PLScKGtvu1OB9yo9MombqroTMuDLgg8sfQ&index=26. Accessed 10th October 2024.

GEM鄧紫棋. "G.E.M.鄧紫棋【無雙的王者】LIVE版 （ 王者榮耀2021共創之夜)", *Youtube,* 2021. Available at: https://www.youtube.com/watch?v=0ZiksZsU6PM&list=PLKVmhoBXRGSWgK6PFJiZ7OBcTZILFwhTS. Accessed 5th September 2024.

Genius. "K/DA "MORE" Official Lyrics & Meaning | Verified", *Youtube,* 2020. Available at: https://www.youtube.com/watch?v=j1RjqonnU7M. Accessed 28th September 2024.

Gibbons, William. "Open Worlds: Globalization, Localization, and Video Game Music", in Melanie Fritsch & Tim Summers (Eds.), *The Cambridge Companion to Video Game Music,* 359–375, 361. Cambridge: Cambridge University Press.

Griffiths, Emma. "The Convergence of Music & Esports: Industry Pros Weigh in on Opportunities, Trends & What's in Store for the Future (Part 1)", *Synchtank,* 2019. Available at: https://www.synchtank.com/blog/the-convergence-of-music-esports-industry-pros-weigh-in-on-opportunities-trends-whats-in-store-for-the-future-part-1/. Accessed 21st August 2024.

HoK Global Esports. "Let's Take a Look at the Opening Ceremony of the KIC2023 Grand Finals!", *Youtube,* 2022. Available at: https://www.youtube.com/watch?v=dOiLoEHyPqI&t=524s. Accessed 5th September 2024.

Hypebae. "Riot Game's Virtual Pop Group K/DA is Ready to Go 'All Out'", *Hypebae,* 2020. Available at: https://hypebae.com/2020/11/kda-riot-games-debut-ep-all-out-virtual-pop-group-league-of-legends-interview-ahri-evelynn-kaisa-akali. Accessed 28th September 2024.

IFPI. "Reports & Resources", n.d. Available at: https://www.ifpi.org/resources/. Accessed 26th August 2024.

Inside Riot. "Celebrating Ramadan in Wild Rift Together under the Crescent", *Riot Games*, 2024. Available at: https://www.riotgames.com/en/news/ramadan-wild-rift-event. Accessed 15th September 2024.

Irrizarry, Larissa. "Alter Egoing: The Shifting Affects of Janelle Monáe", *Journal of the Cultural Studies Association,* 2022, 11(1). Available at: https://www.jstor.org/stable/48748050. Accessed 14th September 2024.

Ivănescu, Andra. "'Pop Stars': The Personas of K/DA, Transmedia Marketing, and Riot Games Music", *Persona Studies*, 2025, 10(1), 42–55.

Jenkins, Henry. "Searching for the Origami Unicorn: *The Matrix* and Transmedia Storytelling" in *Convergence Culture: Where Old and New Media Collide,* 92. New York: New York University Press, 2006.

Kaplan, Andreas M. & Haenlein, Michael. "The Britney Spears Universe: Social Media and Viral Marketing at Its Best", *Business Horizons,* 2012, 55(1), 0–31.

K/DA Fans. "K/DA – ALL OUT Behind the Scenes Full Interview", *Youtube,* 2020. Available at: https://www.youtube.com/watch?v=Hm9uxiQPFBs. Accessed 28th September 2024.

League of Legends. "Heavy Is the Crown ft. Linkin Park (Official Music Video) | League of Legends Worlds 2024 Anthem", *Youtube,* 2024. Available at: https://www.youtube.com/watch?v=5FrhtahQiRc. Accessed 9th December 2024.

League of Legends. "Worlds 2021 Show Open Presented by Mastercard: Imagine Dragons, JID, Denzel Curry, Bea Miller, PVRIS", *Youtube*, 2021. Available at: https://www.youtube.com/watch?v=1OzoFq4Q3_c. Accessed 15th October 2024.

Lee, Julie Yoonnyung & Hemphill, Amelia. "K-pop: The Rise of the Virtual Girl Bands", *BBC,* 2022. Available at: https://www.bbc.com/news/world-asia-63827838. Accessed 28th September 2024.

Maas, Jennifer. "Which Video Games Should Streamers Adapt? New Data Proposes Netflix 'Fortnite' Series, 'God of War' at Apple Over Amazon and More (EXCLUSIVE)", *Variety*, 2023. Available at: https://variety.com/lists/video-game-tv-series-ideas-study/top-cross-visitation-for-peacock/. Accessed 15th October 2024.

McLeod, Ken. "Space Oddities: Aliens, Futurism and Meaning in Popular Music", *Popular Music*, 2003, 22(3), 337–355.

McNally, Paul. "Fortnite's Lantern Fest Returns Bigger Than Ever to Celebrate Ramadan", *Readwrite*, 2024. Available at: https://readwrite.com/fortnites-lantern-fest-returns-bigger-than-ever-to-celebrate-ramadan/. Accessed 15th September 2024.

Muriel, Daniel & Crowford, Garry. "Video Gamers and (Post-)Identity", in Muriel, Daniel & Crowford, Garry (Ed.), *Video Games as Culture: Considering the Role and Importance of Video Games in Contemporary Society*, 174. New York: Routledge, 2018.

O'Brien, Becky. "Bringing the Video Game to Life: Talking with Composer Sean Callery about 'Halo'", *Cinelinx*. Available at: https://www.cinelinx.com/uncategorized/bringing-the-video-game-to-life-talking-with-composer-sean-callery-about-halo/. Accessed 15th October 2024.

Power 4 Band, *X*, n.d. Available at: https://x.com/power4band?lang=en. Accessed 3rd October 2024.

Rama's Screen. "Interview: Composer Dino Meneghin Talks Netflix DOTA: DRAGON'S BLOOD Synthesizer Score", *Youtube*, 2021. Available at: https://www.youtube.com/watch?v=wh-b9sQd2rU. Accessed 14th October 2024.

Rambarran, Shara. "'Showroom Dummies': Live and Simulated Performers, Performances, and Audicenes", in Rambarran, Shara (Ed.), *Virtual Music: Sound, Music, and Image in the Digital Era*, 109–130. New York: Bloomsbury, 2021.

Richardson, John. *An Eye for Music: Popular Music and the Audiovisual Surreal*. New York: Oxford University Press, 2012.

Romero, Pedro. "Linkin Park Q&A Panel | Worlds 2024 Media Day", *Youtube*, 2024. Available at: https://youtu.be/orCSVy2RaFg?si=biCq2GQgy2jmxNN8. Accessed 20th November 2024.

Sánchez-Olmos, Cande & Viñuela, Eduardo. "Transmedia Storytelling, Music and Videogames: The Case of Los Ríos de Alice by Vetusta Morla and Delirium Studios", *Icono14*, 2023, 17(1), 60–82.

Sborgi Lawson, Francesca R. "Music in Ritual and Ritual in Music: A Virtual Viewer's Perceptions about Liminality, Functionality, and Mediatization in the Opening Ceremony of the 2008 Beijing Olympic Games", *Asian Music*, 2011, 42(2), 3–18.

Škripcová, Lucia. "Convergence in Digital Games: A Case Study of League of Legends", *Acta Ludologica*, 2022, 5(2), 86–103.

Stark, Alicia. *Virtual Pop: Gender, Ethnicity, and Identity in Virtual Bands and Vocaloid* (Doctoral Thesis). Cardiff: Cardiff University, 2018.

Stream Wars. "Making of ARCANE – Best of Behind the Scenes, League of Legends, Netflix Original Series (2021)", *Youtube*, 2021. Available at: https://www.youtube.com/watch?v=7rAbZUZCnL8. Accessed 14th April 2023.

Sway. "Eric and Mat talk all things Roblox, SM Entertainment, Genshin Impact, HYBE, New Jeans, Fortnite etc", *Youtube*, 2024. Available at: https://www.youtube.com/watch?v=LawQhrM8F2I. Accessed 15th September 2024.

The Deadline Team. "Next-Gen Xbox One Unveiled with Content Including Spielberg-Produced 'Halo' Series", *Deadline*, 2013. Available at: https://deadline.com/2013/05/xbox-one-unveiled-halo-series-steven-spielberg-505318/. Accessed 15th October 2024.

The Elden Dragon is an NPC in *League of Legends*, a late-game neutral monster that spawns after a series of events, providing a *buff* with amplified damage and an execution effect to the team who slays it.

The International Gaming Syndicate (IGS) began hosting *DotA* competitions in 2004. *DotA 2* was incorporated into the esports scene in 2011, before the game's official launch in 2013. See Felix Bammel, *The History of Competitive DotA*. Amazon, 2022.

Till, Rupert. *Pop Cult: Religion and Popular Music.* London and New York: Bloomsbury, 2010.
Valderrama Santomé, Mónica & Crespo-Pereira, Verónica. "Festivales de música y marketing experiencial: efectos para marca, organizador y espectador", *ADResearch ESIC International Journal of Communication Research,* 2021, 26(26), 64.
Van Bauwel, Sofie & Krijnen, Tonny. "Let's Get Loud: Intersectionally Studying the Super Bowl's Halftime Show", *Media and Communication,* 2021, 9(3), 209–217.
Vicent, Brittany. "10 'League of Legends' Easter Eggs from 'Arcane' Season 1", *Tudum by Netflix,* 2022. Available at: https://www.netflix.com/tudum/articles/arcane-season-1-league-of-legends-easter-eggs. Accessed 7th October 2024.
We Are Collider. "Arcane Netflix Global Experiential Launch", *Campaign Experience Award,* n.d. Available at: https://www.campaignexperienceawards.com/finalists/arcane-netflix-global-experiential-launch-d0004. Accessed 3rd October 2024.
Web Desk. "Linkin Park Rebrands with New Band Members, Announcer Tour and Album", *Geo News,* 2024. Available at: https://www.geo.tv/latest/562840-linkin-park-rebrands-with-new-co-vocalist-announces-tour-and-new-album. Accessed 20th November 2024.
Zen-Wen, Foo. "Every Hidden Reference in League of Legends Worlds 2024 Anthem 'Heavy is the Crown'", *Strafe,* 2024. Available at: https://www.strafe.com/news/read/every-hidden-reference-in-lol-worlds-2024-anthem/. Accessed 9th December 2024.

Esports Music Fandom

6

Esports are inherently social, as they depend on their public to sustain the presence of games, players, and competitions, for which their lore, music, and art are key forms of engagement. The success of the titles that give form to esports is, therefore, strongly reliant on those who primarily inform and socialize them: the fans. The different paths for exploiting the music behind each title are intermingled with the daily practices of users who interact with them, and contribute to the return on the investment of brands in events, promotions, and the launching of commodifiable items. As such, the alternative routes for exchanging, reimagining, and even transgressing official guidelines are placed in the hands of the public—an idea that many companies have grasped, and have started incorporating as part of their marketing strategies.

Music User-Generated Content (UGC) derived from the interaction and engagement with games, has become essential in constructing esports as a global phenomenon, moving beyond brand and official products into alternative contributions. In other words, fan-made initiatives show the community's involvement outside of game ownership, mainly through the continuous reproduction, creation, and reappropriation of audiovisual content. This is done in diverse ways, including "remixes, adaptations, mashups and all kinds of musical creativity,"[1] which allows fans to bring the stories, characters, and game agents of their choice closer to their daily lives, expectations, and experiences. The success of these contributions on social media can be measured by the impact of *influencers*, *YouTubers*, and other public personalities, who have gained recognition and professionalized their activity by sharing video games-based content, as well as through the creative content being uploaded daily on different platforms.

In discussing fandom theory, Jenkins' work[2] must be first mentioned, as it laid the basis for the understanding of fandom as a media-bound phenomenon, developed around convergence, franchising, and the implication of "more than simply a technological shift," which "alters the logic by which media industries operate and by which media consumers process news and entertainment."[3] Despite his theory being first rooted around pre-internet initiatives,[4] many authors have taken it as a compass for their research—also in music.[5] In esports, Jarrett took the author's contributions and incorporated them into the analysis of the global competitive gaming scene:

> Esports is an exemplar of trends in the digital media landscape. When analyzing fandom specifically, it is impossible to overlook esports' background in online-enabled and often non-monetary fan culture. This participatory background is crucial to understanding the business models, co-creative relations, and the multifaceted but fundamentally playful appeal of esports.

DOI: 10.1201/9781032625362-7

In this way, the effect of fandom on the media industry has been responsible for structural changes that directly affect esports. With them, fan-users have moved "from the margins to become a central part of everyday media use and in esports."[6] This has translated into initiatives vouching for the direct participation of fans, from community playlists—e.g., the *League of Legend*'s Riot Games Community Covers Playlist—[7]to on-stage performances—e.g., those featured in contests at BlizzCon.[8] Participatory culture is, as argued by Jarrett, at the very foundation of esports and, as such, takes a strong part in the sharing, reproducing and producing of music around them.

The democratizing model promoted by social media has contributed to the appearance of secondary markets and scenes in which prosumers take a key role in dynamizing the communities around specific titles. Platforms such as YouTube, Deezer, Spotify, Instagram, etc., have allowed fans to extend their options to approach their favorite games and artists, and extend their daily experience around specific games, while these have contributed to the creation of new agents in media and entertainment. This professionalization has implied a progressive separation in UGC content between amateur and professional fans, as the latter have found a lucrative activity in performing, reproducing, and interacting with video game music.

In recent years, the esports and overall gaming industries have increased their reliance on these channels and individuals, as they contribute to informing and expanding their overall lore—e.g., esports teams have incorporated gaming influencers as active brand representatives. With this, they have incorporated some of the trends and suggestions offered by fans into their corporate strategies, or directly as commodifiable products.

This idea is closely linked to the concept of *brandom*, described by Matthew Guschwan in the context of traditional sport,[9] as "the pseudo-fan culture engineered by brand managers eager to cultivate consumer labor and loyalty while preempting the possibility of resistance that participatory fan culture promises."[10] In other words, it implies the mediation of brands in generating "preapproved" fan content, that is in line with the corporate image set for the game. Nevertheless, these globalized tendencies afforded by the internet have also implied a growing need for taking media into account, considering the popularity of streaming platforms—live or not—for sharing and reproducing content. This case contributed to many developers establishing well-defined rules for their communities, despite their impossibility of accessing and reviewing all the content generated around their brands.

For this same reason, this chapter aims to review the trends in fan-created music content related to esports. Acknowledging the vast number of contributions shared online, it does not aim to tackle them all but rather to review their role and significance in the current landscape.

EARLY FAN INITIATIVES

It is hard to establish when the first initiatives of fan content around esports' music—or video games that later became esports—started being uploaded to the internet. The development of streaming platforms was, however, crucial to the elaboration and dissemination of fan content: covers, parodies, and frag movies were posted on platforms such as YouTube as early as 2006, mostly including montages that superposed popular music to footage from the game. Although some titles were already popular at this time, it can be argued that other forms of music content had been uploaded on more rudimental websites, including peer-to-peer networks, personal websites, and forums.[11]

Some of the earlier expressions including music were captured in frag movies, like those produced around *Counter-Strike*—whose first official esports competition was held in 2001, a year after the release of *Counter-Strike 1.0*.[12] Although previous titles like *Frag or Die* (2000) or *Counter Strike Revolution* (2002) served as an inspiration to the online community, it was frag series like *Pure Pwnage* which first introduced themed music to open each chapter, e.g., with *Teh Pwnerer Theme*.[13] This was a 12-second intro constructed on a simple drum-box base, which opened with an off voice calling out "I am the pwnage, bitches," and served to set the mood for the series.

Other initiatives such as *The Leet World*,[14] created by Smooth Few Films, that parodied reality TV shows by placing *Counter-Strike* characters in a house together and having them interact, also counted with their own musical intro. In this case, each chapter opened with a sitcom-like theme that introduced each part, accompanied by a metal soundtrack sung over by a male voice. The creators of the series combined in-game footage with original voice acting, and sporadically included music featuring gun sounds within the episodes.

However, these were not isolated initiatives. Before 2010, they coexisted with other more specific music content, such as parodies—e.g., the *AWP Song*—remixes—e.g., headshot remixes—and custom soundtracks to go with other streamed series, which attests to the immediate popularity of the game among online communities.

Other early competitive games, such as *Starcraft* or the original *DotA*, received similar attention from fans who reimagined their characters, created parodies around the games, or simply used them as inspiration for other original content. An example of this is the *Starcraft*-inspired series *Pimpest Plays*, which featured music tracks to enhance the viewing experience, mostly rooted in metal subgenres—e.g., *Whisper* from Evanescence or *False News Travel Fast* by Sonata Artica.[15] These were superposed to contribute to the gameplay in the videos, and it can be argued that they later informed the sonic identity of the game.

Many fans of popular titles followed these trends, producing original songs since the early 21st century. As reviewing each popular title at the beginning of the decade is out of scope, it is only pertinent to note a few examples, including artists from around the globe, as depicted in Table 6.1. Among the many available, these can be seen as preliminary forms of media convergence involving competitive games, which have maintained continuity to this day.

Other titles released during and immediately after this period had fans following similar initiatives, continuing to engage in music content as a form of interacting with peers and establishing communities to discuss, debate, and reimagine the unfolding of their favorite stories. A quick online search can provide examples around more recent titles such as *Fortnite*, *Valorant*, or *Mobile Legends: Bang Bang*, among others, whose communities have actively participated in expanding their online presence through their own interpretations.

TABLE 6.1 Original Songs Themed around Esports Games

GAME	*SONG TITLE*	*AUTHOR ON YOUTUBE*	*YEAR*
Counter-Strike	OK Let's Go	DJ Dairock	2010
	Strike Down	Rockit Music	2016
	Counter-Strike Rap Battle	Dan Bull & boyinaband	2014
DotA 2	Vi sitter i Ventrilo och spelar DotA	Basshunter	2006
	Dota o Ako	Aikee and Vanessa	2013
	Mundo is a Dr. too	Falconshield	2011
League of Legends	The Legend	Yordles Band	2013
	Pug Life	TFNerds	2012
	League of Legends Rap	Dan Bull	2012
Starcraft II	I Wanna Be A Baneling	HuskyStarcraft & Kurt Hugo Schneider	2012
	Terran Up the Night	Level 80 Elite Tauren Chieftain	2010
	Ghost Assassin	Maduk feat. Veela	2012
Rainbow Six Siege	Rainbows in the Dark	NerdOut!	2015
	Knock Knock	JT Music	2017
	Into the Breach	Defmatch	2015

Among the tendencies that have coexisted in the past two decades music-wise, it is especially pertinent to distinguish between two forms of creative content: parody songs using preexisting popular music, and original music content. These two do not only mark two concurrent directions, but offer two different approaches to music content: one focused on humor, sarcasm, and the regulation of conflicts in the gaming community, and the other centered on creating original pieces that add to the experience of the games from an aesthetically and rhetorically elaborate standpoint.

Parody Songs feat. Popular Hits

Since early on, parody songs using pop culture hits became—and continue to be—a popular trend to appeal to other players, as they serve to allude to common gaming problems, intersubjective knowledge created in and around the game, or amusing associations between in-game scenarios and real life, from a humorous perspective. Among the numerous examples regarding the substitution of popular soundtracks with new lyrics, a good one is the initiative by PlentaKill,[16] a YouTube channel dedicated to creating *League of Legends* parody songs of well-known popular pieces, tailored to the game's community. Their first video, *My Blight*, was published in 2014 featuring Linkin Park's *In the End*, and accumulated more than 1.3 million visits in ten years. Its success was

TABLE 6.2 *The Lazy Song* by Bruno Mars vresus *Lazy Karthus* by Plentakill

THE LAZY SONG	*LAZY KARTHUS*
Today I don't feel like doing anything, I just wanna lay in my bed. Don't feel like picking up my phone, So leave a message at the tone.	This game I don't feel like doing anything, I'm just gonna sit in my base. Don't feel like using all my skills, So I'll just R to get my kills.

followed by other prosperous pieces such as *The Lux* (based on Ylvis' *The Fox*), *Gragas Style* (based on PSY's *Gagnam Style*), or *Lazy Karthus* (based on Bruno Mars' *The Lazy Song*) (Table 6.2).

The lyrics in these songs do not only appeal to the gaming capital of the players,[17] but to their overall popular-culture capital, as it creates a point of convergence in the minds of listeners who put together two separate experiences, to their own amusement.

Instalok was created in 2013 around the same premise,[18] based on the same game. The channel featured songs such as *AP Shaco Pentakill* (based on PSY's *Gentelman*), or *We Are Supports* (based on Lady Gaga's *Applause*), until they ceased their activity in 2021. Other games like *DotA 2* have had channels such as Refresher Parodies[19] do the same in songs like *Timbersaw* (a parody of Pitbull and Kesha's *Timber*), or *The Comeback* (based on Swedish House Mafia's *Don't You Worry Child*); *Call of Duty* has had Poofesure use *Hot Problems* by Double Take, or *Camping and I know it* by FlawedWorld based on LMFO's *I'm sexy and I know it*; to name just a few.

This tendency was also reproduced in other languages to appeal to players in specific geographies. For instance, *Starcraft* became especially popular in South Korea after its release in 1998, which generated a similar dynamic in promoting music content among fans. Some examples of these songs included *마린 일병 구하기* (*Save Private Marine*) by the rap group Honey Family, or a version of the *Nyang Cat* song[20] *스타크래프트1 고양시 패러디 (냥냥송)* (*StarCraft 1 Goyang City Parody (Meow Meow Song)*), both of which are examples of the convergence of internet culture, music, and gaming.

In these cases, the songs often afford a connection between popular music and gaming that is not aimed at the promotion of the other industry per se, but that withholds a social function that, it can be argued, is based on the critique of game dynamics, design, or debates with other members of the community. These, furthermore, can be argued to regulate tensions among players, as they offer a space to reflect on shared experience and to challenge the *status quo* of the game developers, similarly to traditional leisure representations in other contexts of popular culture.[21]

Original Songs by Fans

The success of these initiatives encouraged the composition of original songs around different games, which contributed to professionalizing the work of now music streamers and influencers. Furthermore, these offered a standpoint for music creators to demonstrate their creative abilities and engage with diverse communities, to which they already belonged as prosumers.

Original songs usually deal with the lore, characters, or storyworlds of games, and they tend to be approached from a more artistic perspective than their parody counterparts. Similarly to the previous case, they have been developed around most games on the market, composed in different languages, and around diverse styles. Examples of these include pieces like *EZ4ENCE* by The Verkkars,[22] which became an anthem for the Finnish esports *Counter-Strike* organization ENCE;[23] or *FAKER*, a tribute song for the most popular *League of Legends*' player around the world, Lee Sang-Hyeok "Faker."[24] Nevertheless, most songs do not appeal directly to the competitive side of the games, but to the titles themselves or their related products.

An interesting case for analysis is Matthew Moreland's, better known as ChewieCatt, whose music production has been centered around video games since 2018.[25] The artist has gained around one million followers on YouTube since the beginning of his journey, and has contributed to the music landscape of esports games such as *Call of Duty*, *Rocket League*, and—more extensively—*Fortnite*. Some of his most-watched videos include *Reality* (based on *Fortnite*'s Chapter 2 Season 6), *The Sea* (in reference to *Fortnite*'s Chapter 2 Season 3), or *Shadow of Death* (composed for *Apex Legends* Season 4).

Despite his focus on games and other audiovisual media, Moreland underlines his wish to approach audiences beyond specific titles, and create relatable content for listeners who are not necessarily gamers:

> I try to make, for the most part, every song sound like if someone who has no interest in video games or has no interest in that certain video game in particular, that they can still listen to it and either one, find relatability back to themselves or they can just be like, "oh, this is a really cool song." (...) So I like to make lyrics vague if I can, rather than going into very specific things about the game, because I like it to appeal to a wider range of people that might not like that specific topic or engage in that topic.[26]

The success of his YouTube channel allowed him to launch an independent career with non-gaming or non-*nerdcore* content,[27] which highlights the relevance of convergent products to gain visibility across media for artists. Other creators that have produced original music around esports games include The Living Tombstone, or JT, despite most of their production not being video game-exclusive. Creators such as Derivakat have, however, sporadically contributed to the esports scene in collaboration with official teams. For instance, in 2024, the artist collaborated with team Fnatic and professional player Booster for a seasonal anthem,[28] evidencing the impact of fan production on video games and esports at a corporate level, as talent is progressively incorporated as part of their promotional strategies.

It is also interesting to point out smaller initiatives like musician Marcus Skeen's, which have stood out occasionally for their direct involvement with video game fandom—despite these *one-hit wonders* being harder to find. His contribution was presented as an alternative ego for the game character Aphelios, the imagined main composer for Riot Games' virtual K-pop band HEARSTEEL, which received attention for the already existing fanbase of the band. The artist gave voice to the champion by launching the song *Lost in Silence*, which created momentum in the fan community and was covered by other artists on the platform.[29] To this, followed others like *Polaris* or

Slowburn, which have continued to be popular online, which attest to the fans' interest in engaging with content beyond official launches.

In sum, it can be argued that the continuous stream of creative content annexed to and surrounding esports contributes to the maintenance of the fan scene that scaffolds the whole ecosystem, whether it is envisioned as humorous or serious content. As fan content is inherently positive despite their potential to become subversive—especially in parodies or satiric pieces—it has been progressively acknowledged and incorporated into the marketing strategies of different developers, and will likely continue to hold a strong presence in the international gaming scene.

PLAYLISTS FOR AND BY FANS

The commodification of video game soundtracks, including esports games, has been essential for different companies' diffusion of game music. To this day, game developers and publishers frequently release playlists including official soundtracks as a way to extend the reach and life of their products beyond videoludic content, and upload it on aggregators such as Spotify, Deezer, or Apple Music. The examples are wide and varied: Valve, Epic Games, Supercell, as well as other gaming brands, periodically provide their new releases on these platforms, which allows them to reach thousands of monthly listeners—e.g., the official playlist for *Valorant*, counts with more than two and a half monthly million listeners on Spotify.[30] These contribute to displaying both original soundtracks and those created in collaboration with popular music artists, who also benefit from sharing their joint work.

As described by Díaz Gasca, the metaludical consumption of game soundtracks has been related to "motivators of gameplay experience, sociocultural interactions, and marketing imperatives,"[31] all of which can be applied to esports consumers. The promotion of these music products is, however, not always directed by gaming or esports companies, but rather by the hands of fans who, thanks to the growing expansion of internet options, engage with the music of their favorite titles including them in their own curated lists.

Despite these facilitations, the collaborations between fans and official brands are not new. As described by Ryan Thompson, the model was already set by OC ReMix, which was "amongst the first sites in game audio fandom to host music using the MP3 file format,"[32] which Capcom approached to license some of the uploaded arrangements. This partnership, he argues, "continues to serve as a model for corporations engaging fan communities."[33] This holds true in examples such as the 2024 playlist released by Riot Games for their *Player Days* event around *League of Legends*, which features the arrangements of different artists worldwide, which they titled *Community Covers Playlist*.[34]

Blizzard held a similar initiative with *Overwatch* during what they labeled as the *Summer of Music*, which took place in 2020 and was linked to the launch of the *Overwatch: Cities & Countries* album. The company invited various European artists

TABLE 6.3 League of Legends' Community Covers Playlist by Riot Games

ARTIST	*ARRANGEMENT*
Moisés Nieto	*Welcome to League of Legends*
Eli Bishop (with Kyle Tuttle, Ethan Jodziewicz, Carl Miner, Tyler Andal & Isaac Eicher)	*Taliyah, the Stoneweaver*
Bely Basarte	*The Curse of the Sad Mummy*
Pengfei Du	*Gwen, the Hallowed Seamstress*
GO!! LIGHT UP!	*Get Jinxed*
Ray Chen	*Jhin, the Virtuoso*
Grim Cat	*Caitlyn, the Sheriff of Piltover*
Colin Beasley Dulcimer Gumbo	*Milo, the Gentle Flame*
Tiago Pereira	*Everything Goes On*
ChillOwly	*Pantheon, the Unbreakable Spear*
Minidrum	*Champion Select (Blind Pick Theme)*
Pengfei Du	*Lee Sin, the Blind Monk*
Pangtience	*Gwen, the Hallowed Seamstress*
Carolin "WØNDER" Mrugala	*Still Here*
Moisés Nieto	*Champion Select (Draft Pick Theme)*

to create their own versions of the volume and other *Overwatch* themes, contributing to a sort of participative playlist that was also promoted individually by the music creators themselves through their own channels. The contributors and genres were widely diverse, and included pieces by beatboxers Berywam, rock and metal guitarist Sophie Lloyd, or DJ Sountec. Although these were not explicitly grouped as in the previous case, they constituted a similar form of interaction, as the company requested professional musicians (and fans) to collaborate with them for marketable purposes.

This can also be pointed out in games that assiduously engage with popular music, both in collaboration with industry agents or by their own means. The curation of playlists including real and virtual artists dynamizes their fan communities, providing an extension to the games' and the users' personal experiences. For instance, *Free Fire*'s *Booyah Day*[35] playlists are launched for this specific event each year, and have featured many popular artists on their Spotify channel, like Matuê with *Bang Bang*, Cari Leon with *Modo Insano*, or Phan Mạnh Quỳnh and Hoàng Thùy Linh with *Đợi Chờ Đừng Cáu*. These, furthermore, contribute to the building and maintenance of their international fan communities, following the attention put into the diverse geographies where the game is most popular.

Music Creators and Fan Playlists

Although official playlists and content provided by gaming companies contribute to establishing a reference for fans, their assimilation, and reproduction keep the presence of these games in motion. Many music creators have found a way to professionalize their activity through media such as the aforementioned aggregators and platforms, transforming their fan commitment into their job.

An example of this is that of pianist Moisés Nieto who, through an initial exploration of the intersection of music and gaming, started uploading content online that he arranged on the piano. During the last decade, he escalated his monthly listeners on Spotify to 750 thousand, was included in more than 37 thousand different platforms' playlists, and gained more than 65 thousand users on YouTube.[36] Even if the artist's repertoire is not exclusive to esports games, he has recorded versions of titles like *Clash Royale* or *League of Legends*, which got him featured as the opening and closing acts for Riot Games' *Community Covers Playlist*, as shown in Table 6.3.

The success of the artist in creating his own playlists and contributing content for other fans has implied that he does usually not follow specific trends, but arranges the pieces that are appealing to him and include a relatable backstory:

> I feel like games with more fantasy elements lend themselves to more imaginative, more innovative music. *Counter-Strike* or *Call of Duty*, being shooters with a very realistic aesthetic, don't seem to have such memorable music to me (…) *League*, as it also explains its lore through music, benefits a lot from it, because you can't understand its lore if you don't explore beyond the surface. For example, Amumu's story really resonated with me; it's a very beautiful story. That character and that music really left a mark on me; it's like they used the music to explain his story.[37]

Besides the work of Nieto, others like Grim Cat Piano[38] have covered pieces closer to the international esports scene—for instance, *League of Legends*' collaborative songs such as *Enemy* or *Heavy is the Crown*. Likewise, Rousseau,[39] despite covering a wider range of repertoire, has also worked on pieces like piano medleys for *Fortnite*, contributing to the arrangement and playlist scenes from different geographies. The uploading of such music has, in sum, been a tool for many artists who entered the music industry as 21st-century agents, but it has also contributed to the daily usage of music by the non-musician public who wishes to engage in video game content beyond official products.

Among the many playlists that feature these and other artists, there are also those created to accompany specific games. These may—or may not—include original themes by the publishing companies, arrangements, and other non-related popular music pieces that feel suitable to their gaming experience. For instance, playlists like *Supercell songs* by Spotify user Franjgomez aggregate multiple tracks from *Brawl Stars* and products like The Bad Randoms, while others like *Music for playing Dota 2* by user Taffer, or *Rainbow six siege play list* by Ryder "the wall of defence" include non-game-specific music, curated to set the mood for players. In other words, many playlists designed to accompany players are not based on video game music, but on popular pieces that are associated with the ludic experience. These lists offer a window for analyzing the intersection of popular music artists and gaming, as they contribute to creating the collective imagery around the soundscape of specific games or playing activities.

A rarer case is that of the web app *Mood.gg*,[40] specifically tailored to accompany the *League of Legends*' playing experience depending on the character of choice for each match. The site, created by engineer Farza and discontinued in 2019, included a democratic system for the community to vote on which pieces were better suited to go with characters, which was automatized and allowed listeners to go back to their favorite playlists every time they wished. As described by the author, the song submission system "would also allow users to 'vote' on songs submitted by other users with like/dislike system,"[41] as a means to generate collaborative—rather than unilaterally curated—playlists.

This system allows a deeper insight into the associations created by users between game characters and music, and can help understand the preferences of the fandom behind the title. For instance, character Karthus'—described as "an undying spirit whose haunting songs are a prelude to the horror of his nightmarish appearance—"[42] was linked to songs like *Lucifer* by Avantasia, *Disturbed* by Darkness, or *Grave Digger* by Hell Funeral. Differently, the light-centered character Lux—"the Lady of Luminosity—"[43] was related to pieces like Ellie Goulding's *Lights*, Vanessa Carlton's *A Thousand Miles*, or *Girls Just Want to Have Fun* by Cyndi Lauper.

This was, nevertheless, not the only instance in which fans created personalized playlists for characters in the past. For instance, in 2020 Reddit user DomDomBrah made a Spotify list for each character in *Overwatch*,[44] including 32 characters with four songs each, that had to be introduced manually. These featured pieces like *Jolene* by Dolly Parton or *Kiss My Country Ass* by Blake Shelton for character Ashe—a charismatic and ruthless outlaw—while Gengi—depicted as a Japanese cyborg ninja—was associated songs like *Again* by YUI, or インフェルノ (*Inferno*) by Mr. Green Apple. Similarly, and more specifically to esports, some users have compiled music used by professional gamers during their streams and created playlists for other fans to access. Examples are Amy Jaeger's *SKT T1's Faker's Playlist* on Spotify,[45] and Basu's *S1mple Twitch Stream Playlist*[46] on the same platform and YouTube, both of whom try to recreate the listening soundtracks of two of the best-known esports players in the world.

Thus, the possibility of imagining the music landscapes associated with games, characters, professional players, or events, promotes the engagement of each community with the rest of the titles' fans, and affords a space for self-expression. This can be seen as a form of direct feedback for companies, who in the music preferences of their players, can gain information about their taste, preferences, and associations between different media.

SHEET MUSIC

In some instances, the path to approaching music fandom has also gone through score publishing. In 1992, Square Enix published their first *Piano Collections* compilation, dedicated to *Final Fantasy IV*,[47] which included arrangements of some of their most successful pieces for the piano, under the revision of company composers. Other editions followed around other titles by the same company, such as *Kingdom Hearts*,[48] and the success of the initiative translated into the interest of other brands such as Materia Collective—with games like *Hollow Night* or *Undertale*—[49]who have followed a similar path and launched their own arrangements, prepared for their fans to perform.

In specific reference to esports, arrangement projects were not present until recently, and only appeared along the publication of compilations such as the *League of Legends' Player Days* piano songbook.[50] This volume, available for download for all users as part of their *Player Days* in 2024, features both songs from the game, character songs, and popular themes such as *Legends Never Die,* which fall closer to the competitive scene of the game. Nevertheless, this is not to say that there were precedents in making sheet music available for the community. The volume was prefaced by individual score releases, sometimes along the commentary from the authors which enriched the learning experience for fans—especially musicians.[51] These allowed a deeper comprehension of the music-building process, through statements like composer Jason Wiley's regarding *Leona*'s theme:

> This initial figure, or shall I say "seed," resonated with me. The key of B major along with the open B string pedal on guitar have a bright quality, which feels like Leona. B major is generally considered a very sharp and bright key, and to me it sounds like a super saturated hue of yellow ("pitch to color" could be an entire post by itself!).[52]

To these cases, it must be added all the independent fan uploads on platforms such as *Musescore, MusicNotes*, or *NinSheetMusic*, among others. As described by Summers, it is common for printed scores to be "either produced by music publishers or by the ever-industrious fan communities,"[53] as the latter have widely engaged in transcriptions and arrangements for diverse instruments. Through these means, it is common to find

FIGURE 6.1 First staves of *Call of Duty*'s "Zombies Theme" as arranged by Victormame.

pieces linked to the esports scene, such as anthems for world cups or championships, or promotional songs for competitive events.

For games with esports anthems, such as *Valorant*, it is easy to find multiple arrangements that feature popular music artists as composers. For instance, 2021's championship-made song *Die For You* by Grabbiz, has been adapted to the piano by diverse authors and in different tonalities—e.g., on *Musescore*, user Esprlt arranged it in B minor,[54] while Amy Hao transcribed it in A minor,[55] each with their unique takes. Although some games have not received the same attention, the most popular esports titles, which have most frequently engaged with the music industry, find a direct response from their musician fanbases.

Furthermore, some professional pianists and streamers like Victormame have produced arrangements for fans to engage with, among which esports games-related themes have been included.[56] This showcases the traction created by video game music at a wider level, and its attractiveness to musician fans, those interested in learning, and larger contexts such as music schools and conservatoires.

STREAMED PERFORMANCES

Despite the use of written music, such arrangements are usually not published but kept as tools by music streamers, who perform on social media platforms like Twitch, Kick, or BiliBili. The direct interaction of musicians with fans through these channels has created practices and peculiarities in the production and consumption of music that are based on interactivity, and the reproduction of the repertoire by an only emitting user. Nevertheless, the streaming of video game music, as well as other forms of music, is framed by recurrent arguments around copyright, which imply specific rules for performers.

Twitch, which can be argued as the most popular streaming platform for video games in the Western world—and a key driving force in esports—[57]includes clear policies for content creators in this respect, based on the Digital Millennium Copyright Act (DMCA) and other laws.[58] Although music covers are listed as examples of not-allowed content, there are some exceptions, such as the possibility of performing them if the music is entirely arranged by the performer, they indicate the original author of the theme, and there are no additional tracks or other recorded elements added to the broadcast.[59]

This is similar on other platforms, such as YouTube, both regarding live and non-live performances. In its guidelines, the company states that they "ask rightsholders to consider the applicability of copyright exceptions before they submit copyright removal requests,"[60] but the frequency of demonetization of original content has been a recurrent point of complaint for content creators. In this vein, authors Oliver and Lalchev reinforce how "copyright laws lack clarity and remain uncertain as to what extent they are applicable in the context of the current digital domain."[61] This implies that YouTubers feel restricted on how they can use copyrighted music, while some companies claim that YouTubers are refusing to pay for the copyrights, creating a circular problem.

To bypass potential legal issues, many platforms have issued copyright-free music, and gaming companies such as Supercell have opted to open their repertoire for fans to use in non-commercial activities, with the aim that they can include the companies' soundtracks to go with their gameplays or broadcasted activities. As composer Martin Schjøler describes:

> I think one of our things is that we're very community-driven. And I think technically what it can mean is that we would want to own the music, not so in an evil "we own it" way, but so the community can do with the music what they want. And because the music rights system can be quite complicated. (…) I think that's why *Brawl* is also so crazy: the voice actors, they do weird stuff with the lines and everything because they can just have fun with it. And I think that's a bit more tricky if you have a proper pop artist, because they have their rights and they're protecting their stuff.[62]

Riot Games have likewise published creator-safe playlists on platforms such as Spotify, for streamers to use freely in their online activities,[63] although these exclude collaborative tracks with third parties. Other companies, like label Monstercat—which collaborates with *Rocket League* as their main music provider—have created services for streamers to use their songs purchasing their premium licenses,[64] such as *Monstercat Gold*. These allow free use of a provided music library, the download of original tracks, and access to prereleases, despite the potential retention of collaborative works like in Riot Games' case. Their strict relation to esports, thus, goes through the games themselves rather than through specifically released themes, anthems, or other products.

Live Music Streaming

Regarding original UGC and despite the legal issues withholding potential content, social media has contributed to the professionalization of musicians who entered the entertainment industry as *producer-hosts*. These new agents in the creative (online) landscape are described by Ng and Gamble as combining different roles, from performer, to producer, livestream broadcaster, and community manager, especially within amateur environments.[65]

In this context, it is especially relevant to underline those who have tackled gaming and esports as an integral part of their music production,[66] and used it to explore their hobbies and express themselves, as well as an engagement tool for their listeners. Pianist and streamer Elesky[67] is a good example of the progressive specialization of music content creators on the quoted platforms, as she started uploading arrangements in 2017 on Twitter—now X.com—and quickly became an international referent for gaming and music collaborations. The live performance of video game music on Twitch allowed her to immerse herself full-time in this activity, and has had her featured in events like 2024's Comic-Con in London.[68]

Although her content is not focused exclusively on esports, but in the general entertainment industry—especially video games—her recurrent repertoire includes representative pieces of the international competitive scene.[69] As argued by the artist:

> [*League of Legends*'] Worlds themes are very popular even outside of the Worlds season. I mean, it's true that when a new theme comes out, people request it a lot and so

FIGURE 6.2 Elesky performing live on Twitch.

> on (...) Of course, it also depends on the popularity of the moment with other songs and whether it was released recently—they tend to request it more then. And later, depending on how catchy it is, they keep asking for it. But, for example, Worlds' themes are requested a lot.[70]

Furthermore, some of the songs requested by her fans are not necessarily from titles she had played before, which frequently moves her to approach the games in which they appear. From this process, it can be inferred that the reproduction and interpretation of game content, as well as the dialogues created among music content creators and fans, can act as a catalyst for other members of her community to approach games that had not played before, thus becoming familiar with esports-themes and events.

Other figures in the international scene, such as Lara6683[71]— who also offers transcripts of her arrangements on websites such as *Musicnotes*—[72] follow similar practices that include esports music tangentially, mostly by incorporating video game themes into their repertoires. Nevertheless, most smaller artists' work cannot be closely tracked on platforms, as they do not register their content to be rewatched or are difficult to find due to their small number of followers.

Prerecorded Music Streaming

Prerecorded performances on streaming platforms like YouTube are easier to come across, as they can be found on delay through specific keywords. Fan covers can be easily discovered on this and other platforms—e.g., on TikTok—as other forms of what Jenkins called "textual poaching,"[73] different from those described in previous pages. Constandinides addressed covers as *para-adaptations* in a multilayered dialogue between different media, which he defines as "no-budget user-generated content that creatively 'disturbs' commercial source products, and may eventually achieve a status that surpasses the 'ordinary' expectations of its creator(s)."[74] This is later nuanced by the author when affirming that these include "sophisticated"[75] reproductions, that can be associated with professionalized users with their respective fanbases.

For esport-related content, these performances adhere to the particularities of the social media on which they are posted—in length, style, etc.—as well as in other genres or entertainment niches. For example, many users have approached *PUBG*'s main theme with different instruments and genres on YouTube, including or excluding parts of the original tracks, and mostly appealing to DIY culture. Just to name a few, user Kezia Amelia uses a violin,[76] the Leo Twins perform the song with a guitar and violin,[77] Rishi Raj plays an acoustic guitar,[78] and band Sada Borneo presents an arrangement for ethnic instruments.[79] These examples offer a range of professionalization degrees in the recording of sound and video, translating into between 15 thousand and 1 million views.

Another example of a widely covered song—that can be linked to the previous chapter—is Linkin Park's *Heavy is the Crown*, as performed for the 2024 *League of Legends* World Finals, for which some of the most viewed examples as of November 2024 can be seen compiled in Table 6.4.

Like in the previous case, the range of instruments, genres, and arrangement styles is diverse, and underlines the song's reach beyond the original Riot Games' target.

TABLE 6.4 *Heavy is the Crown* most viewed covers on YouTube.

ARTIST OR YOUTUBE CHANNEL	*TITLE OF THE VIDEO*	*VIEWS (6TH DECEMBER 2024)*
Anastasiia Ivchenko	*I played LINKIN PARK—HEAVY IS THE CROWN on piano in public!*	241,704
Chazy AI	*Heavy Is The Crown (Chester Bennington AI Cover)*	130,492
Lunity	*Heavy is the Crown—Linkin Park (Cover by Lunity ft.*	82,328
Bruno Valverde	*HEAVY IS THE CROWN—LINKIN PARK - BRUNO VALVERDE—DRUM COVER*	56,735
Morphide	*Linkin Park—Heavy is the Crown (Morphide cover)*	51,288
Eddie van der Meer	Heavy Is The Crown ft. Linkin Park—Arcane & League of Legends Worlds—Fingerstyle Guitar Cover	42,020
Ofek Riff Solo	Linkin Park—"Heavy Is the Crown" Guitar Cover with On Screen Tabs (New Song 2024)	39,334
Grim Cat Piano	*League of Legends—Heavy Is The Crown ft. Linkin Park | Worlds 2024 Anthem—Piano Cover / Version*	36,824
Artem Komlev	*Linkin Park—Heavy is the Crown (Instrumental by Artem Komlev)*	35,625
Jackie-O	*League of Legends | Linkin Park—Heavy Is the Crown (Russian Cover)*	33,316

Furthermore, this reaffirms Jenkins et al.'s thesis in *Spreadable Media*,[80] according to whom YouTube videos—as well as those uploaded on other platforms—evidence the engagement of audiences with specific products, and serve as a means to express personal identities and shared interests among peers.

Similar to live streaming, platforms like YouTube or BiliBili offer a space for non-performing fans to interact, give feedback, and contribute to popularizing the secondary markets around esports. Although this can be done in comment sections like in other forums, many fans—including influencers—vouch for creating reaction videos to official and non-official pieces like those quoted above. Authors such as McDaniel have approached this format and underlined it as a creative act through listening, that appeals to users through its *reactivity*. He describes this quality as "an affective response to media that generates further engagement,"[81] that can be thoroughly examined through popular music reaction videos, as they "heighten and exaggerate their visceral experience of music media" and hope to "provoke subsequent reactions among viewers," becoming part of the popular music entertainment panorama.

In the case of esports, video reactions around opening ceremonies at global championships, music videos by esports teams, or roster presentations, offer another good point of reference for fans to engage with that exists at a crossroads between the two industries. For instance, YouTube video reactions around the 2021 *Valorant* World anthem *Die For You*, produced alongside electronic music producer Grabbitz, grasped the attention of gaming and esports influencers—e.g., Michelle Tanina or Gabe Kunda–, but also music producers—e.g., Joey "Lucky Boy" Nato—and overall content creators—e.g., Romeo Snow. The popularity of these videos is frequently proportional to the impact of the esports scene on social media, and they function as an additional attraction around both official and UGC in popular music and esports.

ESPORTS MUSIC AT VIDEO GAME CONVENTIONS

Despite the creation, development, and exchange of most fandom products related to esports and online gaming, events like video game conventions have provided good opportunities for participants to socialize face-to-face. Many conventions have vouched for actively including music in their programs, either as performances by hired bands or as open contests in different categories.

An example of this is BlizzCon, a yearly convention[82] held by Blizzard that offers insight into its work and the expertise of its teams, as well as an evening dedicated to its fans—*Community* Night—and professional performances. Since its first edition in 2005, the event has grown in popularity and modified its format to adapt to the industry's needs and the interests of its fans, becoming what Seo and Jung labeled as "an assemblage of consumption practices"[83] for esports.

Mainly from 2013 to 2019, the convention held talent contests with categories appealing to music—e.g., song contests, talent contests—while later editions tackled it more indirectly or as part of larger categories. For instance, the guidelines released for the 2021 BlizzcOnline—as it was held online—specified that:

> Talents featured in video could include but are not limited to, the following examples: re-enactment of a scene, a sketch, stand-up comedy. A dance routine, acrobatics, or an instrumental or vocal performance, as long as the composition performed is either a Blizzard composition, or an original composition that was 100% written by the qualified entrant.[84]

In their presentation of original content to the community, some of the winners and participants in these events have found a stepping stone for pursuing their art careers. As an example, the 2017 song contest winner, Jay the Bard, presents a good success story in transforming independent fan—*nerdcore*—work into professional activity. His piece, *Tales of Azeroth*,[85] was composed around *World of Warcarft,* as a means to appeal to audiences beyond the specificity of its lyrics, creating an association between his own live path and the characters going through the game.

As stated by the musician, he first participated in—and attended—the contest during that same edition, as encouraged by the previous year's winner Stephanie Jones, and it "opened the door"[86] for him in starting his journey. His first position not only allowed him to approach music and social media content creation professionally, but also got him featured in *World of Warcraft* as an NPC (Non-Playable Character), under his artistic name.[87] Furthermore, the connections created in and since BlizzCon in 2017 allowed him to get in touch with streamers such as Asmongold—a well-known *World of Warcraft* influencer—[88] and contributed to his later participation in esports projects such as the presentation of OTK's esports team, as a voice-over.[89] As stated by Jay, the contest allowed him to start his music career and his professional work alongside the video game industry.

Regarding the criteria for evaluating the performances, the competition judges pointed out that they "just wanted to see what spoke to the community, what spoke to us,"[90] which underlines the attention not only to what is enjoyable for live attendees, but to the overall Blizzard fandom. This idea can also be noted regarding the professional performances hired to dynamize the events, which have featured bands such as Le Sserafim in 2023, Metallica–online—in 2021, and Fitz and the Tantrums in 2019, among others.

Although these events have been separated from specific esports content, including *World of Warcraft* and *Overwatch* competitions, they become relevant as they share the convention space, underlining the multimedia habits of attendees and the close consumption of popular music and video games beyond strictly game music.

On the other hand, some conventions are specifically developed for the convergence of music and video games, and while not all include esports as part of their programs—like VGM—others host LAN Tournaments—e.g., MAGFest—or have featured relevant competitive encounters—e.g., Comic-Con, which has hosted diverse esports competitions. However, these occasions have provided contextualized occasions for featuring esports-themed or esports-games music. In cases like MAGFest or VGM, performers can apply to be featured as guests or be invited to participate, independently of their genres or styles—as long as they include video game-themed content. Despite their distance from esports per se, bands like Pokérus Project—known for their performances of

Pokémon music—can be counted among the participants in these events.[91] Furthermore, spaces like *Jamspace* at MAGFest encourage attendees to collaborate and perform game music, which could potentially include tracks from esports games.

These conventions offer multimedia contexts in which different forms of entertainment share their attendees' attention and vouch for the growing intermediation of niches. More essentially, along with competitive events, they contribute to building users' gaming capital,[92] which is also displayed around and as part of esports.

Music as Drawing: Fan Art

Lastly, other forms of fan art like drawings, paintings, or cosplay, have contributed to exploring esports-related music and characters from a visual perspective. Although this form of self-expression and temporary appropriation of the stories and storyworlds of characters is most relevant on social media like Instagram, Behance, or ArtStation, they have also been present in contests like those organized at BlizzCon or suggested by companies as independent events—e.g., Nouns Esports' *Gaming Art* contest,[93] or *Mobile Legends Bang Bang* Suyou contest.[94]

In the case at hand, these become relevant when depicting esports-band characters or reimagining players, hosts, and casters as actively engaging with music practices.

FIGURE 6.3 HEARTSTEEL Sett and K/DA Ahri as reimagined by Charms Fox (@charms_fox).

Although music characters in games have also been a target—e.g., Sona from *League of Legends*. It is useful to take Riot Games' K-pop bands K/DA and HEARTSTEEL as reference, as they serve as socializers for the community. The intersection of both bands has inspired numerous artists to share their creations online, frequently involved in friendly and romantic situations. Characters Ahri—the lead singer for K/DA—and Sett—the lead singer for HEARTSTEEL—are examples of this, as they have been drawn numerously on diverse media.

Other bands like Pentakill have also been reimagined as interacting with the same brand's bands, creating alternative narratives to the official content provided by the developing company. As already noted by Jenkins in 1992, this presents an assertion of the fans' mastery "over the mass-produced texts which provide the raw materials for their own cultural productions and the basis for their social interactions."[95] The possibilities of iconographic analysis of these artistic demonstrations afford an expansion to the lore which, occasionally, is coopted and commodified as previously shown through arrangements and other strictly music contributions.

CONCLUSION

In esports, as with other media, fandom is "central to the reconfiguration of audience power,"[96] as it does not only involve them in the popularization of esports, but it implies the continuous reproduction, creation, and reappropriation of audiovisual content outside of the mainstream. Although these forms of expression are controlled to an extent by developing and publishing companies, the continuous stream of contributions is rarely overviewed in its totality by the brands, and is rather encouraged by brands as a form of fan engagement.

These dynamics have been afforded by the growing presence of the internet to shape the daily experiences of users, which makes fans direct participants in the global multimedia and entertainment scene. Nevertheless, as stated by Jarrett, there is not a single form of fandom typical to esports, as "the rules of the game, its in-game world and characters, along with the players themselves, their playstyles, their teams, and even the publishers, can all be the object of one's fandom."[97] This includes different approaches to music, that go from the creation of frag movies to the composition of original songs around specific titles.

Furthermore, the democratizing model established by social media has contributed to the appearance of secondary markets around video games and esports, that place prosumers at the center of a continuously growing multimedia gear. Jenkins described this more than a decade ago when stating that fans and other audiences have developed an expertise in distribution technologies,[98] which has afforded the professionalization of their activity as a derivative from primary brands. The participatory culture described by the author thus does not only evolve to shape, share, reframe, and remix media content as large communities and networks, but also as an integral—economic—part of the esports ecosystem, as it adds agents such as *producer-hosts* who take new mediation roles between games and their communities. In recent years, the overall gaming industry has increased its reliance on these individuals, smaller brands, and channels, and many have vouched for incorporating them into their marketing strategies, sometimes as *brandom*—e.g., in the quoted cases including fan arrangements, contests, etc.

Music-wise, multiple forms of multi- and transmedia have emerged that imply the adaptation and reconfiguration of content to the necessities and demands of other fellow users. As earlier described, this can be analyzed in the division of parody music videos and original music compositions, as the first has shown to approach the day-to-day of players through the ubiquity of popular music in a humorous way, while the other aims at providing online communities with original, serious artistic content for their aesthetic and rhetorical enjoyment. These, as the other forms of music creation described in this chapter, create a convergence between popular music and gaming that is not (only) aimed at promoting the industry, but at socializing larger groups of participants, present in the esports ecosystem as users.

The presence of copyright and legal issues has, of course, been a tangent in the debate around music sharing online. The investment in fan activation from gaming companies has implied a progressive negotiation of terms, the inclusion of creator-safe playlists on aggregators, or the release of rights in some cases for fans to engage freely with video game content. Nevertheless, the growing collaboration between video games and popular music creates a somewhat different dynamic, that contemplates the involvement of different parties and rightsholders. For this reason, most public-available music is strictly controlled by developing companies and, exceptionally, involves popular music artists directly. Arrangements of such themes is, of course, a shortcut for including such content in different streaming platforms and formats.

Although esports are also exploited and built through UGC, the music attached to it tends to extend beyond the competitive scene to encompass the games' mechanics, lore, and characters from diverse approaches. These initiatives, if not directly involved with competitions, teams, or players, scaffold the international esports scene by contributing pieces that directly or indirectly circle back to it. The use of transmedia strategies is fundamental in achieving this, as it allows the convergence of esports, music, and overall popular culture in a continuous stream of information that builds the capital around esports games.

In sum, fandom must be seen as a key piece in the assemblage of the international esports—and overall gaming—gears, as it is the communities around specific titles, competitions, and teams, who contribute to their popularization, maintenance, and continuity in time through their public engagement. This has been grasped by many companies, which started incorporating the work of fans in events and competitions, and which increasingly dedicate part of their campaigns and efforts to make them participants in their activities. Music-wise, this has translated into the recognition of music UGC, and even its incorporation is specific games—like *World of Warcraft*. With this, and although the future is uncertain, the participatory culture announced by Jenkins in the 1990s does not seem to be fading and, rather, it can be guessed to increase its incorporation into official products in upcoming years.

NOTES

1 Melanie Fritsch & Tim Summers, "Introduction: Part VI: Beyond the Game", in Melanie Fritsch & Tim Summers (Eds.), *The Cambridge Companion to Video Game*, 389–394. Cambridge: Cambridge University Press, 2021, 391.
2 Henry Jenkins, *Convergence Culture: Where Old and New Media Collide*. New York: New York University Press, 2006.
3 Jenkins, *Convergence Culture: Where Old and New Media Collide*, 15.
4 Henry Jenkins, *Textual Poachers: Television Fans & Participatory Culture*. New York: Routledge, 1992.
5 Carlos Alberto Scolari, "Transmedia Storytelling: Implicit Consumers, Narrative Worlds, and Branding in Contemporary Media Production", *International Journal of Communication,* 2009, 3, 586–606; Cande Sánchez-Olmos & Eduardo Viñuela, "Transmedia Storytelling, Music and Videogames: The Case of Los Ríos de Alice by Vetusta Morla and Delirium Studios", *Icono14*, 2019, 17(1), 60–82.
6 Josh Jarrett, "Esports Fandom", in Seth E. Jenny, Nicolas Besombes, Tom Brock, Amanda C. Cote & Tobias M. Scholz (Eds.), *Routledge Handbook of Esports*, 426–435. Oxon: Routledge, 2024, 427.
7 League of Legends, "Community Covers Playlist | Player Days 2024 - League of Legends", *Youtube*, 2024. Available at: https://www.youtube.com/watch?v=S55wLeTD_EY. Accessed 24th November 2024.
8 Blizzard, "BlizzCon: It's a Wrap", *BlizzCon*, n.d. Available at: https://blizzcon.com/. Accessed 24th November 2024.
9 Matthew Guschwan, "Fandom, Brandom and the Limits of Participatory Culture", *Journal of Consumer Culture,* 2012, 12(1) 19–40.
10 Idem, 26.
11 Nicolas Rogès, "The History of Music Streaming", *Soundiiz Blog*, 2023. Available at: https://soundiiz.com/blog/the-history-of-music-streaming/. Acessed 24th November 2024.
12 Esports Earnings, "CPL World Championship 2001" (Counter-Strike), 2001. Available at: https://www.esportsearnings.com/tournaments/4293-cpl-world-championship-2001-counter-strike. Accessed 25th November 2024.
13 KylePP, "Pure Pwnage episode 1 - "Life of a Pro Gamer" [original web series]", *Youtube*, 2013. Available at: https://www.youtube.com/watch?v=WqWFYOxjZ54&t=42s. Accessed 25th November 2024.
14 SmothFewFilms, "The Leet World, Season 1 Ep 1: Reality Bites (HD)", *Youtube*, 2009. Available at: https://www.youtube.com/watch?v=PAt3aNwNxuA&list=PL94343AEA599BE702. Accessed 25th November 2024.
15 Sideratis, "Starcraft Pimpest Plays 2004", *YouTube*, 2008. Available at: https://www.youtube.com/watch?v=0017BvBApQE&t=114s. Accessed 25th November 2024.
16 Plentakill, "Home", *Youtube*, n.d. Available at: https://www.youtube.com/@PlentaKill. Accessed 25th November 2024.
17 Jarrett, "Esports Fandom".
18 Instalok, "Home", *Youtube*, n.d. Available at: https://www.youtube.com/@Instalok. Accessed 25th November 2024.
19 Refresher Parodies, "Home", *Youtube*, n.d. Available at: https://www.youtube.com/@RefresherParodies. Accessed 25th November 2024.
20 The Nyan cat song was a viral internet meme, originating from a Japanese song titled *Nyanyanyanyanyanyanya!*, composed by daniwellP using the Vocaloid software Hatsune Miku. Nyancat, "Nyan Cat! [Official]", *Youtube*, 2011. Available at: https://www.youtube.com/watch?v=2yJgwwDcgV8. Accessed 25th November 2024.

21 Josep M. Pujol, "Introduction", in *Three Selected Papers on Catalan Folklore*, 7–15. Tarragona: URV, 2013.
22 The Verkkars, "The Verkkars - EZ4ENCE (kannatusvideo)", *Youtube*, 2019. Available at: https://www.youtube.com/watch?v=kPkT0jMjEu8. Accessed 25th November 2024.
23 Counter Strike Wiki, "Music Kit/The Verkkars, EZ4ENCE", *Counter Strike Wiki*, n.d. Available at: https://counterstrike.fandom.com/wiki/Music_Kit/The_Verkkars,_EZ4ENCE#articleComments. Accessed 25th November 2024.
24 SSW, "FAKER | Fanmade Song for Faker", *Youtube*, 2023. Available at: https://www.youtube.com/watch?v=9fXmxITc-jo. Accessed 25th November 2024.
25 ChewieCatt, "Home", *Youtube*, n.d. Available at: https://www.youtube.com/@ChewieCatt/featured. Accessed 25th November 2024.
26 Matthew Moreland "ChewieCatt", Inteview by Interview by Eulalia Febrer-Coll, 11th November 2024.
27 Chewie, "Home", *Youtube*, n.d. Available at: https://www.youtube.com/@chewiex. Accessed 25th November 2024.
28 Derivakat, "COMEBACK - Derivakat x Boaster | FNATIC 2024 Anthem [Official Lyric M/V]", *Youtube*, 2024. Available at: https://www.youtube.com/watch?v=kM1x5oRsSWs. Accessed 25th November 2024.
29 Cristina Guzmán, "Lost in Silence: Musically LARPing as the Unvoiced", *Ludo2024 Thirteenth European Conference on Video Game Music and Sound: 'Sound, Music, and Space'*. Mataró, 11–13th July 2024; Aphelios, "Home", *Youtube*, n.d. Available at: https://www.youtube.com/@ApheliosMusicChannel/videos. Accessed 26th November 2024.
30 VALORANT, *Spotify*, n.d. Available at: https://open.spotify.com/intl-es/artist/3wrFoI9EVjWg6m8xXeWr5t?si=i_AXBKsqQKaWRhkl7cDOLg. Accessed 28th November 2024.
31 Juan Sebastián Díaz Gasca, "Music beyond Gameplay: Motivators in the Consumption of Videogame Soundtracks" (Doctoral Thesis, Griffith University, 2015), 183. Available at: https://research-repository.griffith.edu.au/bitstream/handle/10072/367483/Diaz%20Gasca_2015_02Thesis.pdf?sequence=1. Accessed 15th November 2023.
32 Ryan Thompson, "Game Music Beyond the Games", in Melanie Fritsch & Tim Summers (Eds.), *The Cambridge Companion to Video Game Music*, 409–423. Cambridge: Cambridge University Press, 2021, 411.
33 Idem, 414.
34 League of Legends, "Community Covers Playlist", *Youtube*, 2024. Available at: https://www.youtube.com/watch?v=S55wLeTD_EY&t=415s. Accessed 27th November 2024.
35 Garena Free Fire Global, "Ready to Booyah Your Way? | Booyah Day 2024", October 2024. Available at: https://www.youtube.com/watch?v=QsIldn5qimM.
36 Chartmetric, "Moisés Nieto", *Chartmetric*, 2024. Available at: https://app.chartmetric.com/es/artist/4906. Accessed 27th November 2024; Moisés Nieto, *Spotify*, n.d. Available at: https://open.spotify.com/intl-es/artist/6i5jeqNyrzyfDwIiAfNdyF?si=LZvPf0UyRoSkwZog6GGMFQ. Accessed 27th November 2024.
37 Moisés Nieto, professional pianist and arranger. Interview by Eulalia Febrer-Coll. 6th November 2024.
38 Grim Cat Piano, *Spotify*. Available at: https://open.spotify.com/intl-es/artist/7Ggt1Xiiv381ORbrLiU2Ck?si=tnTe49cRRZKQCBLXtvWjCg. Accessed 27th November 2024.
39 Rousseau, "Rousseau: Modern Series, Pt. 1", *Spotify*, 2019. Available at https://open.spotify.com/intl-es/album/4MWcQGgCw6WZuIC9mCnije?si=X27-QhgvQaiVK4lom2pyLA. Accessed 27th November 2024.
40 Mood.gg, "Welcome to Mood GG", n.d. Available at: https://mood.gg. Accessed 27th November 2024.
41 Farza, "The Story of Mood.gg: How in 4 Months I Went from Knowing Nothing about Web Development to 3 Million Hits and One of the Most Successful Third-Party League of Legends Apps of All Time", *Medium*, 2017. Available at: https://medium.com/@farzatv/the-story-of-mood-gg-5d21f2b19ec3. Accessed 27th November 2024.

42 Riot Games, "Karthus: The Deathsinger", *Riot Games*, n.d. Available at: https://www.leagueoflegends.com/en-us/champions/karthus/. Accessed 28th November 2024.
43 Riot Games, "Lux: The Lady of Luminosity", *Riot Games*, n.d. Available at: https://www.leagueoflegends.com/en-us/champions/lux/. Accessed 28th November 2024.
44 DomDomBrah, "I Made a Spotify Playlist for Every Overwatch Hero", *Reddit*, 2020. Available at: https://www.reddit.com/r/Overwatch/comments/ivg60u/i_made_a_spotify_playlist_for_every_overwatch_hero/. Accessed 28th November 2024.
45 Amy Jaeger, "SKT T1 Faker's Playlist", *Spotify*, n.d. Available at: https://open.spotify.com/playlist/6O1vGJRz7N1AicF0GkGOP6?si=64078b8407e14e57. Accessed 29th November 2024.
46 Basu, "S1mple Twitch Stream Playlist", *Spotify*, 2021. Available at: https://open.spotify.com/playlist/0yIaYLlyEB8XbATA0ZXFqw?si=dff78ac54b434c97. Accessed 29th November 2024.
47 Square Enix, "Final Fantasy IV Piano Collections: Review by Moses Rose", *Square Enix Music Online*, n.d. Available at: https://www.squareenixmusic.com/reviews/moses/ff4pc.shtml. Accessed 29th November 2024.
48 Square Enix, "Piano Collections". Available at: https://www.jp.square-enix.com/music/en/lineup/series/piano_collections/. Accessed 29th November 2024.
49 *Materia Store*, "Sheet Music", n.d. Available at: https://materia.store/collections/sheet-music?srsltid=AfmBOoo2_og4DzKn0KCeGwbV7HLtbO4r-iEscyBb2JDSx_tlvesDd1Y8. Accessed 29th November 2024.
50 Riot Games, *League of Legends Player Days Piano Songbook*. Riot Games Inc., Stellar Sun Songs, EMI April Music Inc, Warner-Tamerlane Publishing Corp., Rebecca Rose Johnson & Sample Sized LLC. Available at: https://cmsassets.rgpub.io/sanity/files/dsfx7636/news/42e3639d9b30c5b54833225bc5e5443e3a0389a6.zip. Accessed 29th November 2024.
51 Ed the Conqueror, "Sheet Music Available Now", *Riot Games*, 2019. Available at: https://www.leagueoflegends.com/en-au/news/media/sheet-music-available-now/. Accessed 29th November 2024; ProtoShredanoid, "/Dev: Rocking on the Rift", *Riot Games*, 2019. Available at: https://www.leagueoflegends.com/en-au/news/media/dev-rocking-on-the-rift/. Accessed 29th November 2024.
52 ProtoShredanoid, "/Dev: Rocking on the Rift".
53 Tim Summers, *Understanding Video Game Music*. Cambridge: Cambridge University Press, 2016, 48.
54 Esprlt, "Die for You", *Musescore*, n.d. Available at: https://musescore.com/user/29293127/scores/8180175. Accessed 29th November 2024.
55 Amy Hao, "Die for You from VALORANT t. GRABBIZ", *Musescore*, n.d. Available at: https://musescore.com/user/43262441/scores/14685508. Accessed 29th November 2024.
56 Victormame, *Música de videojuegos*. Barcelona: Redbook Ediciones, 2024.
57 Jason Smethers, "Streaming Esports", in Seth E. Jenny, Nicolas Besombes, Tom Brock, Amanda C. Cote, & Tobias M. Scholz (Eds.), *Routledge Handbook of Esports*, 404–412. Oxon: Routledge, 2024.
58 Twitch, "Music Guidelines", *Twitch*, n.d. Available at: https://www.twitch.tv/p/en/legal/community-guidelines/music/. Accessed 30th November 2024.
59 Twitch, "Music Guidelines".
60 Youtube, "Copyright", n.d. Available at: https://www.youtube.com/intl/en_us/howyoutubeworks/policies/copyright/#copyright-exceptions. Accessed 30th November 2024.
61 Paul G. Oliver & Stefan Lalchev, "Music Copyright, Creators and Fans: Enemies or Friends in the Digital Domain?", in Ann Harrison & Tony Rigg (Eds.), *The Present and Future of Music Law*, 82–99. New York: Bloomsbury, 2021, 95.
62 Martin Schjøler, Musician and Sound Designer at Supercell. Interview by Eulalia Febrer-Coll. 27th February 2024.
63 Riot Games, "Rito Games Creator-Safe Playlist", *Spotify*, n.d. Available at: https://open.spotify.com/playlist/5hDYD44imzFZEqTfAoco1N. Accessed 30th November 2024.

64 Montsercat, "Monstercat Gold & Content Creator Licenses", 2020. Available at: https://www.monstercat.com/article/monstercat-gold-content-creator-licenses. Accessed 30th November 2024.
65 Jason Ng & Steven Gamble, "Hip-Hop Producer-Hosts, Beat Battles, and Online Music Production Communities on Twitch", *First Monday*, 2022, 27(6).
66 Ng & Gamble, "Hip-Hop Producer-Hosts, Beat Battles, and Online Music Production Communities on Twitch".
67 Elesky, "Home", *Twitch*, n.d. Available at: https://www.twitch.tv/elesky. Accessed 30th November 2024.
68 Elesky, "HUGE SURPRISE!!!," *X*, 2024. Available at: https://x.com/search?q=%40elesky25%20comicon&src=typed_query&f=top. Accessed 30th November 2024.
69 Elesky, "Songs", *Streamersonglist.com*, n.d. Available at: https://www.streamersonglist.com/t/elesky/songs. Accessed 30th November 2024.
70 Elesky, professional pianist and streamer. Interview by Eulalia Febrer-Coll, 15h November 2024.
71 Lara6683, "Home", *Twitch*. Available at: https://www.twitch.tv/lara6683. Accessed 6th December 2024.
72 Lara6683, "Sheet Music", *Musicnotes*. Available at: https://www.musicnotes.com/sheet-music/artist/lara6683?srsltid=AfmBOop__tHiFT3VVxlLh48UE32fryoiSv2hzI7l5Kr_cT-Qq2EdKmRG. Accessed 6th December 2024.
73 Jenkins, *Textual Poachers*.
74 Costas Constandinides, "'You Just Got Covered': YouTube Cover Song Videos as Examples of Para-Adaptation", in Johannes Fehrle & Werner Schäfke-Zell (Eds.), *Adaptation in the Age of Media Convergence*, 111–131. Amsterdam: Amsterdam University Press, 2019, 111.
75 Constandinides, "'You Just Got Covered': YouTube Cover Song Videos as Examples of Para-Adaptation", 114.
76 Kezia Amelia, "PUBGM Theme Music – Violin Cover by Kezia Amelia", *Youtube*, 2024. Available at: https://www.youtube.com/watch?v=FZVlt9jf9y4. Accessed 6th December 2024.
77 Leo Twins, "PUBG Theme | Leo Twins", *Youtube*, 2024. Available at: https://www.youtube.com/watch?v=PCoy3WhMIyQ. Accessed 6th December 2024.
78 Rishi Raj, "PUBG/BGMI Main Theme Guitar Fingerstyle Cover", *Youtube*, 2024. Available at: https://www.youtube.com/watch?v=Ddvqew6GCgw. Accessed 6th December 2024.
79 Sada Borneo, "PUBG MOBILE Theme Song - Sada Borneo", *Youtube*, 2024. Available at: https://www.youtube.com/watch?v=uJhwKabQSH8. Accessed 6th December 2024.
80 Henry Jenkins, *Spreadable Media: Creating Value and Meaning in a Networked Culture*. New York: New York University Press, 2013, 187.
81 Byrd McDaniel, "Popular Music Reaction Videos: Reactivity, Creator Labor, and the Performance of Listening Online", *Journal of New Media & Society*, 2021, 23(6), 1624–1641, 1625.
82 Blizzcon, *Blizzard*, n.d. Available at: https://blizzcon.com/en-us/. Accessed 6th December 2024. The convention was interrupted in 2006, 2012, 2020 to 2022, and 2024 due to diverse circumstances, ranging from the preparation of new game launches to impediments derived from the pandemic.
83 Yuri Seo & Sang-Uk Jung, "Beyond Solitary Play in Computer Games: The Social Practices of eSports", *Journal of Consumer Culture*, 2016, 16(3), 635–655.
84 BlizzcOnline, "The BlizzcOnline Community Showcase Talent Spotlight Submission Agreement", *Blizzcon*, 2021. Available at: https://bnetcmsus-a.akamaihd.net/cms/gallery/QAJ3YVB3IMTV1600377030642.pdf. Accessed 6th December 2024.
85 Jay the Bard, "Tales of Azeroth, Live at Blizzcon (2017 Talent Contest Winner)", *Youtube*, 2017. Available at: https://www.youtube.com/watch?v=cUPFK3SGWis&t=63s. Accessed 28th November 2024; Jason Thomas, "Community Night BlizzCon 2017", *Youtube*, 2017. Available at: https://www.youtube.com/watch?v=Iv_Bhpm3_bM&t=2636s. Accessed 28th November 2024.

86 Jay the Bard, professional musician and streamer. Interview by Eulalia Febrer-Coll. 28th November 2024.
87 Littlefran, "Jay the Tavern Bard Got His NPC in Boralus!", *Reddit*, 2017. Available at: https://www.reddit.com/r/wow/comments/8gerup/jay_the_tavern_bard_got_his_npc_in_boralus/. Accessed 7th December 2024.
88 AsmongoldTV, "Home", *Youtube*, n.d. Available at: https://www.youtube.com/@AsmonTV. Accessed 7th December 2024.
89 OTK, "Introducing: OTK - One True King", *Youtube*, 2020. Available at: https://www.youtube.com/watch?v=i9uLcqNqsQk. Accessed 7th December 2024.
90 Jason Thomas, "Community Night Blizzcon 2017", *Youtube*, 2017. Available at: https://www.youtube.com/watch?v=Iv_Bhpm3_bM. Accessed 7th December 2024.
91 Pokerus Project, "@magfest 2023: Pokerus Project (FULL SHOW)", *Youtube*, 2023. Available at: https://www.youtube.com/watch?v=1yN1lh88hlE. Accessed 7th December 2024.
92 Jarrett, "Esports Fandom".
93 Nouns, "Gaming Art Contest", *Nouns.gg*, 2024. Available at: https://nouns.gg/rounds/gaming-art-contest?utm_source=chatgpt.com. Accessed 8th December 2024.
94 Bikram Chakraborty, "Mobile Legends Bang Bang Suyou Fan Art Contest: Rules and Rewards", *Sporskeeda*, 2024. Available at: https://www.sportskeeda.com/esports/mobile-legends-bang-bang-suyou-fan-art-contest-rules-rewards?utm_source=chatgpt.com. Accessed 8th December 2024.
95 Jenkins, *Textual Poachers*, 24.
96 Jenkins, *Spreadable Media*, 117.
97 Jarrett, "Esports Fandom", 435.
98 Jenkins, *Spreadable Media*, 127–128.

REFERENCES

Amelia, Kezia. "PUBGM Theme Music –Violin Cover by Kezia Amelia", *Youtube*, 2024. Available at: https://www.youtube.com/watch?v=FZVlt9jf9y4. Accessed 6th December 2024.

Aphelios. "Home", *Youtube*, n.d. Available at: https://www.youtube.com/@ApheliosMusicChannel/videos. Accessed 26th November 2024.

Asmongold TV. "Home", *Youtube*, n.d. Available at: https://www.youtube.com/@AsmonTV. Accessed 7th December 2024.

Basu. "S1mple Twitch Stream Playlist", *Spotify*, 2021. Available at: https://open.spotify.com/playlist/0yIaYLlyEB8XbATA0ZXFqw?si=dff78ac54b434c97. Accessed 29th November 2024.

Blizzard. "*BlizzCon*: It's a Wrap", *BlizzCon*, n.d. Available at: https://blizzcon.com/. Accessed 24th November 2024.

Blizzard Entertainment. "Overwatch colabora con creadores de gran talent para el Summer of Music", *Blizzard,* 2020. Available at: https://overwatch.blizzard.com/es-es/news/23473114/overwatch-colabora-con-creadores-de-gran-talento-para-el-summer-of-music/. Accessed 27th November 2024.

Blizzcon, *Blizzard*, n.d. Available at: https://blizzcon.com/en-us/. Accessed 6th December 2024. The convention was interrupted in 2006, 2012, 2020 to 2022, and 2024 due to diverse circumstances, ranging from the preparation of new game launches to impediments derived from the pandemic.

BlizzcOnline. "The BlizzcOnline Community Showcase Talent Spotlight Submission Agreement", *Blizzcon*, 2021. Available at: https://bnetcmsus-a.akamaihd.net/cms/gallery/QAJ3YVB3IMTV1600377030642.pdf. Accessed 6th December 2024.

Chakraborty, Bikram. "Mobile Legends Bang Bang Suyou Fan Art Contest: Rules and Rewards", *Sporskeeda*, 2024. Available at: https://www.sportskeeda.com/esports/mobile-legends-bang-bang-suyou-fan-art-contest-rules-rewards?utm_source=chatgpt.com. Accessed 8th December 2024.

Chartmetric. "Moisés Nieto", *Chartmetric,* 2024. Available at: https://app.chartmetric.com/es/artist/4906. Accessed 27th November 2024.

ChewieCatt. "Home", *Youtube*, n.d. Available at: https://www.youtube.com/@ChewieCatt/featured. Accessed 25th November 2024.

Chewie. "Home", *Youtube*, n.d. Available at: https://www.youtube.com/@chewiex. Accessed 25th November 2024.

Constandinides, Costas. "'You Just Got Covered': YouTube Cover Song Videos as Examples of Para-Adaptation", in Johannes Fehrle & Werner Schäfke-Zell (Eds.), *Adaptation in the Age of Media Convergence,* 111–131. Amsterdam: Amsterdam University Press, 2019, 111.

Counter Strike Wiki. "Music Kit/The Verkkars, EZ4ENCE", *Counter Strike Wiki*, n.d. Available at: https://counterstrike.fandom.com/wiki/Music_Kit/The_Verkkars,_EZ4ENCE#articleComments. Accessed 25th November 2024.

Derivakat. "COMEBACK - Derivakat x Boaster I FNATIC 2024 Anthem [Official Lyric M/V]", *Youtube,* 2024. Available at: https://www.youtube.com/watch?v=kM1x5oRsSWs. Accessed 25th November 2024.

Díaz Gasca, Juan Sebastián. "Music Beyond Gameplay: Motivators in the Consumption of Videogame Soundtracks" (Doctoral Thesis). Griffith University, 2015. Available at: https://research-repository.griffith.edu.au/bitstream/handle/10072/367483/Diaz%20Gasca_2015_02Thesis.pdf?sequence=1. Accessed 15th November 2023.

DomDomBrah. "I Made a Spotify Playlist for Every Overwatch Hero", *Reddit,* 2020. Available at: https://www.reddit.com/r/Overwatch/comments/ivg60u/i_made_a_spotify_playlist_for_every_overwatch_hero/. Accessed 28th November 2024.

Ed the Conqueror. "Sheet Music Available Now", *Riot Games,* 2019. Available at: https://www.leagueoflegends.com/en-au/news/media/sheet-music-available-now/. Accessed 29th November 2024.

Elesky. "Home", *Twitch*, n.d. Available at: https://www.twitch.tv/elesky. Accessed 30th November 2024.

Elesky. "HUGE SURPRISE!!!," *X,* 2024. Available at: https://x.com/search?q=%40elesky25%20comicon&src=typed_query&f=top. Accessed 30th November 2024.

Elesky. "Songs", *Streamersonglist.com*, n.d. Available at: https://www.streamersonglist.com/t/elesky/songs. Accessed 30th November 2024.

Esports Earnings. "CPL World Championship 2001" (Counter-Strike), 2001. Available at: https://www.esportsearnings.com/tournaments/4293-cpl-world-championship-2001-counter-strike. Accessed 25th November 2024.

Esprlt. "Die For You", *Musescore*, n.d. Available at: https://musescore.com/user/29293127/scores/8180175. Accessed 29th November 2024.

Farza. "The Story of Mood.gg: How in 4 Months I Went from Knowing Nothing about Web Development to 3 Million Hits and One of the Most Successful Third-Party League of Legends Apps of All Time", *Medium*, 2017. Available at: https://medium.com/@farzatv/the-story-of-mood-gg-5d21f2b19ec3. Accessed 27th November 2024.

Fritsch, Melanie & Summers, Tim. "Introduction: Part VI: Beyond the Game", in Melanie Fritsch & Tim Summers (Eds.), *The Cambridge Companion to Video Game,* 389–394. Cambridge: Cambridge University Press, 2021, 391.

Grim Cat Piano, *Spotify*. Available at: https://open.spotify.com/intl-es/artist/7Ggt1Xiiv381ORbrLiU2Ck?si=tnTe49cRRZKQCBLXtvWjCg. Accessed 27th November 2024.

Guschwan, Matthew. "Fandom, Brandom and the Limits of Participatory Culture", *Journal of Consumer Culture,* 2012, 12(1), 19–40.

Guzmán, Cristina. "Lost in Silence: Musically LARPing as the Unvoiced", *Ludo2024 Thirteenth European Conference on Video Game Music and Sound: 'Sound, Music, and Space'*. Mataró, 11–13th July 2024.

Hao, Amy. "Die for You from VALORANT t. GRABBIZ", *Musescore*, n.d. Available at: https://musescore.com/user/43262441/scores/14685508. Accessed 29th November 2024.

Instalok. "Home", *Youtube*, n.d. Available at: https://www.youtube.com/@Instalok. Accessed 25th November 2024.

Jaeger, Amy. "SKT T1 Faker's Playlist", *Spotify*, n.d. Available at: https://open.spotify.com/playlist/6O1vGJRz7N1AicF0GkGOP6?si=64078b8407e14e57. Accessed 29th November 2024.

Jarrett, Josh. "Esports Fandom", in Seth E. Jenny, Nicolas Besombes, Tom Brock, Amanda C. Cote, & Tobias M. Scholz (Eds.), *Routledge Handbook of Esports*, 426–435. Oxon: Routledge, 2024, 427.

Jay the Bard. "Tales of Azeroth, Live at Blizzcon (2017 Talent Contest Winner)", *Youtube*, 2017. Available at: https://www.youtube.com/watch?v=cUPFK3SGWis&t=63s. Accessed 28th November 2024.

Jenkins, Henry. *Convergence Culture: Where Old and New Media Collide*. New York: New York University Press, 2006.

Jenkins, Henry. *Spreadable Media: Creating Value and Meaning in a Networked Culture*. New York: New York University Press, 2013, 187.

Jenkins, Henry. *Textual Poachers: Television Fans & Participatory Culture*. New York: Routledge, 1992.

Kyle, P.P. "Pure Pwnage Episode 1 – "Life of a Pro Gamer" [original web series]", *Youtube*, 2013. Available at: https://www.youtube.com/watch?v=WqWFYOxjZ54&t=42s. Accessed 25th November 2024.

Lara6683. "Home", *Twitch*. Available at: https://www.twitch.tv/lara6683. Accessed 6th December 2024.

Lara6683. "Sheet Music", *Musicnotes*. Available at: https://www.musicnotes.com/sheet-music/artist/lara6683?srsltid=AfmBOop__tHiFT3VVxlLh48UE32fryoiSv2hzI7l5Kr_cT-Qq2Ed-KmRG. Accessed 6th December 2024.

League of Legends. "Community Covers Playlist | Player Days 2024- League of Legends", *Youtube*, 2024. Available at: https://www.youtube.com/watch?v=S55wLeTD_EY. Accessed 24th November 2024.

Leo Twins. "PUBG Theme | Leo Twins", *Youtube*, 2024. Available at: https://www.youtube.com/watch?v=PCoy3WhMIyQ. Accessed 6th December 2024.

Littlefran. "Jay the Tavern Bard got his NPC in Boralus!", *Reddit*, 2017. Available at: https://www.reddit.com/r/wow/comments/8gerup/jay_the_tavern_bard_got_his_npc_in_boralus/. Accessed 7th December 2024.

Materia Store. "Sheet Music", n.d. Available at: https://materia.store/collections/sheet-music?srsltid=AfmBOoo2_og4DzKn0KCeGwbV7HLtbO4r-iEscyBb2JDSx_tlvesDd1Y8. Accessed 29th November 2024.

McDaniel, Byrd. "Popular Music Reaction Videos: Reactivity, Creator Labor, and the Performance of Listening Online", *Journal of New Media & Society*, 2021, 23(6), 1624–1641, 1625.

Moisés Nieto. *Spotify*, n.d. Available at: https://open.spotify.com/intl-es/artist/6i5jeqNyrzyfDwIiAfNdyF?si=LZvPf0UyRoSkwZog6GGMFQ. Accessed 27th November 2024.

Montsercat. "Monstercat Gold & Content Creator Licenses", 2020. Available at: https://www.monstercat.com/article/monstercat-gold-content-creator-licenses. Accessed 30th November 2024.

Mood.gg. "Welcome to Mood GG", n.d. Available at: https://mood.gg. Accessed 27th November 2024.

Ng, Jason & Gamble, Steven. "Hip-Hop Producer-Hosts, Beat Battle, and Online Music Production Communities on Twitch", *First Monday*, 2022, 27(6). https://firstmonday.org/ojs/index.php/fm/article/view/12338.

Nouns. "Gaming Art Contest", *Nouns.gg,* 2024. Available at: https://nouns.gg/rounds/gaming-art-contest?utm_source=chatgpt.com. Accessed 8th December 2024.

Oliver, Paul G. & Lalchev, Stefan. "Music Copyright, Creators and Fans: Enemies or Friends in the Digital Domain?", in Ann Harrison & Tony Rigg (Eds.), *The Present and Future of Music Law,* 82–99. New York: Bloomsbury, 2021, 95.

OTK. "Introducing: OTK - One True King", *Youtube*, 2020. Available at: https://www.youtube.com/watch?v=i9uLcqNqsQk. Accessed 7th December 2024.

ProtoShredanoid. "/Dev: Rocking on the Rift", *Riot Games*, 2019. Available at: https://www.leagueoflegends.com/en-au/news/media/dev-rocking-on-the-rift/. Accessed 29th November 2024.

Plentakill. "Home", *Youtube*, n.d. Available at: https://www.youtube.com/@PlentaKill. Accessed 25th November 2024.

Pokerus Project. "@magfest 2023: Pokerus Project (FULL SHOW)", *Youtube*, 2023. Available at: https://www.youtube.com/watch?v=1yN1lh88hlE. Accessed 7th December 2024.

Pujol, Josep M. "Introduction", in Josep M. Pujol (Ed.), *Three Selected Papers on Catalan Folklore,* 7–15. Tarragona: URV, 2013.

Raj, Rishi. "PUBG/BGMI Main Theme Guitar Fingerstyle Cover", *Youtube*, 2024. Available at: https://www.youtube.com/watch?v=Ddvqew6GCgw. Accessed 6th December 2024.

Refresher Parodies. "Home", *Youtube*, n.d. Available at: https://www.youtube.com/@RefresherParodies. Accessed 25th November 2024.

Riot Games. "Karthus: The Deathsinger", *Riot Games*, n.d. Available at: https://www.leagueoflegends.com/en-us/champions/karthus/. Accessed 28th November 2024.

Riot Games. "Lux: The Lady of Luminosity", *Riot Games*, n.d. Available at: https://www.leagueoflegends.com/en-us/champions/lux/. Accessed 28th November 2024.

Riot Games. *League of Legends Player Days Piano Songbook.* Riot Games Inc., Stellar Sun Songs, EMI April Music Inc, Warner-Tamerlane Publishing Corp., Rebecca Rose Johnson & Sample Sized LLC. Available at: https://cmsassets.rgpub.io/sanity/files/dsfx7636/news/42e3639d9b30c5b54833225bc5e5443e3a0389a6.zip. Accessed 29th November 2024.

Riot Games. "Rito Games Creator-Safe Playlist", *Spotify*, n.d. Available at: https://open.spotify.com/playlist/5hDYD44imzFZEqTfAoco1N. Accessed 30th November 2024.

Rogès, Nicolas. "The History of Music Streaming", *Soundiiz Blog*, 2023. Available at: https://soundiiz.com/blog/the-history-of-music-streaming/. Accessed 24th November 2024.

Rousseau. "Rousseau: Modern Series, Pt. 1", *Spotify*, 2019. Available at https://open.spotify.com/intl-es/album/4MWcQGgCw6WZuIC9mCnije?si=X27-QhgvQaiVK4lom2pyLA. Accessed 27th November 2024.

Sada Borneo. "PUBG MOBILE Theme Song - Sada Borneo", *Youtube*, 2024. Available at: https://www.youtube.com/watch?v=uJhwKabQSH8. Accessed 6th December 2024.

Sánchez-Olmos, Cande & Viñuela, Eduardo. "Transmedia Storytelling, Music and Videogames: The Case of Los Ríos de Alice by Vetusta Morla and Delirium Studios", *Icono14,* 2019, 17(1), 60–82.

Scolari, Carlos Alberto. "Transmedia Storytelling: Implicit Consumers, Narrative Worlds, and Branding in Contemporary Media Production", *International Journal of Communication,* 2009, 3, 586–606.

Seo, Yuri & Jung, Sang-Uk. "Beyond Solitary Play in Computer Games: The Social Practices of eSports". *Journal of Consumer Culture,* 2016, 16(3), 635–655.

Sideratis. "Starcraft Pimpest Plays 2004", *YouTube*, 2008. Available at: https://www.youtube.com/watch?v=0Ol7BvBApQE&t=114s. Accessed 25th November 2024.

Smethers, Jason. "Streaming Esports", in Seth E. Jenny, Nicolas Besombes, Tom Brock, Amanda C. Cote & Tobias M. Scholz (Eds.), *Routledge Handbook of Esports*, 404–412. Oxon: Routledge, 2024.

SmothFewFilms. "The Leet World, Season 1 Ep 1: Reality Bites (HD)", *Youtube*, 2009. Available at: https://www.youtube.com/watch?v=PAt3aNwNxuA&list=PL94343AEA599BE702. Accessed 25th November 2024.

Square Enix. "Final Fantasy IV Piano Collections: Review by Moses Rose", *Square Enix Music Online*, n.d. Available at: https://www.squareenixmusic.com/reviews/moses/ff4pc.shtml. Accessed 29th November 2024.

Square Enix. "Piano Collections". Available at: https://www.jp.square-enix.com/music/en/lineup/series/piano_collections/. Accessed 29th *November 2024.*

SSW. "FAKER | Fanmade Song for Faker", Youtube, 2023. Available at: https://www.youtube.com/watch?v=9fXmxITc-jo. Accessed 25th November 2024.

Summers, Tim. *Understanding Video Game Music*. Cambridge: Cambridge University Press, 2016.

The Nyan cat song was a viral internet meme, originating from a Japanese song titled *Nyanyanyanyanyanyanya!*, composed by daniwellP using the Vocaloid software Hatsune Miku. Nyancat, "Nyan Cat! [Official]", *Youtube*, 2011. Available at: https://www.youtube.com/watch?v=2yJgwwDcgV8. Accessed 25th November 2024.

The Verkkars. "The Verkkars - EZ4ENCE (kannatusvideo)", *Youtube*, 2019. Available at: https://www.youtube.com/watch?v=kPkT0jMjEu8. Accessed 25th November 2024.

Thomas, Jason. "Community Night Blizzcon 2017", *Youtube,* 2017. Available at: https://www.youtube.com/watch?v=Iv_Bhpm3_bM. Accessed 7th December 2024.

Thompson, Ryan. "Game Music Beyond the Games", in Melanie Fritsch & Tim Summers (Eds.), *The Cambridge Companion to Video Game Music,* 409–423. Cambridge: Cambridge University Press, 2021, 411.

Twitch. "Music Guidelines", *Twitch*, n.d. Available at: https://www.twitch.tv/p/en/legal/community-guidelines/music/. Accessed 30th November 2024.

VALORANT, *Spotify*, n.d. Available at: https://open.spotify.com/intl-es/artist/3wrFoI9EVjWg6m8xXeWr5t?si=i_AXBKsqQKaWRhkl7cDOLg. Accessed 28th November 2024.

Victormame, *Música de videojuegos*. Barcelona: Redbook Ediciones, 2024.

Youtube. "Copyright", n.d. Available at: https://www.youtube.com/intl/en_us/howyoutubeworks/policies/copyright/#copyright-exceptions. Accessed 30th November 2024.

Epilogue
What's Next?

If scholars can agree on one thing, in esports and in entertainment, it is that the future is uncertain and strongly reliant on changes in technology, the market, and its regulating policies. Different scholars, including Seth E. Jenny and colleagues in the *Routledge Handbook of Esports,* have explored future paths for esports, attesting to the difficulty of addressing specific developments, as they depend "on the perspective of evaluation as well as the specific aspect of the ecosystem being discussed."[1] This also holds true for the wider entertainment panorama in which esports are inserted, and for the potential of their extended collaboration with the music industry. At a non-academic level, mediatic voices in music and gaming, such as Mat Ombler or Eric Tan,[2] have also actively contributed to the analysis of the potential developments for the near future.

Despite most general debates being centered around competition contexts, economics, and marketing—and not necessarily on their multimedia ecosystem—the multi- and transmedia opportunities addressed by the quoted authors attest to the growing need to see esports as more than competitive circuits. That is, they reinforce the need to start considering them and their related products as part of the global entertainment culture.

In this line of thought, recent discussions involving media and esports include topics such as the search for a balance between focusing on game development and mediating it through related products; the growing presence and influence of video games in popular culture, including music, cinema, and other forms of entertainment; the emergence of new markets and the popularization of different music genres, such as C-pop and J-pop; or the continuous growth of music initiatives surrounding esports and the overall gaming landscape. These, alongside the insertion of esports in multiple areas of practice and knowledge, underline the need for understanding the presence of music in esports through an influence that moves beyond their most immediate environment.

The growing transmediation of content exemplified by the chapters in this book, in great measure through the starring of popular artists and brands in competition stages and game products, has become central to esports narratives. As described in Chapter 1, these intersections alter the traditional value chain[3] of music and gaming alike, creating new dynamics that tend toward the homogenization of the multimedia cultural landscape. The participation of Linkin Park in the *League of Legends* World Championship in 2024, for instance, shows this inclination in what can be argued was one of the most significant events in recent years to unite elements from multiple niches under a single roof, contributing to direct contact between esports and music fans.

DOI: 10.1201/9781032625362-8

GAME FOCUS VERSUS MEDIATIZATION

The growth of the esports industry following the COVID-19 pandemic encouraged developers and publishers to invest in their fictional universes and the products related to their imagined lores, to respond to an immediate demand for indoor entertainment. This quick rise, which was crucial to establishing esports as a cultural commodity, was followed by consequential degrowth once sanitary restrictions loosened, which implied that some media projects became difficult to sustain in time.[4] An example is Riot Games' announcement in 2022 of the de-escalation of some of their initiatives to find a balance between developing their main titles and mediatizing content through other means.[5] In this way, some of the efforts and success of the early 2020s began being refocused as a longer-term strategy. Nevertheless, this process was key in helping define the current entertainment panorama and supporting a growing interest in transmediating content to different sectors, including music.

In need of resource management, sponsorships and collaborations continue to be essential to sustain the ecosystem. In-game concerts, for instance, have benefitted from a collaborative model and will presumably continue to do so. According to Gaetano Fazio, CEO of Soho Live,[6] one of the biggest benefits of virtual concerts "is the revenue generated from licensing fees paid by the production partner to the game studio, which can reach significant amounts for larger tours."[7] Furthermore, companies can find other forms of income derived from these events, such as merchandise, the release of soundtracks, etc., which work bidirectionally for the promotion of the involved parties.

The progressive bet on virtual artists to represent brands and labels is related to this, as explored in previous chapters regarding the development of game-character virtual groups. For the last few years, the growth of virtual idols such as Naevis has blended with drawing-based Isegye Idol or PLAVE, among others, highlighting the potential of investing in ully brand-mediated artists, and bringing forward the influence of anime audiovisual aesthetics in the West. In gaming, companies such as Bandai Namco Entertainment have taken an interest in this trend with projects such as Den-On-Bu,[8] bringing forward the relevance of East Asia in taking a leading role in the music *plus* video games industry. Games like *Fortnite* have also embraced it by incorporating the iconic Hatsune Miku as one of their latest collaborations in the researched period,[9] showing an inclination to include existing virtual artists in opposition to developing their own. Nevertheless, it is yet to be seen how big names in game development will respond to the challenge of incorporating external artists *versus* creating their own, how each case will add value to specific titles in the esports landscape, and if fandom dynamics will follow accordingly.[10]

User-generated content initiatives will also likely continue to unfold as brands focus more on user experience and try to integrate their products as transversal forms of experiential marketing into their consumers' (online) daily lives. Some channels or platforms may stand out in this process, as they provide an access point and the means for users to materialize music projects online, such as *Fortnite* or, outside of esports, *Roblox*. This process has been registered mostly by media and industry agents who have started assessing the value of their products based on the revenue generated *for* users and not only *by* them.[11] Will this model provide a path for virtual connectedness among musicians and different music scenes around the globe? Or will it remain a platform for exploiting popular artists and industry-led music experiences? To date, the weight of the debates falls toward the centrality of independent users to shape the market, which can be deemed as a way for developers to delegate part of the mediatization of games to consumers.

ESPORTS IN THE ENTERTAINMENT INDUSTRY

The discussion about focusing on game development rather than complementary content is especially relevant to esports games, which are mostly defined by their competitive core and not necessarily through their investment in music and art. Nevertheless, esports' immersion in general culture and inexorable multimedia nature is progressively situating them closer to the entertainment industry's bullseye.

The growth of initiatives linking esports and music has been exponential in the last few years, as headlines involving popular music artists and bands around competitive titles have become more frequent. This includes smaller collaborations, such as the use of *PUBG*'s IP in movies such as 무도실무관 (*Officer Black Belt*),[12] as well as the insertion of artists in esports products directly, as previously described regarding the collaboration between Le Sserafim and *Overwatch* at BlizzCon, or BTS and *PUBG*, among others.

Furthermore, these agreements have helped shape music consumption to an extent, especially when linked to products that transcend their gaming origins. As an example, artists such as Fever 333, who had an average of "600k monthly listeners on Spotify prior to featuring in the *Arcane* League of Legends soundtrack," were "catapulted (...) to 2.56 million" in weeks after the release of the series.[13] Others, such as rapper and singer Ashnikko, experienced a more reduced yet likewise effective impact, which, in this case, was further potentiated by her performance during the *League of Legends*' 2024 World Championship. Similarly, Monstercat roster artists featured in *Rocket League* have seen steady growth over the years, becoming established in the international EDM scene.[14]

As argued throughout this book, esports games have permeated different layers of the entertainment industry, creating alternative routes to redirect new fans toward their main products and a wider form of expression that reaches beyond competitive arenas. Although this may not be exclusive to esports, as it extends to the overall gaming landscape, their socializing value as sportive community points of encounter favors the dynamization of products that afford community and identity-building processes, which may be less immediate in other contexts. The inclusion of music performances based on popular music in world championships and cup finals is a clear example of this, as they provide a space for the continuous coexistence of music and games, appealing to fans' different cultural experiences, which add to their cultural capital and the overall lore built around competitive gaming culture.

In Chapter 5, I argued that the participation of popular artists in such contexts becomes frequently linked to the expectations and preferences of the games' audiences, including regional featured artists, when appropriate. However, there is a necessary continuous dialogue between the search for innovation and the integration of user preferences, as event producers are active agents in shaping the market. As described by consultant and ex-Riot Head of Music Toa Dunn:

> When I was first working on the development of K/DA (...) in K-pop, Blackpink hadn't really blown up yet. They weren't really big yet on the market, at least not in the Western world. K-pop was big in Korea, and only in really small groups. Around the world, K-pop meant something, but it wasn't mainstream yet. And I remember we did some data [research] (...) So there was this kind of question like, "well, we don't want to just serve Korea, right? This is a global game." And so there was a little bit of hesitation of "should we do this?" This is that creative odds versus business sense. According to the data, you should be like, "no, you shouldn't just do it, you should do one of these other bigger genres." But my hunch was, "Hey, I actually think K-pop."[15]

This attention to the market and the forecast of growing tendencies among the global industry were also key in promoting other virtual bands later on and informing what has become one of the main trends in music and gaming in recent years.[16] In this sense, the music business has attended to the impact of such collaborations and has been growingly interested in closing agreements with developers and publishers inclined to explore transmedia options, including new and rapidly growing markets such as East and South Asia.

EXPANDING MARKETS

Esports continue to rapidly expand in the context of digital capitalism and in sight of the opportunities they offer to connect entertainment products under one umbrella, users from distant countries, and the content they independently generate. Among these, formats such as mobile gaming have become increasingly present, and new publics with growing access to the internet have adhered to them, benefiting and contributing to the heterogenization of the cultural market, bringing music outside of the West into the global pop music mainstream.

To date, this tendency has been mainly supported by industry reports that continuously assess prospective pathways for growth. For instance, Matthew Ball's[17] *The State of Gaming in 2025* report[18] describes the evolution of the market in the last years, which allows forecasting prospections for the immediate future. Among these, he includes the growth of mobile gaming—in addition to PC, console, VR, etc.—and the "investing in and *prioritizing* different cultural events and tones"[19]—among which he accentuates Ariana Grande's *Rift Tour* on *Fortnite*, or the collaboration between BTS and *Free Fire*, among others. The author specifically highlights the strength gained by the Asian market in the last few years, as do interviewees for the IFPI report of 2024 such as Sony Music Entertainment CEO Andrew Chan, who described the relevance of Japanese culture and the existing opportunities to bring it to a global audience, or the flux of artists from India to Canada, "which is both a reaction to something that is happening organically and a proactive turbo-charge to make sure it doesn't just continue but flourishes and finds a wider audience,"[20] among other topics.

Especially in these very regions, mobile gaming has consolidated its presence during the last five to ten years, including adaptations to the market—e.g. *Honor of Kings* or *Game of Peace* in China. Authors like Dal Yon Jin, in *Global eSports*, tackle a progressively shifting trend toward the professionalization of mobile gaming in 2018, although the participants in his study perceived mobile as closer to entertainment than a potential professional outcome.[21] Since then, mobile has become not only an extension or alternative version of other consoles, but has gained its own weight and become one of the driving forces communing with popular music. As stated by Ombler:

> Mobile games make up 50% of the global gaming market, which is interesting because you don't get the media attention that normal games do, despite the fact that a lot of these mobile games are just as big as *Fortnite* or *Roblox*, or anything else. But a lot of players of mobile games [are] predominantly [in] an Eastern market. So there's a really big K-pop thing at the moment where there's loads of music collaborations going on. (...) *PUBG Mobile*, *Free Fire*... they do a lot of stuff with K-pop artists as well. Blackpink have just put out their first mobile game as well, that seems to be doing quite well. So I think a massive growth market for gaming that is currently being done by esports and mobile, but I don't think the wider general gaming audience has caught on to that yet.[22]

This trend has further extended to other Asian geographies, including already present territories such as South Korea and Japan. For example, the Philippines has recently started increasing its international impact in global entertainment, and will likely continue to do so at a wider scale in upcoming years. For instance, music videos like SB19's *Gento* have gathered millions of views on YouTube,[23] raising the interest of corporations such as Sony Music Entertainment, also derived from the worldwide spread of diaspora inclined to consume Filipino artists.[24] This goes hand in hand with the attention of the Asian markets toward their own publics, as they continue to include regional artists in their competitions and esports promotional products.

The so-called C- and J-wave, following the Korean model, also underline the growing influence of the Asian market over the West and the integration of diverse music products in the global cultural landscape.[25] Artists such as Eason Chan—featured in Riot Games' *Arcane*—or CORSAK—featured at the *PUBG Mobile* Club Open of 2019—have rapidly gained popularity in the context of esports, showing the integration of worldwide artists in everyday media. In this sense, it is reasonable to assert that future collaborations in esports games and on esports stages may feature these and other artists as a means to appeal to the global audiences of different titles.

BEYOND GAMING AND ESPORTS

The growth of the symbiosis between the music and gaming industries becomes patent beyond the immediate contexts offered by the videoludic products, as they progressively tend to become integrated into general popular culture. As argued by Tan, "the best games become cultural landmarks" as they "create moments in culture that transcend gameplay."[26] *Fortnite*'s hip-hop season, the bet on well-established popular music artists such as Metallica, Eminem, or Linkin Park in different titles, the inclusion of characters such as Justin Bieber or DJ Alok in *Free Fire*, and their contribution to live events in competitive arenas, all attest to the intent of exploring the potential of music and esports games further from the screen and even the stage that usually responsible for most conversations.

Texts like Jenkins' *Convergence Culture* or Collins' contributions to the discussion of the music industry's role in gaming become as relevant as ever. The tendencies described since the beginning of the century continue to be pertinent, and, in line with a highly digitalized market, music continues to be at the epicenter of the socialization of cultural expressions and exchanges. The global esports scene has been shown to contribute additional layers to an increasingly interdependent industry articulated around media. Esports are thus consolidated not only as an independent niche, but as an integral part of a growing multi- and transmedia ecosystem in which music socializes and articulates the ubiquitous connections of internet-connected users.

Despite music and esports not always being immediate synonyms, and regardless of the distance that can be established from purely competitive settings and the music industry, the extension of the impact of their association is, as of today, key in mediating their dissemination and reach towards wider audiences. What is more essential, their continuous collaboration contributes to shaping the dynamics of the entertainment industry and contributes to giving voice to the users that keep them in motion, affording alternative markets, new music initiatives, and thousands of daily conversations about what we can hear and not only see.

NOTES

1 Seth E. Jenny, Tom Brock, Tobias M. Scholz, Amanda C. Cote, & Nicolas Besombes, "The Future of Esports", in Seth E. Jenny, Nicholas Besombes, Tom Brock, Amanda C. Cote & Tobias M. Scholz (Eds.), *Routledge Handbook of Esports*, 656–670. Oxon: Routledge, 2024.

2 Mat Ombler, Video Games & Music Journalist. Interview by Eulalia Febrer-Coll. 17th September 2023. Eric Tan, Music and Publishing Director for Video Games Companies, former Riot Games and Sony Music employee. Interview by Eulalia Febrer-Coll. 9th July 2024.

3 Ricardo R. Álvarez Vázquez, *The Music Industry in the Dawn of the 21st Century: Networking for a Thriving Music Industry*. Elverum: Kunnskapsverket, 2017; Andrew Leyshon, "Time-Space (and Digital) Compression: Software Formats, Musical Networks, and the Reorganisation of the Music Industry", *Environment and Planning A*, 2001, 33(1), 49–77.

4 Matthew Ball, "Esports and the Dangers of Serving at the Pleasure of a King", *Epyllon*, n.d. Available at: https://www.matthewball.co/all/esportsrisks. Accessed 14th January 2025.

5 Alexander Lee, "Why Riot Games Is Scaling back Its Dream of Becoming 'the Next Disney'", *Digiday*, 2024. Available at: https://digiday.com/marketing/why-riot-games-is-scaling-back-its-dream-of-becoming-the-next-disney/. Accessed 14th January 2025.

6 Soho Live is "A Tokyo-based Company Specialising in the Production of Video Game and Anime Music Concerts", http://www.soho-live.com. Accessed 17th January 2025.
7 Gaetano Fazio, "How Game Studios Can Benefit from Video Game Concerts", *GamesIndustry.biz*, 2024. Available at: https://www.gamesindustry.biz/how-game-studios-can-benefit-from-video-game-concerts#:~:text=Benefits%20of%20video%20game%20concerts,-While%20creating%20video&text=One%20of%20the%20biggest%20benefits,significant%20amounts%20for%20larger%20tours. Accessed 17th January 2025.
8 Lee Gyu-lee, "Virtual Ideols Set to Take over K-pop Scene in 2025", *The Korea Times*, 2025. Available at: https://www.koreatimes.co.kr/www/art/2025/01/398_391094.html. Accessed 23rd January 2025.
9 The Fortnite Team, "Virtual Idol Hatsune Miku beams into Fortnite Festival for Season 7", *Fortnite*, 2025. Available at: https://www.fortnite.com/news/virtual-artist-hatsune-miku-beams-into-fortnite-festival-season-7?lang=en-US. Accessed 21st January 2025.
10 Rafal Zaborowski, "Vitual (Idol) Audiences: Canon, Fanon, and Multivocality in Vocaloid Cultures", in Annette Hill & Peter Lunt (Eds.), *The Routledge Companion to Media Audiences*. Oxon: Routledge, 2024.
11 Jen Larsen, "How User-Generated Content Is Shaping the Future of Gaming and Media", *GamesBeat*, 2024. Available at: https://venturebeat.com/games/how-user-generated-content-is-shaping-the-future-of-gaming-and-media/. Accessed 20th January 2025; Ben Gilbert, "Thunder Only Happens When It's Raining: How Social Media and UGC Could Decide the Future of the Music Industry", *Synchtank*, 2020. Available at: https://www.synchtank.com/blog/thunder-only-happens-when-its-raining-how-social-media-and-ugc-could-decide-the-future-of-the-music-industry/. Accessed 20th January 2025.
12 See Peter Moon, "Being in a Team in Charge of Developing In-Game Collaboration Deals for IP of #PUBG Calibre Allows Me to Get Involved in Several Interesting Conversations and Deals", *LinkedIn*, 2024. Available at: https://www.linkedin.com/posts/petermoon21_pubg-netflix-yoasobi-activity-7250211091132116992-yhMy?utm_source=share&utm_medium=member_desktop. Accessed 20th January 2025.
13 Mat Ombler, "Fever 333 Were Averaging 600k Monthly Listeners on Spotify", *LinkedIn*, 2024. Available at: https://www.linkedin.com/posts/mat-ombler_fever-333-were-averaging-600k-monthly-listeners-activity-7268260797011693568-27w5?utm_source=share&utm_medium=member_desktop. Accessed 20th January 2025.
14 Gavin Johnson, Director of Sync and Partnerships at Monstercat, Interview by Eulalia Febrer-Coll, 13th December 2023.
15 Toa Dunn, former Head of Music at Riot Games. Interview by Eulalia Febrer-Coll. 20th September 2023.
16 Andra Ivănescu, "'Pop Stars': The Personas of K/DA, Transmedia Marketing, and Riot Games Music", *Persona Studies*, 2025, 10(1), 42–55; Nasmedia, "Charting New Territories: How K-pop and Gaming Are Poised for Explosive Growth in the Next Era", 2024. Available at: https://nasmedia.medium.com/charting-new-territories-how-k-pop-and-gaming-are-poised-for-explosive-growth-in-the-next-era-b40e21602a12. Accessed 20th January 2025.
17 Matthew Ball is the CEO at Epyllion, self-described as providing "investment and strategic advisory services, produces television, films, and video games". See Epyllion, https://www.matthewball.co. Accessed 21st January 2025.
18 Matthew Ball, "The State of Video Gaming in 2025", *Epyllion*, 2025. Available at: https://www.matthewball.co/all/stateofvideogaming2025. Accessed 21st January 2025.
19 Ball, "The State of Video Gaming in 2025", 74.
20 Andrew Chan, CEO of Sony Music Entertainment, Greater China. Interview by IFPI Global Music, 2024, 32. Available at: https://www.ifpi.org/wp-content/uploads/2024/04/GMR_2024_State_of_the_Industry.pdf. Accessed 21st January 2025.

21 Dal Yong Jin, "The Emergence and Transformation of Global Esporst: Comparative Perspectives or Korean and Canadian Esports Scenes", in Dal Yong Jin (Ed.), *Global Esports: Transformation of Cultural Perceptions of Competitive Gaming*, 223–239. New York: Bloomsbury: 2022.

22 Mat Ombler, Video Games & Music Journalist. Interview by Eulalia Febrer-Coll. 17th September 2023.

23 SB19 Official, "SB19 'GENTO' Music Video", *Youtube*, 2023. Available at: https://www.youtube.com/watch?v=VZZA_38RUBI. Accessed 18th January 2025.

24 Eric Tan, "The Philippines in the Next Big Music Hub", *LinkedIn*, 2024. Available at: https://www.linkedin.com/posts/erictanhk_the-philippines-is-the-next-big-music-hub-activity-7230597699199193089-Lu39?utm_source=share&utm_medium=member_desktop. Accessed 18th January 2025.

25 Murray Stassen, "J-pop Is Gaining Popularity on a Global Scale", *Music Business Worldwide*, 2024. Available at: https://www.musicbusinessworldwide.com/j-pop-is-now-gaining-popularity-on-a-global-scale/#:~:text=Although%20the%20CD%20has%20thrived,2022. Accessed 12th January 2025.

26 Eric Tan, "The Best Games Become Cultural Landmarks", *LinkedIn,* 2024. Available at: https://www.linkedin.com/search/results/all/?keywords=The%20best%20games%20become%20cultural%20landmarks%20tan&origin=GLOBAL_SEARCH_HEADER&sid=k%3AG. Accessed 18th January 2025.

REFERENCES

Álvarez Vázquez, Ricardo R. *The Music Industry in the Dawn of the 21st Century: Networking for a Thriving Music Industry*. Elverum: Kunnskapsverket, 2017.

Ball, Matthew. "Esports and the Dangers of Serving at the Pleasure of a King", *Epyllon*, n.d. Available at: https://www.matthewball.co/all/esportsrisks. Accessed 14th January 2025.

Ball, Matthew. "The State of Video Gaming in 2025", *Epyllion*, 2025. Available at: https://www.matthewball.co/all/stateofvideogaming2025. Accessed 21st January 2025.

Fazio, Gaetano. "How Game Studios Can Benefit from Video Game Concerts", *GamesIndustry.biz*, 2024. Available at: https://www.gamesindustry.biz/how-game-studios-can-benefit-from-video-game-concerts#:~:text=Benefits%20of%20video%20game%20concerts,-While%20creating%20video&text=One%20of%20the%20biggest%20benefits,significant%20amounts%20for%20larger%20tours. Accessed 17th January 2025.

Gilbert, Ben. "Thunder Only Happens When It's Raining: How Social Media and UGC Could Decide the Future of the Music Industry", *Synchtank*, 2020. Available at: https://www.synchtank.com/blog/thunder-only-happens-when-its-raining-how-social-media-and-ugc-could-decide-the-future-of-the-music-industry/. Accessed 20th January 2025.

IFPI Global Music. 2024. Available at: https://www.ifpi.org/wp-content/uploads/2024/04/GMR_2024_State_of_the_Industry.pdf. Accessed 21st January 2025.

Ivănescu, Andra. "'Pop Stars': The Personas of K/DA, Transmedia Marketing, and Riot Games Music", *Persona Studies,* 2025, 10(1), 42–55.

Jenny, Seth E., Brock, Tom, Scholz, Tobias M., Cote, Amanda C. & Besombes, Nicolas. "The Future of Esports", in Seth E. Jenny, Nicholas Besombes, Tom Brock, Amanda C. Cote & Tobias M. Scholz (Eds.), *Routledge Handbook of Esports,* 656–670. Oxon: Routledge, 2024.

Jin, Dal Yong. "The Emergence and Transformation of Global Esporst: Comparative Perspectives or Korean and Canadian Esports Scenes", in Dal Yong Jin (Ed.), *Global Esports: Transformation of Cultural Perceptions of Competitive Gaming,* 223–239. New York: Bloomsbury, 2022.

Larsen, Jen. "How User-generated Content Is Shaping the Future of Gaming and Media", *GamesBeat*, 2024. Available at: https://venturebeat.com/games/how-user-generated-content-is-shaping-the-future-of-gaming-and-media/. Accessed 20th January 2025

Lee, Alexander. "Why Riot Games Is Scaling Back Its Dream of Becoming 'the Next Disney'", Digiday, 2024. Available at: https://digiday.com/marketing/why-riot-games-is-scaling-back-its-dream-of-becoming-the-next-disney/. Accessed 14th January 2025.

Lee, Gyu-lee. "Virtual Ideols Set to Take over K-pop Scene in 2025", *The Korea Times*, 2025. Available at: https://www.koreatimes.co.kr/www/art/2025/01/398_391094.html. Accessed 23rd January 2025.

Leyshon, Andrew. "Time-Space (and Digital) Compression: Software Formats, Musical Networks, and the Reorganisation of the Music Industry", *Environment and Planning* A, 2001, 33(1), 49–77.

Moon, Peter. "Being in a Team in Charge of Developing In-game Collaboration Deals for IP of #PUBG Calibre Allows Me to Get Involved in Several Interesting Conversations and Deals", *LinkedIn,* 2024. Available at: https://www.linkedin.com/posts/petermoon21_pubg-netflix-yoasobi-activity-7250211091132116992-yhMy?utm_source=share&utm_medium=member_desktop. Accessed 20th January 2025.

Nasmedia. "Charting New Territories: How K-pop and Gaming are Poised for Explosive Growth in the Next Era", 2024. Available at: https://nasmedia.medium.com/charting-new-territories-how-k-pop-and-gaming-are-poised-for-explosive-growth-in-the-next-era-b40e21602a12. Accessed 20th January 2025.

Ombler, Mat. "Fever 333 Were Averaging 600k Monthly Listeners on Spotify", LinkedIn, 2024. Available at: https://www.linkedin.com/posts/mat-ombler_fever-333-were-averaging-600k-monthly-listeners-activity-7268260797011693568-27w5?utm_source=share&utm_medium=member_desktop. Accessed 20th January 2025.

SB19 Official. "SB19 'GENTO' Music Video", *Youtube*, 2023. Available at: https://www.youtube.com/watch?v=VZZA_38RUBI. Accessed 18th January 2025.

Soho Live is "a Tokyo-Based Company Specialising in the Production of Video Game and Anime Music Concerts", https://www.soho-live.com. Accessed 17th January 2025.

Stassen, Murray. "J-pop Is Gaining Popularity on a Global Scale", *Music Business Worldwide,* 2024. Available at: https://www.musicbusinessworldwide.com/j-pop-is-now-gaining-popularity-on-a-global-scale/#:~:text=Although%20the%20CD%20has%20thrived,2022. Accessed 12th January 2025.

Tan, Eric. "The Best Games Become Cultural Landmarks", *LinkedIn,* 2024. Available at: https://www.linkedin.com/search/results/all/?keywords=The%20best%20games%20become%20cultural%20landmarks%20tan&origin=GLOBAL_SEARCH_HEADER&sid=k%3AG. Accessed 18th January 2025.

Tan, Eric. "The Philippines in the Next Big Music Hub", *LinkedIn*, 2024. Available at: https://www.linkedin.com/posts/erictanhk_the-philippines-is-the-next-big-music-hub-activity-7230597699199193089-Lu39?utm_source=share&utm_medium=member_desktop. Accessed 18th January 2025.

The Fortnite Team. "Virtual Idol Hatsune Miku beams into Fortnite Festival for Season 7", *Fortnite*, 2025. Available at: https://www.fortnite.com/news/virtual-artist-hatsune-miku-beams-into-fortnite-festival-season-7?lang=en-US. Accessed 21st January 2025.

Zaborowski, Rafal. "Vitual (Idol) Audiences: Canon, Fanon, and Multivocality in Vocaloid Cultures", in Annette Hill & Peter Lunt (Eds.), *The Routledge Companion to Media Audiences,* 222–233. Oxon: Routledge, 2024.

Index

Note: Bold page numbers refer to tables; *italic* page numbers refer to figures.

FSC
www.fsc.org
MIX
Papier | Fördert
gute Waldnutzung
FSC® C083411

Kolibri 360 GmbH
Ferdinand-Jühlke-Straße 7
99095 Erfurt, Deutschland
produktsicherheit@kolibri360.de